From a biblical basis and a theological foundation to the intentionality of planning a ministry to meet the needs of a postmodern culture, from a historical reminder to the practical legal aspects of a church-based recreation ministry, from organization to Christian ethics in a sports recreation ministry, and from theory to practice—this book has it all. I commend it to you as one of the best and most comprehensive church recreation books I have seen. John Garner has compiled an excellent resource for churches as well as for the classroom.

— Chuck Gartman —
Youth Ministry Professor, Howard Payne University,
Brownwood, Texas

# Recreation and Sports Ministry

## Impacting Postmodern Culture

### John Garner
General Editor

BROADMAN
& HOLMAN
PUBLISHERS

NASHVILLE, TENNESSEE

0-8054-2626-4

Published by Broadman & Holman Publishers,
Nashville, Tennessee

Dewey Decimal Classification: 790
Subject Heading: RECREATION\SPORTS\
CHURCH RECREATION

Unless otherwise stated, all Old Testament Scripture citation is from the Holy Bible, New International Version, © 1973, 1978, 1984 by International Bible Society. All New Testament Scripture citation is from the Holman Christian Standard Bible, © 2000 by Holman Bible Publishers.

3  4  5  6  7  8  9  10  07  06  05

This book is dedicated first to my wife Judy and children Jason and Jeffrey. Your support and encouragement over the years has led to this accomplishment. Judy, to you especially—your sacrifices helped me be able to do what God called me to do. You are indeed a helpmate.

To those who mentored me over the years. To those who ministered to me, gave me a chance, and saw something in me—thank you. I have tried to be faithful to the calling you helped me realize. You shaped my work and this missive in so many ways.

To my fellow authors on this project. Thank you for your patience and persistence. Your contributions to recreation and sports ministry are beyond measure.

Finally, to the men and women who are called to minister using the unconventional tools of recreation and sports. Your work is often misunderstood by church staff and members alike. To you who use recreation and sports as ministry tools, this book is for you and about you. I hope it is an encouragement to you and is honoring to your Kingdom contributions.

*I have become all things to all people,*
*so that I may by all means save some.*
*Now I do all this because of the gospel,*
*that I may become a partner in its benefits.*
1 Corinthians 9:22b–23

— John Garner, general editor —

# Contents

# Contributors

*Editor's Note: This work is a ministry overview. The reader will see a conti-nuity in the overall scope of the work as each chapter supports, reinforces, and expands the others. The editor is indebted to the authors for their consistency as they have examined and explored this ministry area from their chapters' point of view.*

### Dale Adkins, BA, Re.D.

K. Dale Adkins is professor of recreation, park, and tourism adminis-tration (RPTA) at Western Illinois University in Macomb, Illinois. He has presented at the state, regional, national, and international levels, as well as published articles and abstracts. He received his doctor of recreation from Indiana University. Most recently he was president of the American Association for Leisure and Recreation within the American Alliance for Health, Physical Education, Recreation, and Dance. Dale also has served on the board of directors for the American Camping Association.

### Dale Connally, Ph.D., CPRP

Dale is an assistant professor and the director of the Recreation and Leisure Services Division at Baylor University in Waco, Texas. From the University of New Mexico he received a doctorate in education and majored in parks and recreation management. Dale has published articles, abstracts, and ministry resources for use in the church. He lectures and teaches extensively in the field of recreation and leisure services and has presented papers at various outdoor and leisure service symposiums. He is the author of *Games with a Purpose 2* and is actively involved in the Outdoor Network.

### John Garner, BS, MRE

John is director of Recreation and Sports Ministry at LifeWay Christian Resources. He has been working in recreation and sports min-istry for thirty-three years and is the author of more than seventy-five arti-cles in ministry-related newsletters, theological journals, and ministry magazines. He is author/editor of the *Guidebook for Planning Recreation Centers* and the *Operating Manual for Recreation Centers*. John lectures in an adjunct capacity at several seminaries and colleges.

### Judi Jackson, BA, MRE

Judi is a writer, teacher, conference leader, and worship leader based in New Orleans, Louisiana. She graduated from Louisiana State University with a degree in journalism and from New Orleans Baptist Theological Seminary with an MRE in youth education. Judi is an adjunct faculty member at New Orleans Baptist Theological Seminary, teaching in the division of Christian Education Ministries. In addition to teaching at NOBTS, Judi is currently enrolled in the school's Ph.D. program, pursuing advanced studies in Christian education. She coauthored *The Retreat Notebook 2* with her husband.

### Greg Linville, BA, MA

Greg holds a master of arts degree from Ashland Theological Seminary in Ashland, Ohio, and a bachelor of arts degree from Malone College in Canton, Ohio. He was awarded an honorary doctorate of divinity in sports ministry from Briercrest Seminary in April of 1999 and is currently working on his D.Min. degree. He served First Friends Church in Canton as the director of Sports and Recreation for fifteen years. He is currently teaching at Malone College and Graduate School, Briercrest Bible College, and Ashland Seminary. Greg was one of the founders of the association of Church Sports and Recreation Ministers (CSRM), was elected CSRM president in 1999, and now serves as the executive director. Greg is married and the father of two teenage children.

### Rodger Oswald, BA, MA

A graduate of Multnomah Biblical Seminary and College, Rodger is executive director of Church Sports International in San Jose, California. He earned his bachelor and master's degrees from California State University in San Jose. He has served as Christian Education, Missions, and Sports pastor at several California churches. Rodger was instrumental in designing curriculum for an undergraduate degree in sports ministry and establishing a sports ministry department at the Master's College. He lectures and teaches extensively in an adjunct capacity at colleges and seminaries.

### Paul Stutz, BS, MARE

Paul is director of the Recreation/Aerobic Center and professor of church recreation at Southwestern Baptist Theological Seminary in Fort

Worth, Texas. He teaches extensively in the camping and outdoor education field. Paul has served churches in Texas as a minister of Recreation. Paul has served on the Recreation and Sports Ministry Leadership Team for LifeWay Christian Resources and is a lecturer at Rec Lab: The International Conference on Recreation and Sports Ministry.

### *Brad Wesner, BA, MA, MS, Ph.D.*

Brad has worked in Christian camping and served churches in various capacities since 1984. He has had extensive writing and editing experience for educational journals such as *Play and Culture* and has written more than fifty articles for various religious and nonreligious publications, including magazines such as *Parks and Recreation, Church Recreation,* and *Church Administration.* Brad's doctoral work focused on the history of recreation in the American church. Brad's leisure is centered on creative writing, cartooning, model railroading, and his family.

# 1 Introduction to Recreation and Sports Ministry

## John Garner

In 1927 the first issue of *Church Administration* magazine had an interesting lead article. The title was "The Modern Movement for Better Rural Church Buildings." America was in the midst of prosperity—not knowing that the Great Depression was just around the corner. Most of the country was rural. There was a new rural prosperity. Travel was becoming easier. Soldiers had returned from the "Great War." Public schools were being built in rural areas. Churches were doing new ministry actions. Indeed, churches were the center of community life—everything was done there, from worship to socials that gathered folks in their communities.

The interesting part of that article (outline really) was in section 3. In that section, "Some co-ordinate equipment," the listing went like this:

- A well-kept church lawn
- A pastor's home
- A few acres of land
- Part for the pastor's use
- Part for athletic fields
- Garage containing Ford car
- Private light and water system
- A building for community social life[1]

Here was a major denominational publication recommending that a church provide places for athletics and social life. The church was using sports and recreation (socials) to reach people because that was what people were involved and interested in.

In 1889 James Naismith applied to be a student at the YMCA Training School at Springfield. One of the questions asked on the application was, "What is the work of a YMCA Physical Director?" He answered, "To win men for the Master through the gym." In December 1891 Dr. Naismith created the game of basketball. Naismith's invention came during that winter when his supervisor asked him to come up with an indoor game to attract young men during the harsh New England winters—in order to share the gospel on a year-round basis. "Using a soccer ball, two empty peach baskets, a ladder and ten handwritten rules, Naismith introduced his game that would become the most watched and played indoor sport in the world."[2]

In the early twentieth century, famous sports figures were using their sports platform to gather a crowd to share the gospel: The Olympic champion known as the Flying Scotsman, Eric Liddell was using sports as a platform for gathering a crowd and sharing the gospel in 1924. C. T. Studd used his status as a well-known cricket player in England. In America, Billy Sunday, former professional baseball player, became an evangelist and reached millions. Sports and recreation have been used since biblical times to share the message of salvation through knowing Christ as Savior. This was especially evident

> in the post-World War II era as a product of evangelical youth rallies, particularly those connected to the Youth for Christ (YFC) organization. In the 1940s and '50s, YFC discovered what it called "the sports appeal" in attracting an audience—especially among adolescent males—to hear an evangelistic message. On Memorial Day 1945, for example, 65,000 kids came to a YFC rally at Soldier Field in Chicago to hear a gospel message and listen to America's reigning indoor-mile champion, Gil Dodds, give a testimony to his faith in Jesus. . . . By the late 1960s, sports evangelism and ministry was coming to the college campus. Not only do athletes come to Christian college campuses to play and compete, but many of them also come because they perceive athletic participation as a means to ministry—both during and possibly following their days of intercollegiate competition.[3]

If it worked then, how much more open to recreation and sports is our culture now? Popular culture today is saturated with both, thanks in large part to the media. The Olympics, Super Bowl, World Series, X-Games, Iron Man events, the Final Four in college basketball, and the play-off series in professional basketball capture the imaginations of millions of people in America. Socially interactive media events like *Survivor, Who Wants to Be a Millionaire?, Big Brother,* and *Real World* garner large audiences. The next day, water cooler conversations often center on what happened the night before.

Culture is there. The question is, where is the church and how is the church using these tools to reach people? Or perhaps a better question is, will the church see the opportunity to use recreation and sports as ministry tools? The fact is that most churches are not reaching the postmodern culture. Most churches are being ignored by an increasingly non-Christian American culture because people do not see the church as relevant to their lives. But they do see relevance in leisure activities that they pursue at breakneck speed and often at great cost. The church must capture the imagination of a world that is passing it by. If the church can capture people's imagination, it can get their attention. If a church can gain people's attention, it has access to their minds. If a church has access to a person's mind, it can reach his heart. If a person's heart is reached and the message of the love of God through his Son is conveyed, a life can be changed for eternity. As an open-group, open-door strategy to reach people, recreation and sports ministry offers a nonthreatening first touch in lives of all ages.

## Snapshot of American Culture

We live in a leisure-oriented, competition-driven, unseeded culture. Not long ago, it was thought that people would be working shorter hours and have longer weekends to pursue leisure activities. In fact, just the opposite is true. "Today's average married couples labor a staggering 717 hours more each year than a working duo in 1969. The tools that were supposed to free us from the shackles of our desks have bound us to our jobs in ways unimaginable just a decade ago. They are electronic umbilical cords to the workplace."[4] People are working longer hours and being more productive as the competition has gotten more fierce.

Work is pervasive. The "electronic umbilical chords" of laptop computers, cell phones, E-mail, and instant messaging mean that some people never get away from their work. They take work home and on vacation. For many Americans, work has become an addiction. This makes one's leisure time a valued commodity.

Even though work consumes so much of their time, Americans prize their leisure above almost everything. It is not uncommon for workers to negotiate more time off even if they give up some salary to get it. People's time has become more valuable than money. Many Americans no longer work for food, shelter, clothing, and transportation; these are givens for most baby boomers, genXers, and millennials. They work for the weekend, for time off when they can do what they want to do. They will spend considerable time and money in pursuit of fun at the lake or on the golf course; camping; going to baseball, football, or basketball games; mountain biking; jogging; or engaging in a hobby that brings fulfillment to their lives. Billions of dollars are spent on leisure activities each year. The number one retailer of sporting goods sold 5.9 billion dollars worth of sporting equipment in a recent year. In American culture, leisure is a fact of life. Leisure is an expected commodity that is sought, bought, and bargained for. It is important to people in all walks and stages of life, and all indications are that it will continue to grow in importance in the coming years.

"The top four activities of all Americans are watching television, reading, socializing with friends and family, and shopping. The order hasn't changed since 1990. But Americans are spending less time in front of the tube, less time reading and more time hanging out with friends and going shopping."[5] (For more on recreation and culture, see appendix 1, "Recreation and Sports Ministry: Positioning for Impact.")

## From Work Ethic to Leisure Ethic

Gordon Dahl, in "Emergence of a Leisure Ethic," states: "We are beginning to discern the emergence of a leisure ethic. . . . It is an alternative that is being chosen by thousands of today's Americans."[6] Indeed America has moved from a work ethic to a leisure ethic. Most churches and church leaders have not recognized this fundamental shift in our culture. This shift has changed everything except the way the church interacts with culture.

Every Sunday people by the millions pass by the church on their way to the lake, the golf course, the hunting trip, the soccer field, the amateur or professional sporting event, or any number of other leisure pursuits available today. Churches are trying to gather a crowd by doing the same things the same ways they have done them, and they wonder why people are not responding.

A recent Gallop poll found that 90 percent of Americans watch, read about, or participate in sports once a month; 70 percent, once a week. Those statistics are staggering! Sports promoters, advertisers, and athletes have captured the imaginations of most of our culture. They keep the sports engine running at full speed. People are "doing their own thing," and this "thing" is all about leisure. Most often, the way people choose to use their discretionary time does not include the church.

Dahl goes on to say, "Instead of worrying over the hazards of [people] doing their own thing . . . Christians ought to be discovering its opportunities. In other words, we should confidently and consciously affirm the leisure ethic in an audacious exercise of the freedom we possess in Christ, and make our 'thing' the deeds of love, joy and peace which spring from spirits freed of sin and guilt and promised abundance of life."[7] Here you have a view of the church living the abundant life that Christ said was available. As this abundant life is lived out during leisure, it will be attractive to the world. The leisure-ethic lifestyle is both an avenue of abundant life and a laboratory for living for the Christian. The church has relegated itself to "sit on the sidelines," as it were, acting as if recreation and sports were a minor-league event, when in actuality sports is a giant steamroller consuming every person and every dollar those people have. The shift from work ethic to leisure ethic is well understood by this generation. Churches must begin to see the value of offering events and teaching opportunities that appeal to the leisure mind-set. One view is that "the church whose life and destiny have always transcended particular times . . . should be one of the institutions best prepared to adapt and flourish in the world of change and variety."[8]

Figure 1-1 shows the change in our culture since the 1960s.

## Competitiveness Is Everything

Competition on the job has led us to become more conscious of productivity. If I am competitive in my job and produce more services or goods, then I'm often rewarded with more time to use as I see fit. The

|                    | From                                                          | To                                                                                                                  |
|--------------------|---------------------------------------------------------------|---------------------------------------------------------------------------------------------------------------------|
| **Work**           | went to work and came home for R & R                          | 24/7; work everywhere—home, car, plane, hotel                                                                       |
| **Community**      | place to sleep and eat, friends and neighbors                 | place to live and belong, cyber communities                                                                         |
| **Family Vacation**| two weeks of togetherness                                     | two days tacked onto a business trip                                                                                 |
| **Childhood Summers** | neighborhood fun and pickup games at the park              | day-care-like, structured, or highly specialized                                                                    |
| **Youth Sports**   | participate in recreational leagues seasonally                | near year-round competition in one sport                                                                            |
| **Socialization**  | neighborhood chats, family gatherings, or backyard play       | chat rooms, TV talk-shows, or play dates                                                                            |
| **Physical Activities** | traditional team sports (softball, baseball, volleyball, or football) | individual activities, youth adventure (inline skating and snow-boarding), mature fitness pursuits (walking, gym workouts) |
| **Play**           | teams and clubs, fun and relaxation, status and socialization | individual focus, well-being, self-definition                                                                       |

Dr. Ellen O'Sullivan, *Parks and Recreation* magazine, October 2000

*Figure 1-1: Signals of a Shift*

more competitive I can become and the more products or services I produce in a shorter amount of time give me more time to spend doing what I want to do. Being competitive has it rewards.

College and business school graduates are foregoing jobs with higher paying salaries and taking jobs that will allow them more time off. Time is becoming a new form of currency as increasingly time is more valuable than money to workers. When people of this leisure ethic mind-set work, they work hard and are competitive. When they play, they play hard and expect to have the time they need to play. As the most affluent culture in the world, Americans have the money, and they expect to have the time to do what they want to do with their time.

Competition often creeps into the leisure activities. Some Little League teams now require parents to take classes to curb the overly competitive spirit that parents often bring with them to games. Parents are pushing their children to be more competitive so they can win a tournament or a scholarship to college. The joy of participation has given way to the pressure of competition. In one instance, fans and players of a losing team physically beat referees at a high school boy's basketball game. The police had to be called. In a well-publicized instance, a father was convicted of murder for killing another boy's father over a hockey practice.

Competition cannot be eliminated. Indeed, competition can bring out the best in us. In Romans Paul wrote about the athlete preparing for competition and "running the race." Elements of competition are found everywhere. From sibling rivalries, to corporate boardrooms, to sandlot football games, competition is a part of life. It can bring out the best in us, physically, emotionally, and mentally. Games, sports, art shows, bike rodeos, talent shows, and checkers have elements of competition. Life is full of competition. One cannot have a game without competition.

The problem with competition is when it becomes the driving force in the participant's life. Competition can be a powerful motivator, or it can be an all-consuming force that can ruin the participatory experience for the competitor as well as for those who are watching.

The church has a part in teaching the role of competition in a balanced life. The church needs to offer creative alternatives encouraging participation, developing skills, and fostering a love of sports. By seizing the arena of competition and channeling it to be something that builds lives instead of tearing relationships apart, the church can influence this powerful force.

Competition is neither right nor wrong. In fact, competition makes us strive to be better at whatever we do. It is how individuals handle competition that makes the difference. The church can and should handle competition in a new way to make a difference.

## Reaching an Unseeded Generation with Intentionality

We live in a culture that is unseeded with the Word of God. People do not know the Word of God, have not read the Word of God, and are afraid of the Word of God. Most of you reading this book grew up hearing, memorizing, singing, or reading God's Word. Many, if not most, of the genX population know practically nothing about it. They have been told in the media that if you read the Bible, you might go off the deep end. Children are not being taught the wonderful stories and Bible verses that can impress on their hearts the love of God and the salvation brought by Jesus Christ. Churches realize this and are trying to teach the Word of God, but families are too busy going to soccer tournaments, camping, or simply being at leisure to attend Bible study. Because parents will seek to get their children to quality sports and recreation events, churches must seize the opportunity to use quality recreation and sports to teach the Bible. If we believe the Word of God is alive, and if we believe it will not return void, when or where or how we teach it will not matter. What does matter is that we use people's interest in sports and recreation to reach an unseeded generation.

The dictionary defines *intentionality* this way: "from intent, which suggests greater deliberateness; a more settled determination that requires a more carefully calculated plan. Done by intention or design." Intentionality in the recreation and sports ministry context is the purposeful inclusion of sharing the gospel during recreation and sports ministry events. At one time in the history of recreation and sports ministry, a ministry was seen as successful if it had numerous teams or many people involved in recreation classes. This concept was characterized by activity. Activities became ends in themselves, and recreation and sports ministry became activity for activities' sake. Most churches had no strategy for intentional ministry to happen. If someone came to Christ, that was good. If no one came to Christ, the ministry was considered successful simply because the activity was held.

As recreation and sports ministry has matured, intent has changed. The days of rolling out a basketball and having pickup games are over. Programming is the key, and programming is done with the intention of sharing the gospel. Programming is done with or without a facility. Success does not mean having a facility to run. Recreation and sports ministry can be done effectively without a facility.

No longer are churches satisfied with being activity driven. More and more ministries are seeking to be intentional in their recreation and sports ministries.

They are planning their ministries to be intentional by:
- Reaching people by sharing the gospel at every opportunity.
- Maturing believers by discipling them.
- Multiplying ministering Christians by providing avenues for ministry participation.

By designing deliberate but natural touch points for ministry to take place during recreation and sports ministry events, as relationships are built, churches will find that this leisure-oriented generation will respond. The use of sports and recreation activities can be an open door to reach this generation. It is a natural.

How is the church to respond to this leisure-oriented, unseeded, sports-crazy culture? Do we continue on with business as usual? If we do, we will have little positive force in the community. Or do we do as Bob Briner suggests in his book *Roaring Lambs:* "Instead of hanging around the fringes of our culture, we need to be right smack dab in the middle of it."[9] Paul put it this way: "To the weak I became weak, in order to win the weak. I have become all things to all people, so that I may by all

---

## Church and Church Event Attendance: A Matter of Perceived Value

"Who says cocooning is out of style? Americans, it seems, like to hang out at home. According to a Harris Poll, 31 percent of Americans say their favorite leisure activity is reading, up from 27 percent in 1999. They also like watching television (23 percent), spending time with their family (14 percent), and gardening (13 percent). Just 6 percent prefer to catch a flick—down from 8 percent in 1999—and a mere 1 percent prefer eating out. Indeed, personal time seems to be at a premium: Americans spend only twenty hours each week on leisure activities, compared with fifty hours toiling at work" (From: *American Demographics,* March 2001 Indicators: *Time Off* by Gerda Gallop-Goodman).

### Implications for the Church

If Americans' time is at a premium, that says a lot to the church as it endeavors to impact our culture. Here are several observations:

1. If we spend half our time at work, the twenty hours of leisure are magnified in importance.

2. Going to church/church-sponsored events happens in a person's leisure time as a "chosen" activity.

3. Time has a value of its own.

4. People expect certain quality (perceived value) in what they spend their time on. The perception is that if this activity is not going to enhance my life with something of quality/value, I will not spend the time to participate/attend.

5. If going to church is a personal leisure activity, what happens at church must be of the highest quality for people to get their perceived value for the time spent.

6. The church cannot keep doing the same things the same way and expect Americans to respond.

7. Churches who offer perceived quality and value (personal, family, financial, social, relationship, recreation, etc.) are going to attract and have effective ministry opportunities.

means save some. Now I do all this because of the gospel, that I may become a partner in its benefits" (1 Cor. 9:22–23).

## Recreation and Sports Ministry Defined

There are as many manifestations of recreation and sports ministry as there are churches that have either recreation ministry or sports ministry. The term *recreation and sports ministry* has only recently been used in churches. For some denominations, *church recreation* was the term used since the 1940s. For other denominations, *sports ministry* was the preferred terminology. Individual churches may have used the term *recreation ministry* or *activities ministry* to describe the work in their settings. Whatever a church chooses to call this area of work, its nature involves elements of pure recreation and elements of sport—hence the combination of terms in modern times to *recreation and sports ministry.*

For the purposes of this text, the terms shall be defined as *recreation/sports,* any competitive/noncompetitive activity or action that takes place during the leisure time of a group or an individual; and *ministry,* helping people understand their relationship with God, his daily role in their lives, and their need to move from where they are to where they need to be in a right relationship to him. Combining the two results in the following definition: *recreation and sports ministry,* activity that takes place during leisure time with the stated purpose or intention of helping people become aware of their need for a relationship with God, his daily role in their lives, and their place in his kingdom work. This definition, while not specific as to activities involved, encompasses four of the concepts of leisure: (1) time, (2) activity, (3) a state of mind, and (4) as holistic process. (These concepts are discussed later in this chapter.)

## Why Use Recreation and Sports Ministry?

We've discussed the need to use recreation and sports ministry. Now it is important to understand why this ministry should be used.

### Recreation and Sports Events Are Gathering Places for People

Because people are comfortable with recreation and sporting events, they naturally gather at these events. Who isn't familiar with the crowds at basketball and football games? Festivals of all kinds draw huge crowds of people. People understand the nature and action of recreation events. They may not understand what goes on in a church worship service, but they know what happens at a basketball game. By offering recreation and sporting events, the church has a nonthreatening avenue to attract people. Parents will bring their children to the "Fourth of July Extravaganza," which features family-oriented activities, fun, food, and perhaps fireworks. This is a natural way for the church to introduce itself to the community and impact the community for Christ.

Other gathering places are sporting events—amateur and professional. Churches are taking Jesus' example and going where the people are. Christian volunteers often help event professionals by offering to work behind the scenes as parking lot attendees, errand runners, or office workers. Churches are endeavoring to be salt and light in the world, hoping for a chance to share the gospel.

## Recreation and Sports Events Bridge Cultural and Racial Barriers, Building Fellowship

Sports is one of the most universal languages. Every country, every culture plays sports. Christians who use these tools find open doors and multiple opportunities to share the gospel with people from around the world.

Opportunities abound in America to use sports to reach people. Many churches are hosting sports camps and clinics in their neighborhoods or taking teams on the road to play in prisons, being intentional to share the gospel as they go. People will gather for the event. People will listen to the players' testimonies afterward. People will respond to the message of salvation shared in a genuine way.

Here we see the church being what Christ said it should be, unified into one body. The Scripture says, "By this all people will know that you are My disciples, if you have love for one another" (John 13:35).

Recreation and sports ministry can unify and facilitate fellowship within the church. As church members fellowship together, they get to know one another better, barriers are broken down, and lasting relationships are built. Churches that exhibit fellowship and genuine concern find that people want to be a part of such a group. Everyone wants to be more than a number. Recreation events are relationship builders that personalize the church in people's lives.

## Sports and Recreation Ministry Offers Ways for Christians to Live Out Their Abilities, Interests, Talents, and Spiritual Giftedness

Each Christian is gifted by the Holy Spirit for service. Each Christian also has natural abilities, talents, and interests. God brings all of these together to make us who we are. As we learn about our spiritual gifts, we can learn how our personality, natural abilities, talents, and interests complement one another. A person may know how to coach softball but have no idea about their spiritual gifts. Through coaching the church softball team, that person can come to understand that the church is using softball to reach and disciple people. Through leading the team by coaching and ministering to their spiritual needs, he/she is being prepared for other leadership responsibilities within the church.

Sports and recreation ministry is ministry. It is:

- An outreach to nonbelievers.
- A place of discipleship for maturing Christians.
- A training ground for new leaders.

## Sports and Recreation Ministry Offers an Avenue to Gain Visibility in the Community

Through sports and recreation, churches are finding ways to make their presence in the community known. One church wanted the community to know who they were and where they were in case someone ever had a need. They decided to do a large event that involved the entire church. They involved businessmen in the community. They advertised in every media outlet. They moved church from Sunday to Saturday so the event would afford the best opportunity for people to attend. When the event took place, they had thirty thousand people on their church grounds—in a part of the country that is not known for church attendance! They gained visibility in the community that day and shared Christ in a nonthreatening way with each adult. Any church can use sports and recreation to gain visibility in the community. This is possible because in our leisure-oriented culture events help gain visibility as people respond. This has implications for the quality of the events and their perceived value to people.

## Sports and Recreation Ministry Offers a Way to Abundant Balanced Life

People are looking for something to fill the void in their lives. Recreation and sports ministry is often the first touch in a person's life with the church. This ministry area offers a way to develop a relationship with people and to introduce them to the life of the church and a relationship with Jesus Christ. Jesus said, "I have come that they might have life and have it in abundance" (John 10:10).

## Sports and Recreation Ministry Provides a Catalyst for Outreach

A catalyst is a compound added to a chemical that causes the chemical to change its molecular structure while the catalyst remains the same. As a catalyst, recreation and sports activities open doors and enable a church to reach out into a community in nonthreatening ways. Lives are changed, and relationships are developed with intentionality of ministry action.

## Sports and Recreation Ministry Provides an Environment for Fellowship

Recreation and sports events provide informal times of interaction. This leads to a deepening of relationships between participants. These events often are held in a nonreligious setting (basketball court, party, camping), putting guests at ease. As fellowship is strengthened and relationships are developed, doors open for witness and ministry. Among believers, fellowship is a foundation for building respect, unity, and loyalty in the church.

In 1937, Dr. T. B. Maston, a professor of social ethics, wrote in his book *A Handbook for Church Recreation Leaders,* "Churches need to promote play because of what it can contribute to the church as an institution. Play builds the spirit of friendliness and good fellowship. It unifies the group and contributes to a sense of solidarity and loyalty. . . . It [play] erases artificial, superficial differences and divisions in the group."[10]

## Sports and Recreation Ministry Becomes a Tool for Teaching Leadership Skills

Helping people develop leadership skills often starts with their involvement in familiar settings: coaching a team, leading an exercise class, or teaching a crafts class. With training and encouragement, leadership and ministry skills are developed that can also be used while serving on a committee or teaching a Bible study. This is a part of the ministry team's strategy of multiplying ministers.

# A Look at Leisure

Recreation and sports ministry takes place during leisure, when people are not working. This look at leisure considers five perspectives: leisure as time, leisure as activity, leisure as state of mind, leisure as an indictor of social status, and the integration of leisure in a holistic process. Each of these has implications for the church.

## Leisure Viewed as Time

During the agricultural age, work centered around producing food and providing life's necessities. Time was spent meeting the demands of daily existence and getting ready for the next harvest. During the industrial revolution, views of work and time began to change. Industrialization brought about automation. Automation brought about higher productivity; more goods could be produced in less time. Work weeks were shortened, and people found that they had free time.

This newfound leisure was fraught with challenges for culture and the church. The children of working parents needed care. Adults began to spend leisure hours at places that were not reputable in the eyes of the church. Time became something to fill with activity that could be either good or bad. Civic organizations, private businesses, government entities, and churches began to provide for constructive uses for leisure. During this period, playgrounds and national, state, and local parks began to be developed. Churches and YMCAs began to provide places to spend leisure time.

In the Christian context, leisure viewed as time has an element of stewardship. Dahl put it this way: "To a Christian, all of his time is free—his life has been given and redeemed by God—whether it is spent working or playing."[11] Ecclesiastes states that there is a time and a purpose to everything, even leisure time. The Christian has an obligation to be a good steward of leisure time.

Carlton, Deppe, and MacLean state, "Our cultural, moral, and spiritual development is dependent, in large measure, upon uses of leisure."

These writers point out that what we do with leisure is more important than perhaps our culture realizes: "The moral and spiritual forces of our country do not lose ground in the hours we are on our jobs; their battle is during the time of leisure."[12]

Most crime does not take place while people work but when they have time on their hands. The church has a responsibility to provide creative alternatives for leisure time. Paul exhorts us to "redeem the time," to use all time wisely. The church should take seriously the matter of leisure time and use it to bring people to a first-time knowledge of Christ or into a closer walk with him.

## Leisure as Activity

Listing all the activities that one could do in leisure is impossible. Separating what some consider work and others consider leisure is equally impossible. The lines between work and leisure are blurred. Some people will use the Internet for work; others use it for leisure. The same is true for music, crafts, and other activities. Laptop computers allow people to take work home, further blurring the lines between work and leisure.

Geoffrey Godbey put it this way: "In the Christian life, leisure activities should be of a positive nature, be socially acceptable and contribute to healthy personal adjustment, relaxation or enjoyment."[13] He said that whatever we do as Christians in our leisure should contribute to our overall well-being as a person. Paul put it this way: "Whatever you do, do everything for God's glory" (1 Cor. 10:31). Christians should live out their leisure lives as unto God, seeking to please him in every activity. The church should endeavor to provide activities that draw out the best in people and bring them closer to God.

## Leisure as a State of Mind

Going back to the Latin root for "leisure," *licere* meaning "to be permitted or absence of restraint," we see that this view of leisure is not associated with time, work, or location. Leisure is viewed as how one's mind perceives the experience. Leisure can take place anywhere, at anytime, with anyone—at home, at work, or at an event. The state of mind is the focus.

American culture is increasingly experiential in its orientation to leisure. Increasingly our culture reflects leisure as a state of mind. This concept carries both positive and negative connotations. On the positive side, one may see any leisure experience—whether sports, picnics, or worship—as wonderful. One may say afterward, "I really got a lot out of that." On the negative side, being preoccupied may cause one to have ambivalent feelings about the experience. A person might not "enjoy" the leisure experience because of distractions. This view has nothing to do with location or time. It is the experience that counts, and the mind dictates the quality of the experience.

For the church the implications of this view are important. As a state of mind, worship could be viewed as leisure—engaging the body, mind, and spirit to bring refreshment and re-creation. In this view, worship changes our state of mind as we focus on God. Worship becomes a state-of-mind leisure choice. One could argue that worship is the ultimate leisure-choice activity. True worship brings about a re-creativity of mind and spirit.

In the purely recreational setting, this view says that the experience is everything. Postmoderns are looking for the next experience. Interactive media's proliferation, the growth of recreational risk activities, and the popularity of reality TV shows are evidence of this. If a recreation and sports ministry wants to attract people, it should provide interactive experiences that engage both the body and the mind.

## Leisure as an Indicator of Social Status

Throughout history leisure activities indicate social rank. The working class took their leisure where and when they could find it, usually after long hours in the fields or factories. Country clubs were for the rich who could afford the fees. Travel was for the well-to-do who could afford both the time away and the money for tickets, accommodations, and food. The working class, worried about the next crop or whether they would be laid off, rarely spent money or time on leisure pursuits.

Today the division of class by leisure pursuit is still evident. While most people have access to some form of leisure activity, the differences between the upper, middle, and lower classes are real. Distinctions are made by everything from the brand of athletic shoe, to the symbol on a shirt, to the events one attends during leisure and the vacation spots one picks. Some can afford four-star accommodations while others seek campgrounds. Status and image are fostered on society by Madison Avenue as they tell us what to wear, where to dine, and what sports beverage to drink. People seek to convey an image as they choose their leisure pursuits.

Churches in general are impacted by indicators of status. Churches often build recreation and sports complexes for the wrong reasons: to keep up with another church, to keep the kids off the street, or to cure all their financial problems. Churches who do this may hurt themselves in the long run. While properly planned, staffed, and programmed recreation centers can be a valuable tool to facilitate ministry, the church should seek to provide recreation and sports ministry that meets the expressed needs of the people and fulfills the mission of that particular church. The church should provide events and activities that people can afford and that will help that church live out its mission. Churches must be careful not to foster a "country club" attitude in the use of their facilities or programming.

### Leisure Seen as a Holistic Process

This view sees leisure as an integrative whole encompassing all that a person is, experiences, and desires in recreation experiences. This view takes into account the totality of a person's life—work, family, church, education, and other elements that represent a balanced life. The holistic approach perhaps best fits the biblical model of man; life is lived in relationship to others and the world around us. A Christian worldview of this holistic model of leisure would hold that man does not live a compartmentalized life of disjointed events and activities, but that in God's plan for our lives, we are made up of the sum total of our experiences. We are formed by God with a specific set of natural talents, interests, and abilities that make us who we are. And because we are all different, God chooses to give us spiritual gifts to complement our natural abilities and interests for his glory. We use the sum total of all that we are as stewards of leisure to bring glory to God.

## Recreation and Sports Ministry Viewed as Model and Process (M.A.P.)

Instead of recreation and sports ministry, perhaps what we need to talk about is being a kingdom people doing a kingdom work as the body of Christ. Otherwise we may become so wrapped up in trying one new method after another that we lose sight of our God-given direction.

Methods are important, but they never can take the place of following the clear biblical commands to be God's people. We know who we are in Christ and by what he has called us and gifted us to do. The means of doing recreation and sports ministry as kingdom work is not to become more important than the lost persons we are trying to reach or the new Christians we are trying to disciple.

Alan Raughton, director of LifeWay Sunday School in Nashville, Tennessee, says:

> The existence and activity of the church are rooted in God's purposes to bring His kingdom to fulfillment. The kingdom is present wherever the will and reign of God are established in people's lives through the presence of Jesus Christ. Therefore, a biblically sound understanding of church ministry is one with a kingdom focus. It is one where believers see themselves on a kingdom mission: to make disciples of the spiritually lost by bringing them into a right relationship with God through Jesus Christ.
>
> The outcome of faithful obedience will be kingdom growth. Growth becomes God's supernatural work through His people to accomplish His kingdom's purposes. It is the result of God's people obeying His will and His Word in the world in relationship to evangelizing the spiritually lost.[14]

## Defining a Kingdom-Focused Church Model and Process

Biblical principles identify the primary teachings from Scripture that give direction to the scope and work of the church in relationship to its efforts to lead an unbeliever from the condition of being lost without Christ to service as an obedient disciple of Christ.

*The One Great Commission (Matt. 28:18–20)*—The Great Commission defines God's mission for the church, for recreation and sports ministry, and for individual believers. Without the driving force of the Great Commission, any attempt at recreation and sports ministry will be little more than a misguided attempt to use new techniques.

*The Five Church Functions (Acts 2:38–47)*—Recreation and sports ministry acts as a support in the life of the church, or it can act as a lead ministry at times as a part of the following five functions.

1. *Evangelism (Acts 2:38–41)*—In recreation and sports ministry, evangelism must be an intentional part of each event, class, seminar, or workshop. Christian evangelism is the process of sharing the gospel with lost persons and winning people to Christ. In the case of recreation and sports ministry, leaders must be intentional at every point for effective evangelism to take place. Recreation and sports ministry offers the church culturally relevant tools to impact people.

2. *Discipleship (Acts 2:42–43)*—Recreation and sports ministry offers avenues of teaching new Christians about their response to God in love, trust, and obedience, and how to win and train others to do the same.

3. *Ministry (Acts 2:44–45)*—Recreation and sports ministry offers a natural way for Christians to use their gifts, talents, abilities, and interests in ministry to others.

4. *Fellowship (Acts 2:42, 46–47)*—Recreation and sports ministry is a means to facilitate fellowship in the church formally and informally.

5. *Worship (Acts 2:46–47)*—Recreation and sports ministry can facilitate worship that transforms by helping believers to encounter God in worship. This can be done as participants are guided to open-group worship settings or as worship is facilitated on a retreat, at a camp, at a fellowship event, or on the soccer field.

***Relationship to Spiritual Transformation***—Recreation and sports ministry, through its strategies and methodologies, addresses three stages of spiritual transformation in the life of a believer:

1. *Making disciples* represents the efforts to win the lost.

2. *Maturing believers* represents the efforts to disciple new believers and members.

3. *Multiplying ministries* represents providing opportunities for service and missions.

## Ministry Practice Strategies

Church ministry practice strategies are the clear and deliberate intentions and plans of action that are necessary if a church or any ministry area is to achieve its ministry objectives. While primarily seen as a part of a ministry team strategy, a well-balanced recreation and sports ministry will seek to impact all four foundational strategies of corporate worship, open groups, closed groups, and ministry teams.

A *corporate worship strategy* exists to celebrate God's grace and mercy, to proclaim God's truth, and to evangelize the lost. The corporate worship service is an open-group strategy of believers and unbelievers. Recreation and sports ministry complements worship as it directs participants to worship or as it provides worship opportunities at recreation events. (See Acts 2:46–47.)

An *open-group strategy* exists to lead nonbelievers to faith in the Lord Jesus Christ and to build on-mission Christians by providing ongoing, evangelistic Bible study units. Recreation and sports ministry seeks to build relationships between Christians in open groups and nonbelievers for the purpose of getting the nonbelievers into an open-group Bible study. Paul sets the example in Acts 17:10–12.

A *closed-group strategy* exists to build kingdom leaders and to equip believers to serve by engaging people in discipleship that moves them toward spiritual transformation. Recreation and sports ministry impacts closed groups as it provides an atmosphere of relational fellowship and ministry opportunities. Priscilla and Aquila model this strategy in instructing Apollos in Acts 18:24–28.

A *ministry team strategy* exists to build up the body of Christ to accomplish the work of service within the church and to be involved in missions outside the church. Recreation and sports ministry fits the ministry team strategy as it seeks to provide opportunities for Christian growth and intentionally evangelistic ministry using recreation and sports as tools. Examples of these two ministry team concepts—one internal, another external—can be seen in Acts 6:1–3 and 13:1–3.

From a practical point of view, effective recreation and sports ministry strategies are implemented through an ongoing process involving ten essential actions that guide its development. These actions take place in the context of a comprehensive churchwide process rather than as independent actions. This approach underscores the value of developing a holistic plan, the interrelationship of the four church practice strategies, and the collaborative spirit needed by recreation and sports ministry leaders for the good of the whole.

Essential actions for effective recreation and sports ministry as a part of the ministry team strategy include:

1. Commit to the recreation and sports ministry as an important open-group strategy.

2. Minister with purpose.
3. Build ministry leaders through training.
4. Develop soul winners.
5. Intentionally plan to win the lost.
6. Intentionally assimilate new people into open groups.
7. Reach out to all age groups and family types.
8. Guide all leaders to lead/teach to transform lives.
9. Set the right team structure to maximize ministry.
10. Multiply leaders and ministry actions.

## Methodologies

Each strategy is carried out through methodologies. A methodology becomes the ministry's practical application targeted at specific objectives of the strategy and mission statement of the church. Balanced programming in recreation and sports ministry is essential for effectiveness. The programming becomes the way methodologies are carried out. For example, programming for a basketball league or a crafts class becomes a methodology for carrying out the ministry team strategy. Methodologies need to be dynamic as determined by surveys, needs of the church, and opportunities afforded by the local church context and culture.

## Kingdom Results

Four kinds of growth result when a church implements ministry through worship, open groups, closed groups, and ministry teams. The kingdom results are numerical, spiritual transformation, ministry expansion, and kingdom advance.

*Numerical Growth*—The ministry of the recreation and sports ministry should be measurable in membership, baptisms, and attendance levels as it impacts the other ministry areas of the church.

*Spiritual Transformation*—Leaders and participants alike should be spiritually transformed. Nonbelievers are transformed as they come to Christ. Christians are transformed as they grow to be more like Christ— on and off the court.

*Ministry Expansion*—New avenues of ministry are found as the Holy Spirit provides new opportunities and brings new people into the ministry. Recreation and sports ministry will always be expanding as new tools become available. Who knew about X-Games in the 1980s?

***Kingdom Advance***—Recreation and sports ministry affords many mission and ministry opportunities. Any sport/league/workshop/class/fellowship/outdoor education activity/continuing education class or health and wellness event that can be done at a church can be taken on the road and done as a mission/ministry action. Recreation and sports ministry will open many doors and provide many opportunities to reach out as it seeks to advance the kingdom of God.

Recreation and sports ministry is a part of the whole, a ministry team strategy that impacts and builds every other ministry strategy in the church. Relationships with all other ministry strategy areas are vital to the longevity and functionality of the ministry. Recreation and sports ministry is neither more important nor less important than any other ministry area or strategy in the church. As all ministry strategies learn to function as a whole, the church will see people won to Christ, people discipled, and people multiplying themselves in ministry.

## Intentional Ministry

People come to Christ as the Holy Spirit works through others—the right people at the right time bringing them to the point of commitment. After the commitment is made, the process of discipleship is started that lasts a lifetime. As a ministry team's strategy, recreation and sports ministry offers the church a nonthreatening first touch in people's lives. The following outline of the spiritual pilgrimage is typical for most people.

Most of the time, a person does not come to Christ the first time he or she hears the gospel. A process of evangelism happens in a person's life. Often this process involves a decision point or crisis. Alan Tippett, an Australian Methodist missionary, in his book *Verdict Theology in Missionary Theory*, describes the process as one of change that includes a period of awareness, a point of realization, a point of encounter, and a period of incorporation. It is illustrated here in stages that include a recreation and sports ministry encounter.[15]

1. Period of No Awareness of Need for Christ
   The person is unaware of his or her need for salvation.
2. Period of Initial Awareness
   • Perceives need
   • Seeks education, fitness, continuing education, etc.
   • Joins in a recreation activity to meet perceived needs

- Has encounter with believer(s)
- Becomes aware of real (spirit) need
- Sees gospel lived out in a real-world way

3. Period of Deeper Awareness
   - Meets other Christians
   - Continues recreation activity involvement
   - Hears the gospel explained

4. Period of Realization
   - Begins to understand
   - Builds/strengthens relationships
   - Introduced to larger church life (worship)
   - May join a Bible study
   - May join other activities
   - May face crisis or period of questioning past experiences
   - Turns to friends for answers
   - Recognizes the need for change
   - Has a salvation experience
   - Turns to Christ through repentance
   - Prays to receive Christ

5. Period of Discipleship
   - Begins time of spiritual growth (in a closed-group discipleship experience)
   - Takes on role in recreation ministry according to interest
   - Feels prepared to take on larger role in life of church

6. Period of Multiplication
   - Begins to reach out to others using gifts, talents, and abilities multiplying self in the lives of others through involvement in a ministry team

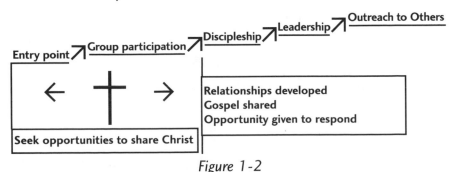

Figure 1-2

Recreation and sports ministry offers one of the best avenues to impact our culture. To the skateboarder, we will offer skateboarding events. To the quilter, we will offer quilting classes. To the fitness minded, we will offer aerobics and nutrition classes. To the basketball player, we will offer opportunities to play the game.

As we attempt to reach these groups, we must be intentional in sharing the gospel at each opportunity. We must be deliberate, with a settled determination and a calculated plan to win people to Christ, using all the tools at our disposal. Otherwise, we become like any other recreation and sports activity supplier. The Christ distinctive must permeate all that we do.

---

### Notes

1. "The Modern Movement for Better Rural Church Buildings," *Church Administration* (October 1927): 2.

2. Kansas Sports Hall of Fame, "Dr. James Naismith," downloaded from http://www.kshof.org/inductees/naismith.html. Accessed on 4 September 2002.

3. James A. Mathisen, "'I'm Majoring in SPORT Ministry': Religion and Sport in Christian Colleges," *Books & Culture* (May/June 1998): 24.

4. Joanne B. Ciulla, *The Working Life: The Promise and Betrayal of Modern Work,* as cited in Alice Stein Wellner, "The End of Leisure," *American Demographics* (1 July 2000): 50.

5. "LeisureTrak," downloaded from http//www.leisuretrends.com. Accessed on 27 January 2002.

6. Gordon Dahl, "Emergence of a Leisure Ethic," *Christian Century* (8 November 1972): 1, 124–27.

7. Ibid.

8. Ibid., 26.

9. Bob Briner, *Roaring Lambs* (Grand Rapids, Mich.: Zondervan, 1993), 31.

10. T. B. Maston, *A Handbook for Church Recreation Leaders* (Nashville: The Sunday School Board of the Southern Baptist Convention, 1937), 33.

11. Gordon J. Dahl, *Work, Play and Worship* (Minneapolis: Augsburg Publishing House, 1972), 61–62.

12. Carlton, Deppe, and MacLean, *Recreation in American Life* (Belmont: Wadsworth Publishing Company, Inc., 1963), 3–4.

13. Geoffrey Godbey, *Leisure in Your Life,* 2nd ed. (State College, Pa.: Venture Publishing, Inc. 1985), 70.

14. Alan Raughton, "Report on Church Ministry Leadership," LifeWay Christian Resources, 2002.

15. A. R. Tippett, *Verdict Theology in Missionary Theory* (Lincoln, Ill.: Lincoln Christian College Press, 1969), 100–103.

# 2

# Biblical Foundations of Sports Ministry: Defining the Phenomenon

## Rodger Oswald

### Cultural/Historical Perspective

The phenomenon of sports ministry as a church tool is sometimes eschewed because some may think the Jewish and/or early church cultures—as well as the cultures in which they existed—did not participate in any form of recreation or sports. Actually, that is not the case. While the Jewish culture certainly rejected the recreational and sporting bent of Egyptian, Babylonian, and Assyrian cultures (all having various forms of leisure activities, various celebrations, and sporting competition relating to preparation for war), archeological discoveries indicate that some leisure time was devoted to "word games" and "board games." Geoffrey Godbey put it this way: "Of all the links between leisure and religion, the common root of celebration is the most important."[1] These same discoveries included finding children's dolls.

Even in Scripture, play is evident as a part of the Jewish culture as Zechariah (8:5) and Isaiah (11:8–9) make reference to boys and girls playing. The leisure aspect of the "garden experience" speaks to leisure within the context of walking through this peaceful environment with God.

Like the nation of Israel, the early Christian community avoided most overt expressions of sporting competition that were replete in the Roman and hellenized cultures around them, but even the forerunners to the Olympic Games were fodder for Paul's metaphorical language in explaining the Christian experience (1 Cor. 9:24–27; 2 Tim. 2:5; 4:7). Jesus also taught, without condemnation of innocent, playful children, that the kingdom of God would be discovered in their innocence and openness.

The reality is that while the Old Testament Jews and the New Testament believers did avoid most sporting activities, play, games, and leisure activities did permeate their cultures, and Scripture does not criticize those activities. Certainly one's motivations, actions, and attitudes within those activities give opportunity for rebuke and/or instruction, but the activities themselves are not condemned.

## Theological Perspective

This is not intended to be a thorough examination of a theological position to justify recreation and sports ministry; however, it seems prudent at least to offer a theological grid through which we can pass the sports ministry in order to establish a logical position, consistent with Scripture, regarding this cultural phenomenon.

*Theology* introduces us to the facts that the God of the Bible is a redemptive God (Gen. 3, 7, 12; Luke 19:10). God is also declared to be a relational God (John 1:12; Heb. 4:16) who is gracious and liberating (Rom. 5:8; Eph. 2:8–9; Gal. 2:16).[2]

*Anthropology* declares that man is a fallen creature (Rom. 3:10–12) with the consequence that he is separated from a Holy God (Rom. 3:23).[3]

*Soteriology's* blessed message is that because God is redemptive and relational, man has the potential to become a child of God (Rom. 6:23; John 1:12; 3:16). With this new identity (relationship), redeemed man now has holy purpose; he has responsibilities that accompany his position (1 Pet. 1:16; 2:9; Acts 1:8). Having been redeemed, man is actively involved in growing in holiness as he becomes a herald of the gospel, a witness of Jesus Christ.[4]

*Ecclesiology* speaks to the issue of the church being God's agency for the Age of Grace (also called the Church Age); however, since the word *church (ecclesia)* is defined as "called out ones," the church is not a building but a worldwide body of believers. While these believers are heaven bound, the earthly call is to congregate in order to worship, to grow into the likeness of Christ, and to participate in the global mission of making Jesus Christ known.[5]

As people participate in these four theological positions, nowhere does Scripture mandate or forbid the use of leisure, recreation, and/or sports. In fact, modern society is demonstrating that redeemed man within the context of a well-organized recreation and sports ministry (usually within a local church) can be an extremely effective tool for communicating Jesus Christ, seeing people come to faith, assimilating them into the local church, and assisting them in their spiritual growth.

## Biblical Perspective

### The Mandate

In attempting to discover the place of sports and recreation in the church, the question must be asked, "Is there a clear mandate that compels the believer?" In other words, is there evidence of an overarching command given by the Lord that applies to all believers? Jesus answered that question in all four Gospel accounts as well as the Book of Acts. In Mark 16:15, Jesus said that the gospel is to be preached to all creation. In Luke 24:47, Jesus said that forgiveness in his name is to be proclaimed to all the nations. In Matthew 28:19, Jesus said that disciples were to be made of all the nations (people groups). In John 17:18, Jesus, as he prayed to his Father, said that he was sending his disciples into the world, just as the Father had sent him. Some feel that Jesus was talking about the Apostles only, but in verse 20 Jesus said, "I pray not only for these [the Apostles], but also for those who believe in Me through their message."

In debate, the preferred speaking position is last since people tend to remember what was spoken last. Perhaps that might give even greater credence to this mandate when one looks at Acts 1:8 and the postresurrection scene when Jesus uttered his last words on earth just before he ascended into heaven: "And you will be My witnesses in Jerusalem, in all Judea and Samaria, and to the ends of the earth."

The mandate is clear: Jesus is to be proclaimed. Jesus is to be preached. Christians are to have a testimony. We are to be witnesses of Jesus Christ into all the world.

**The Means**

While the command of Jesus is abundantly clear, the question remains, who is supposed to do this? It seems to be clear by the calling of disciples (Matt. 4:19; Mark 1:17) that Jesus meant to impact individuals so that they, in turn, could impact others. The apostle Paul certainly understood and taught this same principle (2 Tim. 2:2).

Often this individual responsibility is referred to as a *call*. While the term *call* is used in a more specific way (particularly as applied to pastors and missionaries, for example), there is a sense in which Jesus says to every believer, "Follow me." This can be referred to as the *general* call of those who say they are Christians (followers of Christ) or disciples (those who follow after, learn from, and apply the things that are learned).

Beyond the general call, Scripture clearly communicates a *personal* call. In 2 Corinthians 5:17–20, the apostle Paul described the "new things" that come into the life of one who is "in Christ" (a Christian). One of those new things, according to verse 18, is to become a minister (servant) of the message of reconciliation—to serve the message that, as God has made up with me, he also is willing to make up with you. In addition to being a servant of the message of God's reconciling love, the one who is in Christ is also called on to be an ambassador of Christ—to represent the policies of our sovereign King in the world. The personal passion of this calling is seen in that we would even beg (plead, implore) people to be reconciled to God.

In addition to the general and the personal calls, there seems to be a *specific* call based on the people God uses in the Book of Acts. As the church is birthed and begins to grow, a variety of people are "called" into service to the gospel message. Not all of these people are spiritual giants, graduates of seminaries, or longtime leaders of the church. Using just one example from Acts 15, Paul and Barnabas separated over the issue of taking John Mark with them on the second missionary journey. It is not clear why Barnabas was so adamant about taking John Mark. While it might be a family connection, a case can be made that Barnabas saw in John Mark some quality that, in spite of previous failure, would make him uniquely serviceable for the sake of the gospel. Certainly the Gospel of Mark gives credence to the confidence Barnabas had in him.

While Barnabas took John Mark with him, Paul chose to take a man named Silas. It would be fair to ask, "Why Silas?" While Scripture doesn't answer this question, some conclusions could be reached. Paul is going to preach to Roman citizens. Who better to take than a Roman citizen? Paul was going as a representative of the Jerusalem Council. Who better to take than a member of that council? Paul was going to preach about a living God. Who better to take than a prophet of God?

Providentially, Silas was a Roman citizen (Acts 16:37), a member of the Jerusalem Council (Acts 15:22), and a prophet (Acts 15:32). But think about this: *did* Paul take Silas because he had the right passport, was a member of the right organization, and would serve as a spokesman for God? While the last is certainly a critical component, the first two seem to be circumstantial reasons. Perhaps Paul took Silas because of a "special call" of God to use the distinctives of his life for the sake of the gospel.

The significance of this can be seen in that each person has unique gifts and talents that make that person valuable in distinct situations. While some may be profitable "for the sake of the gospel" because they sing or play an instrument, others will be profitable because they kick a soccer ball, wield a paint brush, hit a baseball, run swiftly, love the out of doors, or shoot a basketball with accuracy. Could it be that this special call creates a platform whereby the athlete has access to other athletes because of a special skill? Could it be that one's talents create an opportunity to impact the millions who watch, read about, or participate in sports on a recreational level? The bottom line is that while there are a general and a personal call, there is also a special call as people use unique talents or abilities to fulfill the mandate given by the Savior.

Of course, God never intended for the individual to operate independently. By command, by his presence, and by the blending of gifts, God intends for the individual to be a part of a greater whole known as the church. While the Greek word for *church (ecclesia)* refers to people who are "the called out ones," the fuller expression of this phenomenon is seen as the "local assembly" that Hebrews (10:25) warns us not to forsake. The birthing of the church in Acts is fleshed out in 1 and 2 Timothy and Titus, and the church that Jesus said he would build (Matt. 16:18) takes shape. As one reads the pastoral Epistles, the ministry of the local church becomes clearer. While some debate the issue of primacy, the local church has three primary functions: first, to provide/create vibrant corporate worship; second, to create an environment and opportunity to grow in faith (often referred to as edification or the process of discipleship); and third, to mobilize in order to fulfill the Great Commission (often referred to as evangelism).

## The Methodology

If the mandate is clear and the means to carry out that mandate is equally clear, the issue, then, is for the church to determine a biblical pattern for carrying out the mandate. At this point it would be wonderful if we could go to Scripture and discover chapter and verse that clearly communicated that X church should employ sports and recreation as a means of fulfilling God-ordained responsibilities. The problem is that chapter and verse cannot be found that condones, charges, or advocates the use of sports and recreation as a part of the church mission. The Bible is equally silent about other issues, yet we find precedence by virtue of biblical principles. For example, the Bible is silent regarding watching of television or going to movies, but God's Word contains principles that guide us as to what to watch, how much to watch, and how much to spend in order to watch.

While the Bible is silent regarding television, it is not silent about the principle of a transformed mind (Rom. 12:2) or the wise use of time (Eph. 5:16). By the same token, biblical principles are germane to the propriety of sports and recreation ministry while carrying out the mandates of Christ.

The following principles are offered to create an apologetic that endorses, liberates, and compels one to consider where this unique ministry ought to fit into one's life or into the ministry life of the church.

## Principle of Divine Diversity

The God of the Bible is a majestic, multifaceted God. He is diverse in his *essence;* he is a triune God—Father, Son, and Holy Spirit.

He is diverse in his *character.* In the Old Testament, the Jews referred to God based on how they personally experienced him and, therefore, called him Jehovah Jirah, God my Provider; or Jehovah Nissi, God my Banner, the one who goes before me; or El Elyon, Almighty God. In the New Testament, John's Gospel refers to Jesus as "the door," "the resurrection, and the life," "the way, the truth, and the life," and "the good shepherd," all ways of communicating his diverse personhood.

In both the Old and the New Testaments, the godhead is seen as diverse in *ministry.* To carry out the will and work of God, God works in diverse ways. In the Old Testament, God walked and talked with Adam; to Moses he was a burning bush, and to the nation of Israel he was the Shechinah Glory—a pillar of fire by night and a cloud by day. In the New Testament, Jesus healed some but not all; he preached to multitudes but discipled a few, focusing on twelve. He preached to many, gently rebuked a few, and intentionally provoked others. The Holy Spirit counsels, convicts, teaches, and comforts. The point is that our majestic God works in a variety of ways. He is creative and diverse.

Genesis 1:26–27 says that man has been created in the image of God. Since Scripture reveals that God is not flesh and bone (Luke 24:39), the question arises: in what way are we like God's image? The answer could be that as our God is diverse and creative, his creation is blessed with that same creative bent, some more than others; but all of creation seems to have the capacity to meet and resolve problems, overcome barriers, and deal with the circumstances of life.

God has granted to human beings the ability to deal creatively with the world around them. Of course, that ability is flawed and frail until a person comes into a relationship with God through Jesus Christ. The created needs to learn to be as creative as the Creator.

With that as the premise, it seems logical that people would discover the most creative ways of carrying out the mandate of Jesus. It seems that Christians, within the context of the church (the means), need to discover the most strategic methodology to accomplish that mandate. The creative bent ought to turn people to sports and recreation not because sports and recreation is so important but because it becomes a means to build relationships with the lost. Through those relationships Jesus Christ can be lived out and proclaimed. The questions ought to be asked: Where are the people of our society? Where do they congregate? The answer is in the gymnasiums and on the fields of sports and recreation.

## Principle of Human Talents

This principle is not to be confused with spiritual gifts. This principle refers to human gifts and abilities that are God given. In Psalm 139, the psalmist praises God for the fact that he is an omnipresent God, so omnipresent that he was even involved intimately in the psalmist's birth (v. 13). The psalmist declares that God created him as a spiritual being (*inward parts* is a Hebrew expression for soul or spirit), as a physical being (*frame* is the Hebrew word for bones), and that God's work was thoughtful and careful (*skillfully wrought* is the Hebrew expression for carefully made; a literal translation of the word means "to crochet; to create delicate lace"). The implication here is that God has made each person exactly as he willed and that creation is "fearfully and wonderfully made."

If we serve a God of order and not chaos, there is logic and purpose behind his every act, even the granting of physical skills and ability. In Exodus 35–36, Moses was following the command of the Lord and having the tabernacle of the Lord built. Those two chapters reveal that God gave the physical ability to those who were to build a dwelling place for God. God gave the craftsmanship to those who were to design and construct this structure. This is an Old Testament picture of the fact that God dwelt "among" his people (Exod. 25:8). In the New Testament, God dwells "in" his people (Gal. 2:20) in order that they might create the ultimate tabernacle revealed in 1 Peter 2:5 when Peter wrote, "You yourselves [we], as living stones, are being built into a spiritual house for a holy priesthood." As God indwells the believer, we, as living stones, fulfill our role as priests, proclaiming "the praises of the One who called you out of darkness into His marvelous light" (1 Pet. 2:9). In doing so we participate in kingdom building, in creating that ultimate spiritual house.

God has blessed every person with certain physical skills and/or abilities, and each person participates in kingdom building when those skills and abilities are used to declare Jesus Christ. When the soloist sings, or the pastor preaches, or the athlete uses his or her sport as a platform for serving the purposes of God, each is fulfilling God's will as it pertains to his kingdom purposes. To fail to use what God has given us through our physical creation denies the very order and sovereignty of God.

## Principle of Liberty

Since this is an attempt to discover the latitude that the church has (individually or corporately) to employ sports and recreation as a ministry tool, the principle of liberty is crucial. If this principle cannot be substantiated, the church ought not consider this type of ministry.

Paul was an advocate of liberty—not license but true liberty in Jesus Christ. He, like Jesus Christ, fought against religiosity or legalism that constrained rather than freed the believer. In fact, in 1 Corinthians 9:1, Paul made his declaration of independence when he said, "Am I not free?"

He was not saying he was free to do whatever he wanted or free to do anything that was unrighteous. He was indicating that he was free from any sort of legalistic posture or man-made rules if they interfered with the proclamation of the gospel. First Corinthians 9:23 says, "Now I do all this because of the gospel." That was Paul's driving desire. It was so important to him that he was willing to fight convention if it meant a greater audience for the gospel. This proclamation of freedom was so strong that he indicated he was willing to be Jewish (those under the Law) or "pagan" (those without the Law) for the sake of their salvation. Paul was saying that he was willing to be culturally relevant even if it meant adapting to another culture at the expense of his own.

When Paul wanted to reach his Jewish brethren, he went to the synagogue in his yarmulke and robe; but when they were unresponsive, he took off the yarmulke and robe and went to the city gates or town square where the Gentiles (pagans) were. He would adapt culturally for the sake of preaching the gospel. Paul went so far as to be willing to go to a specific location to reach a specific portion of his society (the philosophers on Mars Hill) in order to preach Jesus Christ. He was even unconventional enough to rent a pagan meeting place for the sake of preaching Christ.

If Paul can be that free, is it possible that today's church can be equally free and as culturally relevant? If so, the church must go to today's Mars Hill or Halls of Tyrannus. The church must go to the fields of play or the buildings that house competition and games.

Paul addressed the same issue of freedom in Galatians 5. In verse 1 Paul said, "Christ has liberated us into freedom. Therefore stand firm and don't submit again to a yoke of slavery." The freedom Paul addressed is the freedom from man-made rules, in this case the rules that would add Jewish ceremony to salvation by grace through faith alone. Today there are those who condemn sports and recreation ministry, not because the Bible condemns it but because man-made rules have determined that it is wrong. Paul's answer would be that he has been freed from the conventions and rules of men and that he yields to a higher set of rules. The first is that he has been set free by grace. In other words Paul wanted to be set free to proclaim Christ without being hindered by arbitrary rules.

The only question the church must ask is whether something violates the clear teaching of Scripture. There is freedom in Christ, freedom to experience the grace of God in salvation as well as sanctification in order to realize freedom in making Christ known. Some conjecture that sports and recreation ought to be one of these freedoms. In fact, if the apostle Paul were alive today, he might be an athletic musician or a musical athlete because those are two universal languages that would give him greatest access to people in order to proclaim Jesus Christ.

## Principle of Silence

Often when ministry through sports and recreation is challenged, the argument is that Scripture does not clearly say a church should have this type of ministry. The sentiment that silence precludes the use of sports ministry is actually an argument *for* sports ministry.

When discussing this issue, one must agree that the Bible does not promote or indicate that a church should have a sports ministry. By the same token, the Bible does not denigrate, deny, nor state that a church should not have a sports ministry. The reality is that the Bible is silent on the issue, but this silence speaks rather loudly when one carefully examines Scripture.

In dealing with the silence issue, the question must be asked, "Who wrote the Bible?" Using Scripture to answer the question, the answer is that God wrote the Bible (2 Tim. 3:16; 2 Pet. 1:21). Yes, writers were involved, but the reality is that they wrote only what the Holy Spirit prompted them to write, and the Holy Spirit only prompted what God spoke. Therefore, when Paul referred to the Christian experience as running in a race, and the writer of Hebrews referred to one's life as a Christian as an endurance race, and when Paul compared Christianity to an athlete, who really wrote that—man or God? The answer is God.

That, then, leads to another question, this one dealing with God's character. Is he holy? The obvious answer is yes; the conclusion, then, is that what God has written is wholly righteous, without sin, totally holy. Therefore, if something were inherently evil or sinful about sports, a holy God would not have used sports or athletes as a metaphor for the Christian experience. While the Bible is silent, the use of sporting metaphors clearly indicates that God has no problem with sports. Otherwise, he would have added a caveat when those comparisons were used in 1 Corinthians, Hebrews, and 2 Timothy.

## Other Principles

Without going into detail, numerous other principles could be used. For example, the Principle of Tithing or of Stewardship could be used to go along with the Principle of Human Talents. If God has given gifts to the believer, should the believer not use them to bring glory to God? Should the recipient not carefully tend and use everything entrusted to him by God, even the ability to hit a baseball or shoot a basketball, providing those activities were used to glorify and thank God (Col. 3:17, 23)?

Another powerful principle is the Principle of Preparation. Since the Christian experience includes the process of being conformed to the image of Christ (Rom. 8:29) and this process is not completed until the believer dies (Phil. 1:6), how is it possible to develop the character that James (James 1:2–4), Peter (1 Pet. 1:6–7), and Paul (Rom. 5:3–5) describe? All three seem to indicate that trials (problems) will be a part of this refining process. That process is exacerbated by the fact that we are all engaged in spiritual warfare (Eph. 6:10–20; 1 Pet. 5:8), and, like any soldier, we need to go through boot camp. The fields of sports competition are the training ground in secular things so that the competitor might learn to succeed in spiritual battle.

While the Bible is silent on the specific issue of sports and recreation ministry, it is not silent on the call of the individual and the church to carry out the mandate of making Jesus Christ known in our own backyard and then to the whole world. It seems prudent to find the most effective way of doing that without compromising any standard of holiness.

Since sports and recreation are merely games, it seems unfair to classify them as sinful or a wrong pursuit for the individual or the church. What would be wrong is if God has given us a culturally strategic means of reaching people with the gospel and we failed to use it because someone says, "I think it is wrong," or "I think sports is sinful," or "We've never done this before."

Surely the biblical principles discussed (and there are others) grant the individual or the church the latitude to consider this type of ministry. The error would be to fail to implement what God has not condemned on the notion that he has, when that notion is merely man-made.

If the Bible condemns sports or recreation or if the Bible warns against them, the believer and the church should take notice and obey out of respect for God's Word, or as a demonstration of wisdom. However, there is no biblical condemnation, not even a suggestion of condemnation, of sports or recreation. Individuals need to feel freedom to use their athletic gifts, and the church needs to feel freedom to use their athletically gifted, as long as those gifts are used to the Lord, for his glory and for the kingdom's sake.

### Notes

1. Geoffrey Godbey, *Leisure in Your Life: An Exploration*, 5th ed. (State College, Pa.: Venture Publishing, 1999), 162.

2. Lewis Sperry Chafer, *Chafer Systematic Theology*, vol. 1 (Dallas Seminary/Zondervan, 1947), 129, 244, 257, 313.

3. Lewis Sperry Chafer, *Chafer Systematic Theology*, vol. 2 (Dallas Seminary/Zondervan, 1947), 217–23, 360–61.

4. Lewis Sperry Chafer, *Chafer Systematic Theology*, vol. 3 (Dallas Seminary/Zondervan, 1947), 55–72, 223–51, 255.

5. Lewis Sperry Chafer, *Chafer Systematic Theology*, vol. 4 (Dallas Seminary/Zondervan, 1947), 16, 21, 149–51.

# 3 Visions and Re-Visions: A History of the Modern Church Recreation and Sports Movement in the United States

Brad Wesner

Today most Americans take recreation for granted in the church setting. From church softball teams to church picnics, the congregation just wouldn't be a church if it weren't for recreation. Believe it or not, though, the American church has not always been so favorable toward recreation.

The modern church recreation and sports movement in the United States has roots extending through the Old Testament, pagan cultures, and church history. In the United States, church recreation developed in three stages. The first period, the Era of Apathy and Disgust, began with the colonization of New England in 1620 and continued through 1872. Although the church generally frowned upon recreation during this period (if it noticed recreation at all), modern church recreation leaders drew upon unique pieces of philosophy from this period to justify the church's eventual incorporation of recreation.

The Era of Apathy and Disgust closed in 1872 with a dramatic win by antirecreation leaders. In 1872, the Methodist Episcopal Church passed legislation banning all amusements in general and many by name, including dancing, theatergoing, and horse racing. Other denominations had already passed similar bans. The Presbyterian Church singled out dancing and theater in an 1843 ban, which it reaffirmed in 1865. The Provincial Council of Baltimore, the voice of the bishops of the Roman Catholic Church, banned the theater and novels in 1869. The Episcopal

Church targeted "gaming," "amusements involving cruelty to the brute creation," and "theatrical representations" in an 1817 ban. And numerous Southern Baptist congregations established rules banning dancing. It was the Methodist ban, though, that had the greatest influence. Because of the ban's wording and because of Methodist influence in society, the Methodist ban received attention in other denominations and was so widely disseminated in secular culture that it could not be ignored.[1]

Although intended to stop recreation, the ban inspired recreation within the church! Recreation proponents in various denominations organized themselves and set out to establish a philosophy of recreation. After the pendulum had swung to the extreme right, a new era got underway, and the church's view of recreation became much more liberal. From 1873 to 1918, from the beginning of the ban to the end of World War I, church recreation moved through an Era of Acceptance.

In 1919, the church took the next step, moving from merely accepting recreation to actively promoting recreation. In fact, both the Methodist Church and the Southern Baptist Convention established recreation offices at the national level and strove to teach local congregations how to best use recreation. Although the church had periodic setbacks—for instance, both the Methodist Church and the Southern Baptists discontinued their departments of recreation—we continue to live in this era of recreation promotion.

## Pre-American Roots of the Church Recreation Movement

Although Americans may have shaped church recreation and led the modern church recreation movement, the roots of church recreation extend to both ancient Israel and ancient Greece. Leisure in the modern sense did not exist in biblical times, but scriptural writers clearly distinguished between work and rest. Moses stated, "Six days do your work, but on the seventh day do not work, so that your ox and your donkey may rest and the slave born in your household, and the alien as well, may be refreshed" (Exod. 23:12). Moses also set aside a sabbatical year, one in seven, when even the land was unattended, and he declared that after seven sabbath years, people set aside the fiftieth year as the Year of Jubilee (Lev. 25:4). As part of the Year of Jubilee, the church held special religious feasts. Later, as clergy developed ancient Judaism, they added more days of feast and festivity.

Meanwhile, from the Greeks, clergy learned about building and planning for leisure. The Greeks constructed parks, stadiums, and theaters and supplied these facilities with programs. Greek programs and philosophy greatly influenced the early apostles. Paul of Tarsus compared the Christian life to athletic events (1 Cor. 9:24; Gal. 2:2, 5:7; 2 Tim. 4:7; and Heb. 12:1). He also used Greek dualism to compare the flesh to the spirit regarding the desire for pleasure (2 Tim. 3:1–5).[2]

The apostles and other leaders of the early Christian church established patterns later generations referred to as guideposts. Many Christians, appalled at the pleasure-seeking Romans, reacted by banning recreational activities. Clergy also banned sports, drama, and other recreation because of the activities' close association with pagan religions. For instance, Romans, like their Greek predecessors, often honored a god at a sporting event. In 744, Pope Zacharias pronounced the first Christian churchwide ban on recreation. In time, an "implicit, if not avowed, doctrine of the church" claimed that amusements substituted for prayer and meditation, and, as such, were sinful.[3]

During the Middle Ages, monks and clergy continued to perceive recreation as sinful, claiming such activities took the mind from God and from preparation for the next world. However, for multiple reasons—too many laborers, not enough work, and the belief that people needed time away from work to do good deeds—the powerful medieval Christian church instituted 170 annual holy days, holidays from regular activities. These feasts, such as the Feast of Visitation and the Feast of the Immaculate Conception, included considerable merrymaking. Jews, too, celebrated special feast days, such as Hanukkah and Passover. In addition to feasts, clergy also promoted recreation in the forms of painting, literature, dance, music, and drama, usually stressing a religious theme.[4]

During the Middle Ages, clergy contemplated the concept of recreation. They accepted Augustine's notion that God and rest were one; therefore, if one knew God, one had a permanent state of leisure. They also accepted his argument that Christians could incorporate much of pagan culture, including its forms of recreation, since something pagan was not necessarily unholy. Clergy readily accepted Thomas Aquinas's view that clerical occupations were superior to other occupations, dividing labor into sacred and secular compartments. Clergy were also influenced by Aquinas's adaptation of Aristotle's belief that the contemplative life supercedes the active life and that leisure in this sense was desirable. In *Summa Theologia,* Aquinas gave dignity to rest: "Rest is taken in two senses; in one sense, meaning a cessation from work, in the other, the fulfilling of desire." Although both Augustine and Aquinas taught physical pleasure belonged to beasts, not people, both furthered leisure within the church.[5]

Martin Luther, an Augustinian friar who founded both Lutheranism and the Protestant Reformation, combined Augustine's and Aquinas's ideas, arguing that all work, whether contemplative or active, by clergy or by laity, was equal in God's sight. In fact, he deemed all of life as sacred; people could use any wholesome activity, including free-time activities, for God's glory.[6]

Luther also challenged the idea of pleasure being sinful. Prior to the Reformation, monks degraded their bodies in an attempt to glorify their soul; they considered the pleasures that recreation provided for the body as sinful. Luther argued against degrading the body: "God has indeed created body and soul and desires both to be allowed and give recreation but with proper measure and purpose." Luther also spoke out for participation in recreation. In a 1534 letter, he wrote, "To have pleasure in sins is of the devil, but participation in proper and honorable pleasures with good and God-fearing people is pleasing to God." In *Table Talk,* a book of Luther's discourses assembled in 1848, Luther quipped, "Our loving God wills that we eat, drink, and be merry."[7]

Roman Catholics also spoke in favor of recreation. In 1609, St. Francis De Soles, in *Introduction to the Devout Life,* argued in favor of playing games: "Those games in which the gain serves as a recompense for the dexterity and industry of the body or the mind . . . are recreations in themselves good and lawful." In 1695, St. John Baptist De LaSalle, in *The Rules of Christian Manners and Civility,* wrote that holidays had God's blessing and followed the precedent found in the Old Testament: "God, who knows the weakness of our nature, authorizes us to take that rest and refreshment which are necessary to keeping up the strength of mind and body. In the brightest days of the church, the fruitful, though still anointed by pristine fervor, devoted certain days to rest and rejoicing."[8]

The Jewish people also turned their attention to recreation in the Middle Ages and Reformation, particularly to swimming. In the *Sculchanara,* a sixteenth-century compilation of laws governing the life and behavior of Jews, rabbis instructed every father to teach his son to swim. Although opponents of recreation interpret this rule as implying a lifesaving precaution, recreation proponents interpret it as a Jewish push for family fun.[9]

In 1618, England's King James issued an edict, later known as the *Book of Sports,* which made Sunday sports and recreation lawful following Divine Service. Noting that commoners could not enjoy sports on Sunday when they had free time and that they worked all other days, he approved archery, leaping, vaulting, dancing, May games, and other activities. However, he did prohibit bear and bull baiting, considering them too cruel for Sunday. Much of the negative Puritan philosophy regarding recreation stemmed as a rebellion to this document.

## Era of Apathy and Disgust

The American colonists imported a religion that contained a wide range of opinion concerning recreation. Regardless of one's denomination, social life outside the family frequently revolved around church meetings. Some colonists, though, celebrated religious holidays such as Passover and Christmas with feasts that contained both secular and religious elements.

Most early religious Americans approved of participation in play when done for God's glory and one's individual salvation. However, they believed that play for the sake of play, just like work for the sake of work, was incompatible with the Scriptures. Although they often considered it spiritually dangerous to have a good time, colonists opposed most recreation for patriotic and economic reasons, not religious ones. The colonists were generally comprised of dissonant groups who had struggled to cause reforms in England. Unsuccessful, they had come to the colonies, carrying with them their scorn of their opponents' lifestyles, including their recreational activities. Most imported holidays celebrated English national history, and on the whole the Puritans had little fondness for the motherland. Too, due to harsh climate, little time remained for celebrations. In New England the civic body, often synonymous with the religious body, legislated against the more secular and/or highbrow activities, jailing citizens who danced around May poles, decorated Christmas trees, danced at weddings, conducted sports events, or gave theatrical performances.[10]

Colonial society recognized the need for archery and similar survival skills, and clergy did little to prohibit these leisure activities. Inadvertently, the church also offered recreation through community projects such as cornhuskings and barn raisings and through service projects such as quilting bees. Although these community gatherings accomplished tasks for the social good, they also provided the occasion for feasts, games, and social recreation.

Around the Revolutionary War, clergy accepted recreation as a part of secular society, first in the South and then in the North. Climate conditions and social factors, not theologies, account for most of the differences between Southern and Northern clergy perceptions of recreation. Temperatures plunged during New England winters, and therefore time Southerners could spend in leisure activities Northerners had to spend shoveling snow. Too, although some genteel citizens settled in the North, the slave-holding aristocracy who had the time, wealth, and taste to patronize the arts generally settled in the South. Northern clergy also maintained tighter control over their flocks than Southern clergy did; whereas a Southern parson might ignore his parishioners ventures' with questionable recreation activities provided it was not habitual, Northern clergy generally had something to say.[11]

As Americans moved west, clergy developed programs to cope with frontier life. In the name of education and community service, they allowed the first professed recreation program, the lecture, into the church in 1818. These lectures became formalized in 1826 when Josiah Holbrook, an American educator, established the first lyceum, a lecture series named after the ancient lyceum, the park near Athens, Greece, where Aristotle lectured in 400 B.C. Holbrook followed this Mulburry, Massachusetts, lecture series with other series in nearby towns, establishing circuits for lecturers. A local lyceum committee, usually closely allied with the church, coordinated the lectures. Often having the only auditorium in town, clergy found themselves hosting the lectures.[12]

Following the Civil War, clergy frequently spoke against the growing amusements, believing that, though scriptural writers did not specifically condemn amusements, amusements remained conducive to immorality. Fearful that the eager rush of society after such diversions as dancing, cardplaying, theatergoing, and sports would corrupt its members, clergy sought to banish these pastimes by stigmatizing such diversions as so potential for evil that no one could participate in them.

Although the effort to do away with recreation continued long past 1872, the 1872 ban by the Methodist Episcopal Church represents the pinnacle of the success of recreation opponents. At the 1872 quadrennial conference of the Methodist Episcopal Church, the Committee on the State of the Church, chaired by Daniel Curry, framed and secured passage of a bill that amended the *Discipline* chapter on "Imprudent Conduct" to include "dancing, playing at games of chance, attending theaters, horse races, circuses, dancing parties, or patronizing dancing schools, or taking such other amusements as are obviously of misleading or questionable moral tendency."[13]

The legislation, passed 179 to 75 on the twenty-eighth day of the monthlong conference, contained several flaws that opponents exploited until successfully repealing the ban in 1924. Although few could argue with Curry's goal to "arrest, if possible, practices which portend so much evil to the Church and to the world," the ban provided the catalyst to focus the church's attention on recreation, and it forced proponents of recreation to state their case carefully.

As the twentieth century prepared to open, recreation became a hot issue within the American church. Both pro- and antirecreation leaders of later generations used early American thoughts and deeds as a springboard. For instance, prorecreation leaders focused on the Puritan goals of a better society, while antirecreation leaders focused on the Puritan bans of many recreational activities. As the Era of Apathy and Distrust closed, the future of the church's relationship with recreation was at a fork in the road, and its leaders could choose only one of the four prongs: to promote recreation, merely to accept recreation, to be apathetic toward recreation, or to oppose recreation. Which prong they would choose, though, was unclear.

## Era of Acceptance

Although the Methodist Episcopal Church's 1872 ban reached the most people and received the most attention, other groups of Methodists, including the General Conference of the Methodist Protestants and the Methodist Episcopal Church—South, as well as other denominations, such as Presbyterians, Catholics, and Baptists, had bans as well. Despite antirecreation forces having enough votes initially to pass their legislation, pressure to repeal the bans soon came from both internal and external sources.

Supporters of the 1872 ban answered the mounting cries to repeal it. They argued that God remained the same from year to year, and, if the activities in the 1872 ban were sinful then, they were still sinful in the present time and would remain so in the future. They claimed that specifying recreation activities by name eliminated any doubt in parishioners' minds of the activities' harm. However, even those in favor of keeping a ban soon realized the folly of this argument for specifying sinful amusements, for "the devil is constantly devising new amusements."[14]

Delegates gave the ban more attention each passing general conference. The front page of the *Daily Advocate* called the amusement debate "the hottest issue" of the 1900 General Conference! In 1924, the general conference voted to overturn the ban and return to John Wesley's advice of using one's conscience concerning amusements. With the ban overturned, the amusement question quickly faded as an issue at the general conference.

The overturning of the ban signaled approval of the growth of recreational programs throughout the denomination. Most of these early programs, though, failed. Due to the stigma of theatergoing and dancing, leaders could not provide high-class recreation such as Shakespearean plays and balls, and therefore church recreation programs were perceived as second-rate by the general public. Too, most church recreation leaders had no training, resulting in sloppy productions of material many members already found suspect.

Church recreation leaders of this era made the mistake of focusing too narrowly. The leaders tended to focus on one form of recreation, usually physical, to the exclusion of other forms. Muscular Christianity—sometimes called Muscular Judaism when offered in the synagogue setting—received its name because leaders reconciled a robust physical life with Christian morality and duty. They claimed the church had to focus on both morals and muscles, since the body serves as the temple of the Spirit, and they maintained that physical strength built character and righteousness, making the believer fit for God's work.[15]

For both theological and practical reasons, clergy-led recreation appeared to be a passing fad. However, with the advent of World War I, a need arose for clergy-led recreation, both on the home front and on the war front. Clergy answered the call, and many received valuable training in leading recreation through the Young Men's Christian Association (YMCA). As rationing forced people to stay in their own community, church-led programs grew popular. Church-led recreation activities were soon accepted as a part of society, and church members began to plan annual recreation activities. For instance, urban congregations often had fairs and bazaars in the fall and strawberry festivals in the spring, while rural congregations had an annual picnic each summer. By the time the war ended, church recreation wasn't only accepted; it was expected!

As the need for recreation grew within the church, the church developed facilities to meet recreational needs. The most famous and widely used architectural design was the Akron Plan, drafted by Lewis Miller and Jacob Snyder in Akron, Ohio, as part of a national experiment approved by the Methodist Episcopal Church. The plan for the Akron Methodist Episcopal Church greatly aided the church recreation movement through its "collapsible walls." One could pull the curtainlike folding walls out to form many rooms, or one could collapse them so that the many rooms became one auditorium. Although Lewis and Snyder intended the individual rooms as classrooms for the Sunday school and the auditorium as a meeting place for all classes to come together to open the Sunday school session, congregations soon realized that the auditorium had gymnasium and fellowship hall possibilities and that the individual classrooms had club room possibilities. The plan received wide use throughout Protestant congregations through the 1910s, until leaders replaced it with architectural plans that provided permanent classrooms, libraries, kitchens, banquet rooms, and gymnasiums.[16]

Although clergy continued to be antagonistic toward much commercial recreation, they approved of most recreation provided by voluntary associations such as the YMCA and public agencies such as park districts. Although the church often tied doctrinal training into its own recreation programs, the church developed a two-way working relationship with these other agencies regarding recreation. In 1912, the Playground Association of America reported that the church either directly created or inspired 40 percent of the playgrounds inaugurated in 1911. By the 1930s, many municipal departments organized church athletic leagues, supplied leadership for parties and picnics, gave program suggestions, and trained the church's recreation leaders. In exchange, public recreation departments often freely used church facilities.[17]

In the Era of Acceptance, leaders established church recreation as one facet of multifaceted church programs, such as a rural congregation's youth program or an institutional church's outreach. The scope of the recreation programs varied, depending on facilities, leaders' skills, and church atmosphere. During this era, programs grew more sophisticated, more elaborate, and in the eyes of some, more bawdy. Although a minority perceived the growth of recreation in the church setting as a fulfilling of their prophecies of the church's decay and of recreation's addictive qualities, the majority saw the dawning "of the day when the devil will no longer monopolize the grand opportunities in recreation that the Church should control."[18]

## Era of Promotion

In the Era of Promotion, leaders sought to guarantee the long-term partnership of religion with recreation. Clergy of this era were unlike the clergy of the past era: To them recreation was not a sideshow, a way to raise money, or bait; it was serious ministry! Congregations no longer perceived their recreation leaders as entertainers or purveyors of amusement but rather as overseers of one of society's most vital cultural responsibilities.

At the turn of the century, leaders had designed most all-church recreation programs to meet bills generated elsewhere in the congregation. Oyster suppers, strawberry festivals, and ice cream suppers paid for themselves and other programs. These recreational activities were "offered more for the sake of filling the church's pockets than for meeting a need of the people," for leaders designed them to get "money out of people who had given all they thought they could" and to get donations from people whom leaders could not normally ask to give, such as members of other denominations.

In the Era of Promotion, though, recreation programs required more money to operate than they generated! Although the money did not go for individual gain by anyone in the congregation, clergy had to meet expenses such as upkeep of the fields and halls, the rental of equipment, the janitor's salary, and the guest leader's fee. The new programs also meant building new physical plants, including office space, art galleries, lecture halls, club rooms, and gymnasiums.

After the church accepted the philosophy that "recreation and secular activity fall well within the scope of Christian life if they are disciplined in that direction," leaders realized recreation directors would have to be trained and supervised. They turned to a combination of laypeople who could afford to donate the time to supervise activities and professionals who had the expertise to oversee the programs.[19]

As the 1920s began, both secular and religious officials expressed dissatisfaction with society's recreation, claiming that "somebody put a wreck in recreation" and "took the unity out of community." The push for congregations to offer recreational activities came from both outside and inside the church. Externally, the push came from leaders of public recreation. For instance, Howard Braucher, president of the National Recreation Association, said, "Make wider use of recreation in connection with Sunday schools, young people's societies, and other organizations so as to give a richer life to the members of the churches. Hold institutes for training church membership as volunteers to give recreational leadership in their own homes, in their neighborhoods, and in all organizations where they belong."[20]

Meanwhile, the push also came internally from Protestant, Catholic, and Jewish officials. The Right Reverend Doctor William T. Manning, bishop of New York, Protestant Episcopal Church, said, "The instinct for play is as divinely planted in human nature as the instinct for worship." The Reverend Doctor Harry E. Fosdick, a Baptist, pastor of Riverside Church, New York, stated, "The spirit of play, which is the crown of work and of home life, is also the crown of religion." Norman Richardson, professor of religious education at Northwestern, a Methodist Episcopal school, wrote, "The subject of play has come to be one of the most serious matters which the Church can possibly take into consideration." Dr. Ahba Silver, rabbi at The Temple of Cleveland, Ohio, wrote, "The Church is interested in leisure because it knows that no culture, no civilization, no spiritual religion is possible without leisure, for culture requires leisure."[21]

Denominational leaders began to set forth principles of recreation, including standards of recreation program excellence. As they established principles, they grew bureaucracies at both the local and the national levels to share and enforce the principles. They also produced an explosion of books detailing recreation philosophy and suggesting acceptable recreation activities within the church. As congregations recognized recreation as a viable, necessary ministry, they no longer left recreation to chance. Recreation professionals emerged, seminaries began to offer recreation courses, and denominations provided hands-on workshops.

In 1914, the general conference of the Methodist Episcopal Church—South suggested the need for a denomination-wide church recreation program. As a result, the denomination formed a position on its national General Epworth League Board, the board in charge of overseeing youth activities, and assigned the position the duties of overseeing a national church recreation program among youth. The League waited until the completion of World War I to hire Elvin Harbin, an ordained Methodist minister who had established a national reputation as a youth leader. Although lectures, camps, potlucks, quilting bees, fairs, and other forms of church recreation existed decades before Harbin's birth, national recreation leaders such as Joseph Lee, Howard Braucher, and Charles Brightbill still regarded Harbin as the founder of church recreation, for he solidified recreation as a legitimate ministry, set standards, and provided the field with a philosophy.[22]

Convinced that most parishioners could not innately perform recreational services but could be taught to be recreation leaders—"Recreation leaders are not born. They are made. They are made by study, hard work, and a deep appreciation of the importance of recreation as a factor in human welfare"—Harbin founded the Southwide Leisure Time Conference, a recreation laboratory in which participants heard lectures about the philosophy of church recreation and in which they gained hands-on experience in drama, storytelling, crafts, games, and numerous other forms of church recreation. After the Methodist Episcopal Church—South merged with the Methodist Episcopal Church and the Methodist Protestant Church to become the Methodist Church, Harbin was named director of Leisure-Recreation Ministries on the newly formed Board of Education, and he promptly established four other regional hands-on training centers.[23]

Church recreation was also introduced as a formal course in colleges, universities, and seminaries. Boston University, which formed the Department of Religious Education in 1918 and the Department of Young People's Work in 1920, offered the first course in church recreation. Lynn Rohrbough wrote the first thesis on church recreation in

1925, a handbook of recreation leadership in the church setting, which he later published as *Handy*. In 1926, Rohrbough introduced the term *church recreation* to describe church-centered recreational programs.

Lynn Rohrbough became an ordained Methodist and established the first clearinghouse for church recreation, Church Recreation Service, in 1924. Through his ecumenical co-op, later renamed Cooperative Recreation Service, he also made and sold traditional table board games from around the world. Through his business, Rohrbough sought to train recreation leaders, improve standards of recreation, and publish wholesome recreational materials not available elsewhere. The Methodist Church frequently recommended the books he published, but when Rohrbough turned his attention to songbooks, the Methodist Church increased its own production of materials, which it sold to its own congregations, other denominations, public schools, and recreation agencies.

Methodists weren't the only ones establishing formal church recreation training. T. B. Maston taught the first Baptist seminary course in recreation in 1922 at Southwestern Baptist Theological Seminary in Fort Worth, Texas. Agnes Pylant, his former student, and William Marshall, Wayland College president, then established a church recreation department and a degree program at Wayland College in 1949.

The Southern Baptists, at their national publishing house, established the Church Recreation Department, originally known as Church Recreation Service. Chester Swor, the catalyst, delivered the speech "Our Youth of Today" to the Southern Baptist Convention in 1942, hoping to stimulate interest in recreational activity by suggesting that congregations provide wholesome alternatives to unwholesome activities, particularly for youth.

In January 1943, the Executive Committee of the Sunday School Board approved the creation of Church Recreation Service. However, although the Convention gave approval, the Sunday School Board undertook no implementation. Swor, upset that the Board had not implemented the plan by 1948, addressed the Convention again, bluntly asking that the Sunday School Board establish a Church Recreation Department. The Convention overwhelmingly favored accepting Swor's recommendation. The department began to function in February 1954 with Agnes Pylant as director.[24]

The Church Recreation Department sought to "meet the challenge of leisure through an accelerated program of promotion and leadership training" and then to have congregations do the same in their community. Because of a limited number of personnel, Pylant focused most of the department's energy on writing, believing this would allow the staff to reach the most people. Along with producing *Church Recreation Magazine,* Pylant and her staff wrote numerous books, brochures, and articles. They also offered consultation and hands-on training.[25]

Both the Methodist and the Baptist recreation office peaked, entrenched, and declined. In 1968, the Methodist Church merged with the United Brethren Church, and in 1972 the resulting United Methodist Church eliminated the recreation director by splitting his duties among other departments, notably camping and youth work. The national church recreation departments had worked themselves out of a job; they had so infiltrated recreation into the church setting that church authorities felt the need for a specific office to promote recreation was no longer valid. Perhaps one exception to this was among Southern Baptists, where the work continued to flourish.[26]

The Methodist Church and the Southern Baptist Convention were the only two major denominations to undertake establishing a national chair of recreation. Other denominations expected groups such as the National Council of Churches to oversee recreation education. The National Council of Churches did get involved in several recreation programs, including camping, drama, and social recreation. It even sponsored some recreation services, such as placing recreation leaders in public parks. However, on the whole, it sought to train leaders rather than provide services. Leaders of the National Council of Churches perceived the Council as a catalyst, planning ministries that local leaders would eventually control. Unfortunately, they sent mixed signals of their intentions, and many denominations—particularly the Lutherans, Presbyterians, and American Baptists—ceased to expand their recreation programs because they thought the National Council would oversee recreation education.[27]

Southern Baptists have continued their work in church recreation. In 1964, under Bob Boyd's direction, they began their annual training conference called Rec Lab, which has grown into the longest-lasting and largest training experience in the field of recreation and sports ministry. In 1971, Ray Conner became director of the Church Recreation Department until his retirement in 1993. Under his direction the department added staff for all ministry areas of recreation-producing ministry resources and holding conferences for all denominations. Perhaps the best known area of work under Conner's direction is that of a recreationally oriented youth camp called Centrifuge, which under its first director, Don Mattingly, became an international camp experience for more than sixty thousand teenagers each year. From Centrifuge grew the sports camp Crosspoint and several other mission and sports-related camp experiences for children and teenagers. Southern Baptists are active in the work today as LifeWay Christian Resources houses and staffs the program of Recreation and Sports Ministry from its Nashville offices.

Church recreation took another blow when two television evangelists, Jimmy Swaggart and James Bakker, succumbed to temptation. Ironically, Jimmy Swaggart, pastor of the Family Worship Center, an Assembly of God church in Baton Rouge, Louisiana, claimed he opposed modern recreation. He even considered Christian aerobics inappropriate, referring to Christian aerobics as modern dance. Although he officially opposed much church recreation being offered in other denominations, Swaggart had a great influence on Pentecostals in getting those congregations to accept church recreation.

Swaggart, the cousin of rock star Jerry Lee Lewis, introduced the Assemblies of God to both a new form of music and a new medium. Swaggart followed in the footsteps of early American congregations that had often blended secular tavern songs with new words to create religious hymns, and he introduced a honky-tonk form of gospel music. To spread his music and message, Swaggart turned to radio and television. Although early Assemblies clergy banned the radio and the television, Swaggart recognized their potential for spreading the gospel, and in 1969 he launched a radio program. He also launched a series of albums, selling more than twelve million. His use of the media not only spread the gospel, but also an acceptance of radio, television, and recorded music as acceptable Christian diversions. Swaggart's influence waned in the late 1980s.[28]

James Bakker was another Assemblies of God television evangelist who greatly furthered the church recreation movement and then left his ministry position in disgrace. Bakker took the previously established concept of the Christian campground and combined commercial recreation with religion, opening a "Jesus" theme amusement park, Heritage USA, in Fort Mill, South Carolina, in 1985. The park was designed to compete with Disneyland, Six Flags, and other large theme park chains. A high-tech Passion play emerged as the twenty-three-hundred-acre park's most popular attraction. Other activities for guests included spiritual counseling, weekly baptisms in the hotel swimming pool, typical resort recreations, and the opportunity to watch the Jim and Tammy Faye Bakker broadcasts in person. Heritage USA initially experienced considerable success. In 1987, it attracted more than six million people, trailing only Disneyland and Disney World in attendance. However, Jim Bakker, accused of selling thousand-dollar partnerships that promised lifetime lodging rights at his theme park to far more partners than could actually be accommodated, turned administration over to Jerry Falwell, a Southern Baptist television evangelist. In 1990, following Hurricane Hugo's destruction and facing bankruptcy, Falwell closed the park. In December 1990, Morris Cerullo, another television evangelist, bought the park with the long-term goal of reopening it as New Heritage USA, something that has yet to happen.[29]

The church appears to be on the verge of a new era in its relationship with recreation. Budget cuts and internal reorganizations have done away with national recreation offices. Older youth, who formerly received many leisure services, have become leisure service providers in theme parks, fast-food outlets, and similar commercial settings, and many no longer make time to participate in church recreation. Previously stable programs such as the quilting bee are declining in popularity, reflecting a lack of interest among parishioners. Those who led church recreation in the twentieth century are retiring. Sadly, recreation is so ingrained within the church that most people are apathetic toward learning more about it, for they cannot picture the church without it, and yet, because they do not learn more about it, its potential is barely realized.

The Era of Promotion is coming to an end. A new era is about to get underway. As someone interested in leading church recreation, you have a voice in the forming of the new era. You now have an understanding of the past, of how the field got to where it is today. As you now know, the church has often formed a vision for recreation, and then it has recast that vision. You are a part of today's revisioning process. Where will you lead the field?

Church recreation has ties to both religion and secular culture. Religion and culture share a two-sided relationship, for culture influences the approach to religion, and religious attitude influences culture. As Washington Gladden, a Congregationalist and a proponent of church recreation observed, "Religion cannot be kept alive without alliance with social forces; the social forces cannot be kept in healthful operation without the aid of religion. Because of the interdependency between the Church and culture, religious groups can not ignore recreation, nor can the Recreation Movement ignore the church."[30]

---

### Notes

1. *Minutes of the General Assembly of the Presbyterian Church in the United States of America* (New York: Fanshaw, 1843); J. T. Crane, *Popular Amusements* (Cincinnati: Hitchcock and Waldin, 1869).

2. R. Kraus, *Recreation and Modern Society,* 3rd ed. (Glenview, Ill.: Scott-Foresman, 1984).

3. D. Van Dalen, E. D. Mitchell, and B. L. Bennett, *A World History of Physical Education* (New York: Prentice-Hall, 1953); W. Gladden, "Christianity and Popular Movements," *Century,* 29.3 (1885): 384–92.

4. J. Huizinga, *Homo Ludens: A Study of the Play Element in Culture* (Boston: Beacon, 1950); R. Lee, *Religion and Leisure in America: A Study in Four Dimensions* (New York: Abingdon, 1964).

5. J. Kelly, *Leisure* (Englewood Cliffs, N.J.: Prentice-Hall, 1982).

6. H. D. Lehman, *In Praise of Leisure* (Scottsdale, Pa.: Herald, 1974).

7. E. Lueker, ed., *Lutheran Cyclopedia* (St. Louis: Concordia, 1955); R. L. Woods, ed., *The World Treasury of Religious Quotations: Diverse Beliefs, Convictions, Comments, Dissents, and Opinions from Ancient and Modern Sources* (New York: Hawtorn, 1966), 738–39.

8. H. L. Mencken, *A Dictionary of Quotations on Historical Principles from Ancient and Modern Sources* (New York: Knopf, 1942), 443, 1,011.

9. National Recreation Association, *Proceedings* (New York: National Recreation Association, 1937); E. Berlatsky, "Recreation and the Faiths: A Look at the Jewish Philosophy at Work," *Selected Papers Presented at the Forty-Second National Recreation Congress* (New York: National Recreation Association, 1961), 181–83; S. W. Baron, *A Social and Religious History of the Jews,* vol. 2, 2nd ed. (New York: Columbia, 1952).

10. R. M. Boyd, "Footprints of Fellowship," *Church Recreation* (February 1964): 4; S. Bayne, "Christian Doctrine of Play," *Proceedings, National Recreation Congress* (New York: National Recreation Association, 1952), 26–31.

11. G. Eisen, "The Concept of Time, Play, and Leisure in Early Protestant Religious Ethic," *Play and Culture,* 4 (1991): 223–36; Kraus, *Recreation and Modern Society.*

12. J. Holbrook, "Exchange Lyceum," *Western Christian Advocate* (30 September 1842): 96.

13. *Journal of the Delegated General Conference of Methodist Episcopal Church* (1872): 379–80; G. P. Mains, "Our Special Legislation on Amusements: Honest Doubt as to Its Wisdom," *The Methodist Review* (May 1892): 375–89.

14. G. P. Mains, "Special Legislation," 388; C. W. Harman, "Amusement," *Daily Christian Advocate,* 14 (1900): 355.

15. E. E. Hale, "Public Amusements and Public Morality," *Christian Examiner* (July 1857): 47–65; T. W. Spalding, *The Premier See: A History of the Archdiocese in Baltimore, 1789–1989* (Baltimore: Johns Hopkins University, 1989).

16. D. Egbert and C. Moore, "Religious Expression in American Architecture," *Religious Perspectives in American Culture,* J. Smith and A. Jamison, eds. (Princeton, N.J.: Princeton, 1961), 361–42; G. Lundburn, M. Komarovsky, and M. McInerny, *Leisure: A Suburban Study* (New York: Columbia University, 1935); L. Miller, "The Akron Plan," *Seven Graded Sunday Schools: A Series of Practical Papers,* J. Hurlbut, ed. (New York: Hunt & Eaton, 1893), 11–32.

17. R. Cutting, *The Church and Society* (New York: Macmillan, 1912); C. J. Vettiner, *Rural Recreation for America* (Louisville, Ky.: Rural Recreation for America, 1949); J. E. Griggs and L. J. Moore, "Men's Ministry," *Perpetuating Pentecost: A History of the First 75 Years of the Southern Missouri District of the Assemblies of God,* B. Newby, J. E. Griggs, and S. D. Eutsler, eds. (Springfield, Mo.: Southern Missouri District Council of the Assemblies of God, 1989), 81–85; A. V. Sapora, personal interview, 3 February 1993.

18. W. Fay, "What Attitude Should the Church Take Toward Amusements?" *Homiletic Review,* 24.1 (1892): 84–87; W. B. Hale, "Another Year of Church Entertainments," *Forum* (December 1896): 396–405.

19. F. Eastman, "Rural Recreation Through the Church," *Playground* (October 1912): 232–38; Hale, "Another Year," 396–405; B. Guenther, chair, Commission on Church Architecture of the Lutheran Church—Missouri Synod, *Architecture and the Church* (St. Louis: Concordia, 1965), 51.

20. C. M. Bowman, *Guiding Intermediates* (New York: Abingdon-Cokesbury, 1943), 13.

21. Ibid.; N. Richardson, *The Church at Play: A Manual for Directors of Social and Recreational Life,* 2d ed. (New York: Abingdon, 1922), 27.

22. D. R. Braden, *Leisure and Entertainment in America* (Dearborn, Mich.: Henry Ford Museum and Greenfield Village, 1988); L. H. Gulick, "Play and the Church," *Playground,* 3.36 (1910): 29–30; W. Mutch, "Recreation and the Sunday School," *The Encyclopedia of Sunday Schools and Religious Education,* vol. 3, J. McFarland and B. Winchester, eds. (New York: Nelson, 1915), 864–66; R. H. Hipps, letter to researcher, 2 September 1992; C. Brightbill, *Man and Leisure: A Philosophy of Recreation* (Englewood Cliffs, N.J.: Prentice-Hall, 1961).

23. E. O. Harbin, *The Recreation Leader* (New York: Abingdon-Cokesbury, 1952), 7.

24. Robert M. Boyd, "Recreation and the Faiths: A Look at the Southern Baptist Church Philosophy at Work," *Selected Papers Presented at the Forty-Second National Recreation Congress* (New York: National Recreational Association, 1961), 184–87.

25. Ibid., 198.

26. R. H. Hipps, telephone interview, 28 December 1992.

27. Ibid.

28. M. M. Poloma, *The Assemblies of God at the Crossroads: Charisma and Institutional Dilemmas* (Knoxville: University of Tennessee, 1989).

29. K. L. Woodward, "A Disneyland for the Devout," *Newsweek* (11 August 1986): 46–47; S. A. Forest, "You Can't Say Morris Cerullo Has No Faith: Can the Televangelist Cleanse the Soul of Heritage USA?" *Business Week* (31 December 1990): 59.

30. W. Gladden, *The Church and Modern Life* (Boston: Houghton-Mifflin, 1908).

# 4 The Recreation and Sports Minister as a Professional

## Dale Connally

## Recreation and Sports Ministry as a Leisure-Services Provider

Leisure services is a broad field whose practitioners seek to help clients improve their quality of life through meaningful leisure experiences. Leisure services are typically provided by organizations attached to government entities and both profit and nonprofit corporations in the private sector. Churches and other religious organizations who sponsor recreation and sports ministries are often categorized as a leisure-service provider in the nonprofit private sector.[1]

In his study of research and other writings concerning the use of recreation and sports in churches, Ernce concluded that there is no conflict between the church and leisure services when leisure services are provided from a Christian perspective.[2] Both historical and survey research supports the notion that recreation and sports ministries of various denominational churches are a bona fide leisure-services provider. In fact, several recreation and sports ministers have also been influential in the secular leisure-services professional organizations.[3]

## Recreation and Sports Ministry as a Profession

*A body of academic knowledge and technical skills*—To understand the unique niche that recreation and sports ministry fills in the leisure-services profession, the initial step is to explore the composition of a traditional profession. One element of a profession is a body of academic

55

knowledge and technical skills that is integral to practitioners. Shivers, in *Introduction to Recreational Service,* suggests that recreation and sports professionals need a liberal arts program that includes social sciences, educational theory, and enough culture education to build a theoretical base for more specific course work in leisure services.[4] Kraus and Edginton have identified several key elements of leisure-services curricula: recreation history and philosophy, program planning, fiscal and risk management, public relations, and research skills.[5] External agencies including the National Recreation and Park Association (NRPA) and the American Alliance of Health, Physical Education, Recreation and Dance (AAHPERD) are actively involved in identifying key issues to be addressed in academic preparation programs in leisure services.

*Academic institutions*—Another element of a profession is academic institutions and other organizations to help facilitate the learning of necessary knowledge and skills. Academic programs are offered at the associate, undergraduate, and graduate levels at public and private colleges and universities across the United States. Seminaries also provide course work to prepare ministers for recreation and sports ministry. Numerous other organizations offer training events specifically designed to educate and train recreation and sports ministers. An even larger group of secular professional organizations offers educational conferences highlighting several niche markets within the leisure-services field. Appendix 1 lists several secular and religious training events and professional organizations that may be useful for a recreation and sports minister.

*Referent authority*—An additional element of a profession is referent authority from the public. It is not clear whether the general public views leisure services as a true profession. On one hand, we are living in an age when the vast majority of Americans view their leisure pursuits as essential to their quality of life and are willing to pay for service. Studies have shown that people are aware of and appreciate individual providers of leisure services. However, there is less evidence that people value leisure services as a true profession.[6] Monetary remuneration is often viewed as a barometer of referent authority. Theoretically, the higher the average salary, the more valued the profession. The salaries of leisure-services professionals are generally viewed as average, compared to other service occupations. There are other financial indicators beyond salaries that may indicate public perception of leisure services.

The last two decades have brought relative economic prosperity to the United States. However, publicly funded leisure-services providers have had to deal with shrinking budgets and rising costs. Such a lack of financial support implies that leisure services may be near the bottom of the public sector pecking order. A somewhat similar pecking order exists in most churches. Compared to other ministers on a church staff, most recreation and sports ministers face, at best, average salaries and budget appropriations. Moreover, recreation and sports is often the only ministry in a church that is expected to raise its own revenue.

In a study of the ministry as an occupational labor market, the researchers suggest that pastors who minister at larger churches are at the pinnacle of the church job ladder. Few pastors plan to leave the pastorate to pursue other ministry positions. In other words, many of them would view it as a step backward to move from the pastorate to become a recreation and sports minister.[7] The dichotomy of the recreation and sports minister offering relevant programs that are valued by church members and integral to vibrant congregations, yet facing financial challenges, is not unique. Public school teachers, traditionally viewed as among the most honorable professionals, are often relegated to low salaries and woefully inadequate funding for instructional programs.

***Ethical practice***—The fourth element of a profession is a collective agreement on ethical practice. Ethics are actions based on values. The leisure-services profession has several core values: contributing to the quality of life for individuals, advocating for the rights of all people, helping people make wise decisions in leisure, and promoting environmental stewardship.[8] Leisure-services professionals seek to help individuals develop intellectually, physically, socially, and spiritually. Leisure professionals also focus on leadership and moral character development. These values have led to the National Recreation and Park Association adopting a code of ethics (see fig. 4-1) for leisure-services professionals. Several denominations have developed codes of ethics as a guide for their ministers,[9] while others are hesitant to do so in light of individual and local church autonomy.

Recreation and sports ministers share the core values of the leisure-services profession and add a unique perspective. Recreation and sports ministry does not view programming as an end but rather as a means to foster spiritual growth to believers and nonbelievers. Ministers enter the recreation and sports field out of a sense of calling by God to perform such service. McDuff and Mueller suggest that calling's importance to the ministry field may be unique. They also propose that some sense of calling, not necessarily divine, is a critical factor that separates professional and nonprofessional vocations.[10]

*Paternalism*—A tenet of the most highly recognized professions is the concept of paternalism. In simple terms, paternalistic behavior occurs when a professional performs an act, either commission or omission, for the advancement of an individual. The act may be performed without the consent of the individual. Lawyers and doctors are frequently trusted to commit acts of paternalism. The leisure-services field is extremely hesitant to embrace and practice paternalism. Leisure, by definition, depends on the free will of an individual. Recreation and sports ministers who serve in an environment that values the priesthood of the believer and the free will of the individual are uncomfortable committing acts of paternalism.

Recreation and sports ministry does, however, exhibit one trait essential for paternalism. Paternalistic behaviors occur in situations when a professional has authority over persons who have a need that the market in general will not meet—the unemployed, older adults, and single parent families, for instance.[11] While having no legal connection or obligation, people in these categories who are in need often look to the church as a source of caring support and transformation.

*A common set of standards*—A final element of a profession is a common set of standards for professionals. Such standards address certification, accreditation, and licensing. Certification is the process of identifying individuals with the needed expertise to function within a profession. NRPA and AAHPERD collaborate to offer the Certified Park and Recreation Professional (CPRP) certification. Criteria for the certification include certain levels of education, a national examination, and continuing education.[12] The CPRP is highly valued in the public sector but rarely recognized or desired in the private sector, including recreation and sports ministry.

Accreditation refers to the credentialing of individual academic programs or leisure agencies. Most college, university, and seminary programs seek general accreditations such as the Southern Association of Colleges and Schools (SACS) or the Association of Theological Schools (ATS). More specifically, leisure-services academic programs and leisure

---

## National Recreation and Park Association (NRPA)*

The National Recreation and Park Association has provided leadership to the nation in fostering the expansion of recreation and parks. NRPA has stressed the value of recreation, both active and passive, for individual growth and development. Its members are dedicated to the common cause of assuring that people of all ages and abilities have the opportunity to find the most satisfying use of their leisure time and enjoy an improved quality of life.

The Association has consistently affirmed the importance of well-informed and professionally trained personnel to improve continually the administration of recreation and park programs. Members of NRPA are encouraged to support the efforts of the Association and profession by supporting state affiliate and national activities and participating in continuing education opportunities, certification, and accreditation.

Membership in NRPA carries with it special responsibilities to the public at large and to the specific communities and agencies in which recreation and park services are offered.

*As a member of the National Recreation and Park Association, I accept and agree to abide by this Code of Ethics and pledge myself to:*
- Adhere to the highest standards of integrity and honesty in all public and personal activities to inspire public confidence and trust.
- Strive for personal and professional excellence and encourage the professional development of associates and students.
- Strive for the highest standards of professional competence, fairness, impartiality, efficiency, effectiveness, and fiscal responsibility.
- Avoid any interest or activity which is in conflict with the performance of job responsibilities.
- Promote the public interest and avoid personal gain or profit from the performance of job duties and responsibilities.
- Support equal employment opportunities.

*Source: http://www.nrpa.org/story.cfm?departmentID=37&story_id=181.

---

*Figure 4-1: Code of Ethics*

agencies may be accredited through NRPA and AAHPERD. Schools submit evidence in terms of liberal arts program, content of leisure-services course work, field experiences, faculty credentials, and workloads. Agencies submit self-assessments of programs and personnel. Peer review follows for both academic programs and agencies as outside experts judge whether standards have indeed been met.[13] Agency accreditations are rare in the recreation and sports ministry domain. However, many Christian camps follow a similar procedure to become accredited through the American Camping Association.

Licensing, as it pertains to leisure services, refers to standards set by governmental agencies to oversee areas of professional practice. The common areas addressed by leisure-services agencies include, but are not limited to, food preparation and service, transportation, and youth camping. The agency responsible for licenses in each area varies by state but generally involves departments of health, transportation or police, and health or human services, respectively.[14] Licensing is an important element in a risk-management plan for recreation and sports ministers. Ministers must work to make sure that their kitchens and food service areas meet standards, that drivers are properly licensed, and that day or resident camps meet state standards.

Given these elements of a traditional profession, is leisure services in fact a profession? Shivers believes leisure services is a quasiprofession that has made progress in the last couple of decades but still has some growth to accomplish. The education that is required is a major weakness. Some entry-level positions are still available for individuals with no college education. In addition, many people are in supervisory and upper-level management who have little or no formal education in leisure services.[15] This tendency is mirrored in the recreation and sports ministry. Churches do not universally require seminary education, and a specific concentration or degree in leisure services or recreation and sports ministry is rarely required.

As mentioned earlier, accreditation or certification is not universally required in either the secular or sacred leisure or ministry professions. The current CPRP certification addresses knowledge and skills that are somewhat related to the ministry field. The NRPA accreditation process is currently aimed more toward public sector leisure providers than recreation and sports ministry. The development and strengthening of faith-based professional organizations that could offer ministry-appropriate certifications and accreditation would help recreation and sports ministers pursue a higher level of professionalism.

Due to its link to clergy, recreation and sports ministry is perhaps situated a bit stronger along the professional continuum than other niches within the leisure-services profession. The clergy in general has a long history of being viewed by society as a profession. Torkildsen identifies ministers, lawyers, and medical doctors as members of the "original professions."[16] Wesner concludes that during the last century more and more churches recognized recreation and sports ministry as a valid clerical profession.[17]

There is certainly evidence that the leisure-service profession *may* or *may not* meet the complex criteria for a traditional profession. However, from an individual minister's perspective, one must not view the professionalization of leisure services as a pointless struggle to achieve a static set of criteria necessary for the public to view leisure services as a profession. In other words, one should not forsake meeting people's needs through recreation and sports ministry in a professional manner just because there is not unanimous judgment that the leisure-services profession is in fact a profession. Indeed, one must view professionalization as a developmental process. The continuous upgrading of individual ministers' academic preparation, lifelong learning, and professional practice is necessary to strengthen the profession and to be efficient, effective ministers.[18]

## Burnout among Recreation and Sports Ministers

One of the more popular maladies that may hinder both the efficiency and effectiveness of recreation and sports ministers is burnout. Fichter views burnout as feeling overwhelmed with work, coupled with a great deal of emotional stress.[19] Burnout attacks all aspects of a person. Physical symptoms commonly include sleep disorders, chronic fatigue, headaches, and other minor illnesses.

Mental symptoms include withdrawal from work and family, dogmatism, and a general lack of motivation. The burnout victim's emotional experiences entail frustration, anxiety attacks, and a debilitating sense of feeling overwhelmed by work. Without effective coping mechanisms and support systems, the minister suffering from burnout may sink into a situational depression that can greatly diminish the impact of one's job performance.[20]

Several theories seek to explain the causes of burnout. Olsen and Grosch propose that affected ministers often possess a narcissistic personality that craves an inordinate degree of admiring appreciation from congregation members. This craving is often exacerbated by the sense of calling ministers experience. A vicious cycle ensues as a minister senses a divine plan and executes the plan. The congregation showers the minister with accolades, often exaggerated and excessive. Both the minister and the congregation raise their expectations, and the cycle begins again.[21]

Apart from this narcissistic pattern, Olsen and Grosch also believe that the pressures and demands of congregational life in opposition to a minister's family life can lead to burnout. As a minister's family grows in number and maturation, the family's needs for guidance from the minister as parent also grow. Conversely, as the minister feels pressure at home, yet is thriving on the accolades of congregation members, a dichotomy emerges. The minister may be viewed as a hero at church yet as something much less flattering at home.[22]

Grenz theorizes that ministers' burnout may be influenced by spiritual issues. Many ministers have an erroneous view of work and leisure. Traditional ministers mistakenly view leisure as a mere precursor to more productive work. The contemporary minister often sees work as a necessity in order to afford the materialistic leisure common in today's leisure culture. Christians do not work to earn leisure. Instead, they work as a sign of gratitude for the leisure God has provided.[23]

Grenz also states that many Christians have corrupted the relationship between God and man, especially between God and ministers. Some ministers have come to think that God's work cannot be accomplished without them. This is a limiting view of God, often prompting individuals to seek more responsibility than they can effectively fulfill.[24]

Developing a realistic view of one's ministerial responsibilities is one way to prevent burnout. Ministers must also work with congregations to help members support and appreciate the ministers' work appropriately and to form realistic expectations for ministers.[25] Ministers should maintain active hobbies and recreational pursuits, and they should schedule meaningful time with their families.[26]

Ministers can help prevent burnout by examining their individual personalities and problem-solving approaches. To avoid burnout one should learn to view change as an opportunity and challenge, not a danger. One should also exert locus of control to help minister responsibly and within one's abilities.[27]

Another successful coping mechanism is to seek God's presence during times of adversity.[28] This would seem like a foregone conclusion for ministers; however, Rodgerson and Piedmont find that ministers sometimes tend to compartmentalize their religious practice as work, often failing to apply religious problem-solving approaches.[29] While a vibrant Christian faith does not fully protect one from burnout, a minister should seek God's help to develop and maintain effective ministries. Effective ministries may already be the rule rather than the exception. Fichter reports that only 6 percent of the priests surveyed were candidates for burnout. The overwhelming majority of the respondents are healthy ministers with vibrant ministries.[30]

## Professional Development for Recreation and Sports Ministers

Stych identified four types of learners with respect to vibrant lifelong learning for ministers.

*Laggards* firmly resist innovation. They tend to be creatures of habit, outdated in their skills and approaches to ministry. Occasionally, their archaic approaches may even present safety hazards to participants physically and/or emotionally. They do not value continuing education and usually only participate in learning experiences when mandatory.

*Maintainers* are slow to accept change. Their involvement with continuing education is sporadic at best. They are suspicious of both nontraditional ministers and nontraditional ministry.

*Progressive managers* strive to improve professional practice but are drawn to more traditional, proven methods. They value continuing education, especially more traditional offerings. They embrace technology as a ministry tool.

*Visionaries* seek to improve professional practice. They are willing to pursue nontraditional approaches to lifelong learning and ministry. They are drawn to learn within and beyond their field and are not afraid to take risks.[31]

Seeking formal education is one way for the progressive managers and visionaries better to prepare themselves to use recreation and sports as effective tools for ministry. Formal continuing education may range from taking individual courses to seeking additional undergraduate or graduate degrees. Seminary education is highly valued for some recreation and sports ministers, especially those called to serve in traditional local churches.

Informal continuing education experiences are an alternative to formal academic course work. Traditionally, informal continuing education includes attending seminars and conferences, personal reading, and networking.[32] Ministers should seek informal learning experiences within their denominations, from other denominations, and from secular sources for maximum effectiveness. Learning outside the recreation and sports realm in areas such as technology, science, or vocational pursuits may also enhance one's ministry.[33]

Brown suggests four emerging approaches to informal continuing education that may be implemented by recreation and sports ministers.[34] First is the use of technology and the educational objects technology offers. For example, the Internet is a tremendous tool for locating recreational equipment suppliers and related information. Descriptions of games are also available on-line. Tremendous amounts of data relating to sports participation and sports ministry are available.

Another emerging approach is a form of networking known as skill exchanges. For instance, one recreation and sports minister might have a background in soccer but lack skills in hunting. She might partner with a fellow minister, offering to hold a soccer clinic at his church. In exchange, he might lead a hunting seminar at her church.

Peer matching is another approach to informal continuing education. An example might be an ecumenical group of recreation and sports ministers from several neighboring communities who meet together on a regular basis. The meeting could include social time as well as structured individual ministry case studies shared for group problem solving.

The final approach involves links to educators at large. This could include using academic professionals, from both secular and faith-based institutions, as consultants. Such consulting provides valuable educational dialogue. An overloaded minister can often profit from an uninvolved perspective. Consultations also provide professors with real-world experiences to keep course work relevant for their students.

Another informal approach to professional development is mentoring.[35] There is much to be gained from partnering seasoned recreation and sports ministers with those just entering the ministry. Such a relationship can often shorten the learning curve for a young professional. Experienced ministers can also become energized from meaningful relationships with enthusiastic, creative young ministers.

The focus of lifelong learning is often related to producing a tangible product as a result of learning. For example, a recreation and sports minister returning from a conference might be expected to develop new sports leagues or implement new recreational programs. Purdum, on the other hand, stresses the spiritual importance of lifelong learning. Continuing education should go beyond academic study, also providing time for reflection, self-assessment, and spiritual renewal. Continuing education should move beyond being a mere professional expectation. Germane lifelong learning helps one to be a good steward, fully utilizing the gifts and talents God has entrusted to his ministers.[36]

Lifelong learning should enhance the ministry potential and professionalism of recreation and sports ministers. Shivers proposes three premises to guide the practice and conduct of responsible leisure-services professionals.[37] Each premise will be accompanied by implications for the recreation and sports minister. The first premise is a preoccupation with public welfare. From a study of lifelong learning for Pentecostal ministers, Lavallee states that the primary reason for seeking informal continuing education was a desire to meet the needs of church members.[38] All recreation and sports ministers should remember that ministry's purpose is to meet the needs of the people we serve.

The second premise is a continual search for truth. Ministers are in a position to discover and share truth. This should be viewed as a tremendous opportunity *and* responsibility. Historically, the clergy has been well educated and well informed. This must continue to be the case in the rapidly changing Information Age.[39]

The third premise is a dedication to ethical practice. Because of the holistic nature of recreation and sports ministry, individual ministers must continually strive to uphold the highest personal and professional ethics. The central tenets of our ministries should be relevance and excellence.

Recreation and sports ministers must diligently explore the variety of lifelong learning experiences that are available to help them reach their ministry potential. Purdum describes the challenges of reaching one's ministry potential and the role of vocational professionalism. (For more information, see appendix 2, "Sources for Lifelong Learning and Networking.")

Ministers' days are spent within the bosom of the church, but our ministries are with people whose everyday lives are completely secular.

This is a challenge to our sense of call and the priesthood of all believers. True integrity of vocation is directly linked to a clear-eyed exploration of all the ways in which God might be calling us to live and work.[40]

Through such exploration, recreation and sports ministers will continue to be valuable contributors to both the mission of the church and the goal of advancing the leisure-services profession.

*Notes*

1. Christopher R. Edginton, et al., *Leisure and Life Satisfaction: Foundational Perspectives,* 3rd ed. (New York: McGraw Hill, 2002), 282–84.

2. Keith D. Ernce, "Church Recreation in the Southern Baptist Convention as a Leisure Consumer, Leisure Provider and Member of the Leisure Services Delivery System" (Ph.D. diss., University of New Mexico, 1987), 132.

3. Brad E. Wesner, "Visions and Revisions: An Exploratory Investigation Sketching the Origins and Growth of the Evolving Relationship Between the Church and Recreation, 1872–1992" (Ph.D. diss., University of Illinois at Urbana-Champaign, 1995), 162–64; Ernce, 132.

4. Jay Shivers, *Introduction to Recreational Service* (Springfield, Ill.: C. C. Thomas, 1993), 524.

5. Richard Kraus, *Recreation and Leisure in Modern Society,* 6th ed. (Sudbury, Mass.: Jones and Bartlett Publishers, Inc., 2001), 320; Edginton, et al., 372.

6. Kraus, 318.

7. Elaine M. McDuff and Charles W. Mueller, "The Ministry as an Occupational Labor Market," *Work and Occupations* 27 (2000): 108.

8. Edginton, et al., 373–74.

9. "The Covenant and Code of Ethics," downloaded from http://www.abc-indiana.org/Region/Polity/codeethics.html. Accessed on 27 February 2002. "Code of Ethics," downloaded from http://www.aapc.org/ethics.htm. Accessed on 21 February 2002. "Code of Ethics for Elders," downloaded from http://www.wcg.org/lit/church/ministry/codeethics.htm. Accessed on 27 February 2002.

10. McDuff and Mueller, 107.

11. M. J. McNamee, H. Sheridan, and J. Buswell, "Paternalism, Professionalism and Public Sector Leisure Provision: The Boundaries of a Leisure Profession," *Leisure Studies* 19 (2000): 200–04.

12. "Education and Professional Standards," downloaded from http://www.nrpa.org/department.cfm?departmentID=2&publicationID=11&Sub_DepartmentID=22. Accessed on 27 February 2002.

13. "What Is Accreditation?" downloaded from http://www.nrpa.org/story.cfm?story_id=128&departmentID=2&publicationID=11. Accessed on 27 February 2002. "Agency Accreditation," downloaded from http://www.nrpa.org/department.cfm?departmentID=2&publicationID=11&Sub_DepartmentID=233. Accessed on 27 February 2002.

14. Kraus, 327.

15. Shivers, 541.

16. George Torkildsen, *Leisure and Recreation Management,* 3rd ed. (London: E & FN Spon, 1992), 435.

17.  Wesner, 163.

18.  Elizabeth Purdum, "Sanctifying Ministers Through Lifelong Education," *Dialog* 38 (1999): 277.

19.  Joseph H. Fichter, "The Myth of Clergy Burnout," *Sociological Analysis* 45 (1984): 376–77.

20.  Sarah B. Watstein, "Burnout: Buzzword or Reality," *ATLA Proceedings* 40.01 (1985): 112.

21.  David C. Olsen and William N. Grosch, "Clergy Burnout: A Self Psychology and Systems Perspective," *Journal of Pastoral Care* 45 (1991): 297–98.

22.  Ibid., 301.

23.  Stanley J. Grenz, "Burnout: The Cause and the Cure for a Christian Malady," *Currents in Theology and Mission* 26 (1999): 427, 429.

24.  Ibid., 430.

25.  Olsen and Grosch, 302.

26.  Ibid., 303.

27.  Gary L. Harbaugh and Evan Rogers, "Pastoral Burnout: A View from the Seminary," *Journal of Pastoral Care* 38 (1984): 103.

28.  Ibid., 104.

29.  Thomas E. Rodgerson and Ralph L. Piedmont, "Assessing the Incremental Validity of the Religious Problem-Solving Scale in the Prediction of Clergy Burnout," *Journal for the Scientific Study of Religion* 37 (1998): 523.

30.  Fichter, 379.

31.  Brad E. Stych, "Improving Workshop Use with Ministry Professionals," *Christian Education Journal* 15 (1995): 46–47.

32.  Edginton, et al., 389.

33.  Purdum, 278–80.

34.  George Brown Jr., "Lifelong Learning and Ministry," *Reformed Review* 50 (1997): 163–64.

35.  Purdum, 280.

36.  Ibid., 277.

37.  Shivers, 544–47.

38.  Nil N. Lavalee, "A Study of Continuing Learning Among Pentecostal Ministers," *Eastern Journal of Practical Theology* 10 (1996): 31.

39.  Kenneth G. Davis, "From Anecdote to Analysis: A Case for Applied Research in Ministry," *Pastoral Psychology* 46 (1997): 104.

40.  Purdum, 280.

# 5 Organization of Recreation and Sports Ministry
## John Garner

Every church uses recreation and sports ministry. Every church. It may not be well organized, but all churches do it. Banquets, parties, fellowships, sports teams, church picnics, drama, camping, and special celebrations are a part of the life of most, if not all, churches. People enjoy and need this fellowship and activity. Churches that seek to meet these needs offer opportunities for social, mental, physical, emotional, and spiritual growth. A well-organized recreation ministry with a balanced program will offer opportunities for growth in all these areas to all ages. Doing this with a vision of reaching, winning, and teaching the lost requires kingdom-oriented thinking and planning.

A recreation and sports ministry that reflects kingdom thinking will support and help the church carry out the Great Commission of "going unto all the world." Kingdom planning seeks to minister to all participants, believers and nonbelievers alike, by creatively using the tools of crafts, socials, camping, sports, wellness/fitness, drama, music, and continuing education—anything that can be done in one's leisure time to impact lives with the gospel. As these tools are thought through, planned for, and used wisely, opportunities arise for evangelism, discipleship, fellowship, ministry, and worship. This kind of kingdom thinking will result in numerical and spiritual growth along with the expansion of ministry opportunities and missions advance.

Churches that use recreation and sports must do so with the intention of developing relationships with the lost and building the fellowship of the church. As these are done, new church leaders are found and trained, and nonbelievers are reached. Perhaps because there is nothing religious about recreation and sports ministry, to be effective there must be extra caution and a high degree of organization and planning to facilitate effective intentional ministry.

No one can get things accomplished or minister in chaos. The scriptural admonition of 1 Corinthians 14:40 is, "Everything must be done decently and in order." The mechanism that allows everything to run smoothly is organization. Organization provides framework, stability, direction, and accountability. Organization also minimizes conflict, duplication, and wasted effort. In a ministry team environment, a good organization involves:

*Enlisting*—Finding the right person for each job.

*Empowerment*—Trusting the people with responsibility and authority to get a job done–their way.

*Nurturing*—Growing people in a job to become more than they thought they could be, thus providing training for larger leadership roles in the future.

*Developing relationships*—Fostering trust and interdependence among ministry team members.

*Coaching*—Helping ministry team members be effective.

*Intentionality*—Making sure that the gospel is presented at every opportunity.

An organized recreation and sports ministry team seeks to allow a wide population of individuals to express their talents, gifts, interests, and abilities in ways that bring personal satisfaction and corporate good. This helps accomplish the work of the church through its members' involvement as outlined in 1 Corinthians 12:12–31. Each part of the body (church) has distinctly different functions. Lived out through well-organized, scripturally based, philosophically sound ministry, the final outcome of an organized recreation and sports ministry team effort will see many kingdom results.

The organizational structure of recreation and sports ministry of a church must establish and support a Christ distinctive in each activity/ministry action. This will set the ministry apart from other recreation efforts by community, private, or other nonprofit entities. Part of this distinctive is creating an atmosphere in which ministry and fellowship are planned for and intentionally happen. Another part of this Christ distinctive is for discipleship to be planned for as personal involvement by members happens. Personal service opportunities abound in recreation and sports ministry. The organizational structure must provide for member involvement. As evidenced by Oswald earlier, every church member can minister according to his or her giftedness, talents and abilities, or interests. This is the concept of ministry teams.

Scripture guides us as we endeavor to develop a functioning organization that:

*Seeks every opportunity to reach the lost*—"I have become all things to all people, so that I may by all means save some" (1 Cor. 9:22).

*Honors God at each event*—"Whatever you do, do everything for God's glory" (1 Cor. 10:31).

*Relates to the whole person*—"Jesus increased in wisdom and stature, and in favor with God and people" (Luke 2:52).

*Creates an atmosphere of happiness*—"A cheerful heart is good medicine" (Prov. 17:22).

*Teaches use of gifts, talents, interests, and abilities*—"Do not neglect the gift that is in you" (1 Tim. 4:14).

*Develops the fellowship of the church*—"By this all people will know that you are My disciples, if you have love for one another" (John 13:35).[1]

These six principles should guide those planning recreation and sports ministry for all ages in the church.

## Steps to Organization for Effective Recreation and Sports Ministry

There are nine basic steps to assure success in providing an effective base for recreation and sports ministry. Each step builds on the one before and sets the stage for the one to follow.

### 1. Establish Church and Staff Support

Recreation and sports ministry must have the support of the pastor, staff, and church in general. This is one ministry that will touch all other ministries and all ages. As the leader of the church, the pastor must understand the concept and support it. No ministry will succeed if the pastor is not behind it. He must see how it can be used as a tool for both discipleship and evangelism. Staff members need to understand how this ministry will support and complement their ministries. There is no room for competition between this ministry and others in the church. Done right, recreation and sports ministry undergirds and complements all other ministries. Recreation and sports ministry funnels prospects to the worship services, to the choirs, to the youth and children's ministry, as well as to the Bible study ministry of the church.

Natural support for "recreation and sports" will be in evidence. Everyone likes to play; however, church members must understand that this will not be activity for activity's sake. They can be involved in recreation and sports ministry as an intentional ministry and can invite their friends with confidence that all who participate will come under the influence of the gospel at some point anytime an event, class, seminar, league, or gathering occurs. Enlisting church member support will take time and continuous training as to why a church would want to get itself organized for recreation and sports ministry.

The leader charged with helping teach recreation and sports ministry principles will need an understanding of how the Great Commission and the five functions of the church—evangelism, discipleship, ministry, fellowship, and worship—are lived out through the open and closed groups as outlined in the model and process in chapter 1 of this book. They will also need to understand how their work will impact the kingdom results of numerical growth, spiritual transformation, ministry expansion, and kingdom advance of the church.

## 2. Provide Leadership That Has a Vision for Using Recreation and Sports as Ministry Tools

The church must find leadership that has a vision and understanding of how recreation and sports can be used as an intentional ministry tool. This leadership can be a full-time staff member, a part-time staff member, or a volunteer. This person must understand the key role he or she is going to play in teaching the church how to use recreation as a ministry tool. There is nothing religious about recreation and sports ministry. It is neither good nor bad: recreation is morally neutral; sports is morally neutral. The key is what you do with these tools. The leader will need to possess an understanding of and insight into the use of these secular tools in the life of the church. Left on their own, these tools will not lead a church to do ministry. However, as the leader trains the activity leaders to be intentional by providing ministry resources, encouragement, and guidance, these activities can be the instrument opening the door for evangelism and discipleship.

A mistake some churches make is thinking that because the church sponsors an activity it will take on a spiritual dimension. The organization as led by a person called of God to this unique ministry area will constantly have to remind itself why they are doing this ministry, what needs to happen, and how to get where the church wants the ministry to go. For the evangelic church, reaching and discipling people must be primary.

Various sized churches with different staff situations must determine who is responsible at the administrative level for recreation and sports ministry. There may be a natural growth progression as a church grows from one size to the next with differing needs.

*For the small church*—When the pastor is the only staff member, a gifted and skilled layman may be asked to develop the recreation and sports ministry. This director should have full responsibility for the recreation and sports ministry. He or she should be empowered to call ministry team meetings, set calendar dates, and work with the pastor in overall coordination of the ministry. Communication with the pastor and the church ministry leadership team is important during formative, implementation, and development stages. Periodic conferences will keep things compatible with the pastor's and the church's concept of the direction the ministry should take.

*When a second staff member is added to the small church model*— Recreation supervision and administration usually passes to the new person on staff. The staff member with recreation as one of many responsibilities may choose to continue the "director plan," as the pastor did. He will depend on a ministry team and lead teams to help get the job done. Having multiple staff assignments, the minister will delegate much of the programming and authority for quality ministry in all areas to take place. Many churches with active programs (even with a gym, open for programmed hours) work successfully with this arrangement.

*Adding a full-time recreation and sports minister*—As the church grows numerically and ministry expansion demands that a professionally trained person be added to the staff, the church will seek a full-time recreation and sports minister. The church will usually begin to plan a comprehensive program and/or a complex drop-in facility. This person's role will be to coordinate a wide-ranging ministry to all ages in all leisure–services areas. He or she still should depend on the recreation and sports ministry leadership team, volunteers, and possibly paid staff for successful ministry and operation of a facility.

In all these situations the personality of the church and the personality of the minister will determine the design of the ministry team and its effectiveness.[2]

## 3. Set Up a Ministry Team Structure

The recreation and sports ministry team is made up of people who have an interest in using recreation and sports. This natural interest can be married to the heart of a Christian so that people see how God can use their natural ability as a tool for ministry. Christians want to serve God. Most of us think that unless we preach, lead music, teach a Bible study, or become a missionary we can't serve God. The recreation and sports ministry team allows folks with interests in leisure activities a place to serve God, the church, and the community.

Figure 5-1 illustrates how a ministry team might function. The pastor is the exofficio member of each ministry team. In larger churches a staff member may be the liaison between the church staff and the ministry team. Ministry team members function on two levels, one long term and the other short term. The first level is the longer-term level. The team members on this level would serve a two- to three-year rotating term. This rotation system assures continuity from year to year. Each ministry team member would have an area of specialization or interest that they would represent on the team. Often these leaders are called coordinators. This level makes up the policy-making and advisory part of the overall team. All policies directly related to recreation and sports ministry come from this body. If a church has a recreation facility, often this body will give guidance to the facility ministry. However, sometimes a church will have a facility ministry team to give attention to the unique needs that a facility brings. Coordinators give the overall direction to the ministry.

> *The recreation and sports ministry leadership team is a policy-making and guiding body.*

These persons should: (1) be committed Christians, (2) be active church members, (3) have a ministry concept of recreation and sports,

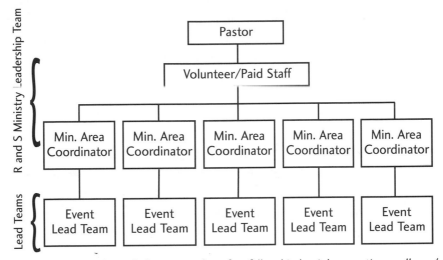

Ministry areas might include arts and crafts, fellowship/social recreation, wellness/fitness, outdoor education, sports, age groups, retreats, community outreach, trips, drama, and music.

*Figure 5-1: Ministry Team Structure*

(4) understand the inner workings of the church, (5) be dedicated to reaching and growing people for God, and (6) have the time necessary to serve.[3]

The recreation and sports ministry leadership team should be made up of people with diversity of interests. Members should not all be professionals or all sports oriented. They should represent all membership elements in the church as this ministry team touches every ministry area of the church.

The functions of the recreation and sports ministry leadership team include:

- Advise the staff member associated with recreation and sports ministry.
- Develop and protect the purpose, philosophy, theology, and policies for the recreation and sports used as ministry tools.
- Receive and consolidate calendar dates, leadership enlistment, and budget recommendations from ministry area coordinators.
- Be responsible for long-range planning. Serve as a sounding board for new ideas in light of the ministry team assignment of the church.

- Focus recreation and/or sports events on evangelism of the unsaved, outreach to prospects, and in-reach to inactive church members.
- Ensure that every aspect of the ministry (1) honors God, (2) is in harmony with the church's purpose/mission statement, and (3) channels people into open and closed groups as appropriate.
- Be vigilant to see that ministry is the purpose of the committee and program's existence.
- Provide a balanced calendar to ensure that the ministry is well rounded, functional, and not dominated by any person or program area.
- Provide a proper atmosphere where intentional ministry can happen.
- Maintain facilities, maximize their use, and project needed improvements.[4]

The ministry team should appoint or elect a chairperson to work with the staff member, coordinate/lead the meetings, and act as a sounding board and advisor to the staff member.

*Lead teams serve for short terms to carry out an activity or event, then are dissolved. Teams are usually made up of persons with interest in particular areas of ministry.*

When a particular ministry action is planned, the coordinators pull together a short-term lead team to help plan and implement the event. The lead team is made up of highly motivated members who have an interest in a particular activity area. They come together for a short time to plan and help with the event. After the event is over and evaluated, the lead team then dissolves. The next time that event is to be done, the lead team members may change. Most lead teams function for six to eight weeks. This concept works because people will give short periods of time to something that interests them. No long-term commitments are needed, calendars can be scheduled, and other activities planned around the event. Short-term commitments are here to stay.

## 4. Develop a Biblically Sound Theology of Recreation and Sports Ministry

For a church to have an organized recreation and sports ministry that is effective and supports the mission of the church, the ministry must have a solid foundation in Scripture. While other chapters in this text will go deeper into Scripture and theology, this chapter provides an overview of the basics of what a church will need to know and understand as a rationale for organizing a recreation and sports ministry according to Scripture.

Throughout Scripture God speaks of labor/work and rest or leisure. Where he does not speak directly, he gives principles for living. As the church moves to organize a ministry using recreation and sports, it must teach its members why they are doing this type of ministry. This is not a one-time event. Because our culture is so leisure oriented, the natural tendency is to equate recreation with fun and games and not ministry opportunities. Members must be reminded often as to why a church is using recreation and sports, lest they take the natural or secular view and see recreation and sports ministry events as activity for activity's sake.

Five basic understandings mark the beginnings of a biblical worldview of recreation and sports used as ministry tools:

1.  God provides meaningful labor (work).
2.  God commands the Sabbath or rest.
3.  Man has corrupted God's good gifts—work and leisure.
4.  Foundations for this culture.
5.  Jesus provides the example.

Each of these concepts is based on Scripture in principle or by example for the church to consider.

***God provides meaningful labor (work).*** Some basic Scriptures for this statement include:

"All hard work brings a profit, but mere talk leads only to poverty" (Prov. 14:23).

"That everyone may eat and drink, and find satisfaction in all his toil—this is the gift of God" (Eccles. 3:13).

"The sleep of a laborer is sweet, whether he eats little or much" (Eccles. 5:12).

"The thief must no longer steal. Instead, he must do honest work with his own hands, so that he has something to share with anyone in need" (Eph. 4:28).

"Seek to lead a quiet life, to mind your own business, and to work with your own hands, as we commanded you, so that you may walk

properly in the presence of outsiders and not be dependent on anyone" (1 Thess. 4:11–12).

In these passages we find the principle that work is provided by God
as a gift. Work is something that brings meaning and satisfaction to life.
In some cases, work provides something to share with others. In other
instances the principle is living a quiet life not dependent on others. Profit
is a worthy motive for work, and hard work is said to be sweet. Whatever
we do, as North Americans, our work provides for us food, shelter, clothing, transportation, and the means for our leisure. This aspect of work is
one of our primary motivations; our work supports our leisure.

Work has a way of bringing a sense of accomplishment and fulfillment. God in his infinite wisdom has provided work to enrich our lives.
The Christian response to work should be one of thankfulness and stewardship as we live out our gifts, talents, interests, and abilities in the workplace. In the workplace Christians meet the world. Christians must live in
an attractive and consistent way to attract the unbeliever. This is the reason for stewardship of our labor, "so that you may walk properly in the
presence of outsiders" (1 Thess. 4:12).

***God commands the Sabbath or rest.*** Scripture background for this
concept is well known:

> "By the seventh day God had finished the work he had been
> doing; so on the seventh day he rested from all his work. And God
> blessed the seventh day and made it holy, because on it he rested from
> all the work of creating that he had done" (Gen. 2:2–3).

> "For six years sow your fields, and for six years prune your vine-
> yards and gather their crops. But in the seventh year the land is to
> have a sabbath of rest, a sabbath to the LORD. Do not sow your fields
> or prune your vineyards" (Lev. 25:3–4).

> "Then He told them, 'The Sabbath was made for man, and not
> man for the Sabbath'" (Mark 2:27).

> "He said to them, 'Come away by yourselves to a remote place and
> rest a little.' For many people were coming and going, and they did
> not even have time to eat" (Mark 6:31).

Rest is fundamental to the well-being of humankind. We have God's
example of his "resting" after creation. Every seventh year, the land was to

rest and lay fallow and man was not to work that field for a year. Jesus pointed out that the Sabbath was made for man's good. Jesus also called his disciples to get away to a quiet place and get some rest.

The concept of rest was created and sanctioned by God for man's good. It provides a time to "re-create" our inner being and rejuvenate our bodies. Our fast-paced culture places a premium on leisure pursuits, often to the detriment of much-needed rest. Leisure education taught by the church and times of rest provided by the church can help people put this rest principle to work in their lives. A rested person performs better, feels better, and in turn can minister more effectively. We must learn how to lead the church to "come away [with Jesus] to a remote place and rest a little," for God commands the Sabbath.

The dilemma the church faces is how to help Christians understand the need for godly rest in such a fast-paced and competitive world. Rest is not only the cessation of activity but can include diversionary activities, anything that gets one out of his or her work routine—reading, biking, hobbies, conversation, trips, lawn work, or going to Bible study or worship. All of these can bring refreshment and new focus to life, the purpose of rest. Some might call this rest "recreation," and they would be right. This Sabbath rest (restful leisure) re-creates the mind, body, and spirit, preparing people to serve God and their fellow man through the meaningful work God has called us to do.

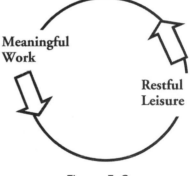

Figure 5-2

*Man has corrupted God's good gifts—work and leisure.* Scripture also supports this understanding:

"Go to the ant, you sluggard; consider its ways and be wise! . . . How long will you lie there, you sluggard? When will you get up from your sleep? A little sleep, a little slumber, a little folding of the hands to rest—and poverty will come on you like a bandit and scarcity like an armed man" (Prov. 6:6, 9–11).

"She who is self-indulgent is dead even while she lives" (1 Tim. 5:6).

"At the same time, they also learn to be idle, going from house to house; . . . saying things they shouldn't say" (1 Tim. 5:13).

People find ways to corrupt God's blessings and the good gifts he has provided to us. A person does this by putting his work before God and family and by making the pursuit of leisure the main goal in life. While work is given by God, and it blesses us, people put work before everything and anyone else. Often people, Christians included, get their sense of worth and self-esteem from what they do at work rather than their relationship with Christ. Dr. Ellen O'Sullivan wrote in *Parks and Recreation* magazine: "The average married couple works 717 more hours each year than in 1969."[5] We are working more hours to be more productive. However, work will not bring true satisfaction to life, but a life lived in balance will. God has provided work, so in essence it belongs to him. We are to be stewards of work, not slaves to it.

So it is with leisure. Leisure is made to be the end rather than the means to an end—that end being restful leisure that prepares us for meaningful work. Our leisure-oriented culture has convinced us that having leisure is the main point to life. The pursuit of leisure is not bad. How it is used makes all the difference. The pursuit of leisure as the focus to life results in an unbalanced life. The corruption of leisure has led us to almost an addiction to leisure itself—not the joy, peace, and fulfillment of the abundant life that Christ talked about in Scripture. Living for pleasure has led many individuals and nations to ruin. While not approaching their look at leisure from a Christian context, Carlson, Deppe, and MacLean state: "Leisure itself is a two-edged sword; it carries no guarantee for Utopian happiness. It may bring opportunity for enjoyment of art, music, and science; for the development of health, strength and satisfaction; or for the acquisition of inner resources that lead to contentment. Conversely, it may bring idleness, boredom, overindulgence, deterioration or corruption. . . . The wise use of the gift of leisure is the challenge of our time."[6] They are right—the wise use of leisure is not only a challenge for our time; it is a challenge of Christian stewardship.

***The Bible lays a foundation for this culture.*** Both the Old Testament and the New Testament have references to sports:

"This is what the LORD Almighty says: 'Once again men and women of ripe old age will sit in the streets of Jerusalem, each with cane in hand because of his age. The city streets will be filled with boys and girls playing there'" (Zech. 8:4–5).

"Do you not know that the runners in a stadium all race, but only one receives the prize? Run in such a way that you may win. Now everyone who competes exercises self-control in everything. However, they do it to receive a perishable crown, but we an imperishable one. Therefore I do not run like one who runs aimlessly, or box like one who beats the air. Instead, I discipline my body and bring it under strict control, so that after preaching to others, I myself will not be disqualified" (1 Cor. 9:24–27).

In these passages we find play and athletics mentioned in the Old Testament and the New Testament. In the Zechariah passage, men and women outside in the street and children playing in the streets carry an image of almost a Mayberry type of harmony and fulfillment. The land is safe, the people are fulfilled, and God is blessing. In the New Testament passage, runners preparing to run a race is one analogy, while boxing is used as another example of Paul taking culturally relevant happenings and using them to teach a spiritual lesson.

Our culture is as varied as the people who make it up. Impacting this culture will take a variety of methods targeting various age and interest groups. The interest in leisure is overwhelming. Senior adults have time and money to spend on leisure pursuits. High school students participate in an ever-increasing array of activities. Children's activities are found everywhere, provided by all types of organizations. Sports organizations cannot handle the crowds of children that come to them to play.

The principle here is that we can use all the tools at our disposal to influence the culture around us. Paul's example of "speaking the language" as he does in 1 Corinthians 9 shows us the way to capture the imagination of our culture with language they understand.

***Jesus provides the example.*** When Jesus changed the water into wine at the wedding feast, when he attended a banquet in his honor, and at other times, he affirmed fun and fellowship.

On the third day a wedding took place in Cana of Galilee.
Jesus' mother was there, and Jesus and His disciples were
invited to the wedding as well. When the wine ran out, Jesus'
mother told Him, "They don't have any wine."

"What has this concern of yours to do with Me, woman?" Jesus asked. "My hour has not yet come."

"Do whatever He tells you," His mother told the servants.

Now six stone water jars had been set there for Jewish purification. Each contained twenty or thirty gallons.

"Fill the jars with water," Jesus told them. So they filled them to the brim. Then He said to them, "Now draw some out and take it to the chief servant." And they did.

When the chief servant tasted the water (after it had become wine), he did not know where it came from—though the servants who had drawn the water knew. He called the groom and told him, "Everybody sets out the fine wine first, then, after people have drunk freely, the inferior. But you have kept the fine wine until now" (John 2:1–10).

Then Levi hosted a grand banquet for Him at his house. Now there was a large crowd of tax collectors and others who were guests with them. But the Pharisees and their scribes were complaining to His disciples, "Why do you eat and drink with tax collectors and sinners?" (Luke 5:29–30).

In these passages we find Jesus giving his blessing to parties and banquets. Jesus enjoyed people. He had a message for them, and he went to where they were to deliver the message. The church should follow Jesus' example and go to were the people are—at the ballpark, golf course, lake, football game, Olympics, fishing hole, park, crafts fair, party, stock car races, rodeo, school carnival, and theme parks. Wherever people are, the church needs to be there, taking the presence of Christ. If a church wants to reach families in the summer, where will it find them in the evenings? At the ballparks with their children.

Jesus was outside the synagogue with the people teaching great spiritual truth using tools and things they understood: sports analogies, agricultural object lessons, a little boy's lunch of fish and bread, and sometimes a miracle, often with people some did not like very much. The principle is plain enough to see: go where the people are and use tools they understand to teach them the love of God, the sacrifice of the Son, and the presence of the Holy Spirit.

Applying biblical concepts is key to good organization for recreation and sports ministry. Understanding these things will keep a focus on ministry and not activity. The Bible is the basis for all ministry. The principles and guidance it gives will keep one focused on the main things: reaching people, discipling believers, and multiplying ministering Christians.

## 5. Develop a Mission Statement

A mission statement for the recreation and sports ministry of any church must complement the church's mission statement. Each mission statement will be different for each church based on the church's local culture and church practice.

When developing a mission statement, the ministry team under the direction of the pastor or staff will:

1. Consider the church mission statement.
2. Seek mission statements from other churches.
3. Develop a philosophy of ministry based on Scripture.
4. Seek input from members and staff.
5. Seek to include the concepts of evangelism, worship, discipleship, ministry, and fellowship, which result in numerical growth for the church, spiritual transformation of participants, expanded ministry opportunity, and advancement of the kingdom of God.

A vision statement for recreation and sports ministry might include the following thoughts:

*Vision*—Recreation and sports ministry seeks to be a Great Commission and Great Commandment ministry that builds the kingdom of God by using recreation and sports as ministry tools. This ministry seeks to "become all things to all people, so that I may by all means save some" (1 Cor. 9:22). We will use these tools to evangelize the lost, disciple believers, minister in Christ's name, facilitate worship, and encourage fellowship.

*Desired results*—In doing this ministry, a church should expect to see visible, tangible results in the areas of numerical growth as people are intentionally evangelized; spiritual growth as Christians are discipled; ministry expansion as Christians use their gifts, talents, and abilities in recreation and sports settings; and kingdom advance as recreation and sports are used to capture the imaginations of a leisure-oriented culture outside the walls of the church.

## 6. Educate the Church

Because there is nothing religious about recreation activities or sporting events, the recreation and sports ministry team must begin to educate the church about what recreation and sports ministry is and what it is not. This is not a one-time event. Education must be done continuously as new people come into the church. Church members must be reminded why you do this ministry and what the results are expected to be.

One of the jobs of the recreation and sports ministry team will be to see opportunities to share the story about what is happening in the ministry. This can be done through several means: newsletters, promotional mailings, reports to the church, flyers, handouts, personal stories about involvement in the ministry in a recreation and sports ministry newsletter, and other opportunities as they are made available.

Upon election of the ministry team, the team members should be in Bible study classes and at other meetings helping the church understand the recreation and sports ministry vision and expected results. If possible the pastor should preach a sermon on the use of recreation and sports as the church expects to see this ministry done. The story should be told often, pointing out the results in the lives of participants and the growth of the church.

## 7. Use Surveys to Assess Needs and Opportunities

One of the keys for establishing a well-organized recreation and sports ministry is to find out what the people want in such a ministry. In order to provide the most comprehensive and well-rounded ministry, a series of surveys will need to be done.

A recreation and sports ministry survey is a way to get information that will help ensure success. The process involves three types of surveys: property survey, community survey, and membership survey.

***The property survey***—This survey involves looking at everything on the church property that might be used for recreation and sports ministry activities. The survey will involve looking for inside space suitable for activity and looking at outdoor areas that may host an event.

*Survey indoor space.* When looking for space inside, look for large open spaces for larger groups, such as a fellowship hall for an all-church gathering. For a smaller group, perhaps the dining room is available for crafts classes as water is readily available, or by moving tables and chairs for aerobics ministry classes. Sunday school rooms can be used for continuing education classes, such as computer classes or tutoring.

Look for suitable space for various age groups. Preschool play days could be centered in the preschool Sunday school area, where furniture fits them. A senior adult stretching exercise class could be held in a room on the first floor that has good air exchange. A large Sunday school department might serve well as a game room if storage is available so that the games can be put away on Sunday. Whatever the need, many areas of a church can also be used for recreation events, classes, workshops, or tournaments. Survey all areas inside, and ask, "What could we do in this space?"

*Survey outdoor space.* Churches usually have a lot of usable outdoor space. Parking lots can be used for many activities: carnivals, bike rodeos, cookouts, basketball, roller hockey, and volleyball. Grassy areas can be used for picnics, ice cream socials, watermelon cuttings, fairs, day camping, adventure games, and VBS recreation.

Of course, safety is an issue when using outdoor areas. Make sure traffic can be blocked if you are using a parking lot. Make sure grassy areas have no broken glass, holes, or any other safety issues. Particular attention should be paid to overhead power lines, ditches, and the grade (slope) of the area.

Outdoor recreation areas need to be adjacent to or have water and rest rooms available. A survey of outdoor areas on your church property will open up new space for recreation and sports ministry.

***Community survey***—This survey will look at what is available in the community that may be used by the church for recreation and sports ministry activities. Look for places of business, parks, farms, and other places that could host your group. Bowling alleys could host a church bowling league. Local, state, or national parks could be used for day camping, outdoor worship services, cookouts, camp outs, and picnics. Craft shops can often be used to host crafts classes. Shop owners will usually let outside groups hold classes in their shop provided you purchase your materials from them. Schools often let churches use or rent their facilities for basketball or volleyball leagues. City recreation departments often will host church softball leagues. Lakes offer the opportunity for water ski outings or other outdoor activities. Some campgrounds have adventure recreation and ropes courses available for church use.

Communities have a host of usable sites for recreation and sports ministry activities to take place. A survey of any community will turn up many potential sites.

*Membership survey*—The most useful survey is the membership survey. From this survey one gains knowledge of what the membership is now doing, would like to do, or could provide leadership for. This survey is taken of the entire congregation, from junior high through senior adults. The recreation and sports ministry leadership team will assist in taking the survey. The procedure is as follows:

1.   Enough surveys are printed for the entire congregation. (See sample survey in appendix 3.)

2.   Work with the pastor and church staff to set the time period for this survey—usually three consecutive weeks.

3.   Survey the largest population available. For most churches this will be the Sunday morning Bible study time. An option would be to mail out the surveys. However, it has been proven that the best response comes from Sunday morning Bible study units. Mail surveys to homebound members, those who work with preschoolers and children on Sunday morning, and inactive members.

4.   The recreation ministry leadership team will divide up the Bible study organization, and each team member will take several classes/groups to conduct the survey.

5.   Each Sunday during the allotted time, leadership team members are in their assigned Bible study units to take the survey.

6.   The survey should take a maximum of ten minutes. The members are asked to check appropriate boxes on the survey form to indicate:

☐   I am now taking part in this activity.

☐   I am interested in this activity.

☐   I have experience and could help lead this activity.

NOTE: These three answer categories will help the programmer identify potential participants—those who check "now taking part in" or "I am interested in this activity." Potential leaders come from "I have experience and could lead this activity." (See the sample survey in appendix 3.)

7.   When the allotted weeks are up, the leadership team tallies the surveys. If the church uses a computerized membership system, this can be done in a membership database as coded fields in each member's pro-

file. If the membership is not computerized, or no member profile fields are available, a database can be set up in Access or Excel.

8. From the information gathered, you will find potential participants, and potential leaders, and can begin programs.

The job of the recreation and sports ministry leadership team will be to tally the surveys; decide which activities to start first, as indicated by the most interest found on the survey; to check the church calendar to choose the optimum time to begin the chosen activity to avoid conflicts with other ministry areas; to enlist leaders (indicated on survey); to publicize the event; to purchase any needed materials/supplies; to conduct sign-ups; to hold the class, activity, or workshop; to evaluate the event; and if successful, schedule the next time you will host that event. If it was not successful, your evaluation will point out weaknesses so that they may be remedied next time.

Surveying should be done every three to five years or as needed. New members should be surveyed as they join a Bible study group or the church. New participants and new leaders will be found.

Consider these keys to successful start-up events:

- Start slowly. Pick the top three to five events/activities. Do only what can be done well.
- Publicize well.
- Check the calendar. Make sure not to conflict with church or community events.
- Provide the budget and work within budgeting constraints.
- Find a qualified lead team of interested supporters to help carry out the event.
- Train event leaders to have a ministry mind-set. The leadership team has the responsibility to teach those who lead events to use their area of interest as a tool for sharing the gospel. While this may seem elementary, it must be an intentional part of the planning process, or the event will be just an activity and not ministry.
- Do everything with quality.
- Evaluate the process.

## 8. Work within Existing Calendaring and Budgeting Frameworks

The recreation and sports ministry leadership team will work with the assigned staff member to see that the ministry operates within existing guidelines for calendaring and budgeting. (For sample budget worksheets, see appendix 5, "Event Cost Projection"; appendix 6, "Non-Event Cost Projection Worksheet"; appendix 7, "Total Cost Projection Worksheet"; and appendix 8, "Recreation and Sports Ministry Budget Accounts.")

## 9. Provide a Balanced Ministry Calendar for All Ages

Each person who gives leadership to recreation and sports ministry has his or her favorite areas or interests. The tendency of many ministry/program providers is to have an abundance of what they like, leaving out large segments of potential participants. The sports enthusiasts will naturally have a tendency to provide program ministry in sports. The outdoors person will want to provide outdoor experiences because they see potential for activity and ministry there. The leader may not realize that this is happening. A conscientious effort must be made to provide a balanced calendar for all ages—preschoolers to senior adults—in the appropriate programming areas.

• • • • • • • • • • •

**Programming—**
*providing, planning, staffing recreation activities that meet the objectives of the church and the expressed needs of the people.*

• • • • • • • • • • •

Programming is the key to keeping people involved. It is the reason they want to participate. Done creatively, programming will keep a ministry from becoming boring. Programming comes directly from the survey, meeting the needs of constituents.

### *Program Planning*

• Start with activities that have the most potential participants, according to the survey. The programmer should pick three to five of the most requested events.
• Work within the church calendar and budgeting system.
• Go all out to ensure success, especially if this is a new ministry.
• Promote. Create the buzz with creative, imagination-catching advertising.
• Make the event feel larger than life, something that you would not want to miss. Desktop publishing makes promotion much easier than it used to be.
• Equip to get the best results. Purchase only institutional quality

equipment, use visuals to create an atmosphere for socials, provide top-quality basketballs for games.

- Train leaders to have an intentional ministry mind-set. Recreation and sports events are not religious in nature. Leaders must be trained to use the event, practice, or game for the gospel's sake. Provide printed helps for leaders.

***Programming Formats***

- Open play/drop-in
- Clinics: one-day events
- Workshops: one- or two-day skill enhancement
- Classes: several sessions, basic to advanced
- Leagues/tournaments
- Clubs/affinity groups
- Special events

A helpful tool is a programming grid. Using the grid (see sample in appendix 4, "The Programmer's Evaluation Cube") the leader gets a quick view of what is being offered in all areas and for all ages. When he or she sees that the programming calendar is overbalanced in one direction or is leaving out one or more populations, the calendar can be adjusted to achieve balance.

## 10. Evaluate Progress

Any organization goes through stages:

Stage one is conceptualization. In this stage the idea is born and the vision shared with others to see if it is viable.

Stage two is preparation. Here, getting ready with the right infrastructure is important. With the right foundation in place, the idea can be implemented.

Evaluation is the last stage, and it is often omitted. Organizations that do not evaluate successes and failures are setting themselves up for ineffectiveness if not outright failure. The evaluation process is concerned with the collection of qualitative and quantitative information. The leadership team will evaluate each activity and, at the end of the programming year, evaluate the overall ministry. Areas to be evaluated include:

- Administration—Was the administration of the event/year well organized, staffed properly, planned well, and promoted adequately? Did it stay within budget?

- Leadership/staff—Was the staff knowledgeable and adequately trained not only in the skill being taught but in intentional ministry? Did we leverage our people resources to the best advantage?
- The overall program—Did the program meet its goals and impact lives? Did the program complement the vision statement of the church and ministry area?
- Facilities—Were the facilities adequate, well lighted, and comfortable?
- The future—What can we do in the future to enhance this event? Do we keep or drop the event?

Evaluation is the process of making what just happened better the next time around. Talking over and evaluating the five areas above and getting input from participants will give keen insight into the value of an event.

Organizing for recreation and sports ministry is necessary because of the sophistication of our culture and the importance of doing whatever we do with quality. The days of simply rolling out a ball cage into the gym and calling that ministry are long gone. Recreation and sports ministry is a multifaceted and multilayered ministry tool. Recreation and sports ministries that exhibit professionalism, quality, and grounding in God's Word as foundation stones of their organization will bring honor to Christ and people into the kingdom. If we take Scripture seriously, we must heed the Word of God when it says, "Everything must be done decently and in order" (1 Cor. 14:40).

---

**Notes**

1. Adapted from Wendell Newman, *Organizing for Recreation,* John Garner, ed. (Nashville: Convention Press, 1986), 8.

2. Ibid., 9–18.

3. Ibid., 12.

4. Ibid., 13.

5. Ellen O'Sullivan, "Play . . . for Life," *Parks and Recreation,* October 2000. Downloaded from http://www.findarticles.com/ef_O/m1145/10_35/66682725/print.jhtml. Accessed 27 August 2002.

6. Ronald E. Carlson, Theodore Deppe, and Janet R. MacLean, *Recreation in American Life* (Belmont: Wadsworth Publishing Company, Inc., 1963), 3–4.

# 6 Recreation and Sports Administration in a Ministry Setting
## Dale Adkins

The challenge for the minister of recreation and sports in the twenty-first century is knowing how to manage the human, physical, and fiscal resources in order to do ministry. No longer can a minister merely "shoot from the hip" in order to lead a church effectively; he or she must be able to articulate clearly how the entrusted resources will be organized, used, supervised, and evaluated for ministry. The accountability that is needed and demanded by congregations today with respect to ministerial leadership requires that good administrative practices be understood and implemented for today's recreation minister.

It becomes important at the outset to clarify the purpose of administration within the context of recreation and sports ministry. Administration is about people. The church possesses resources (facilities, equipment, finances, people). Most important is the notion that the church is people. The church is called to reach people and multiply people to be "fishers of men." The church can exist without a lot of physical assets, but its foundation is Christ. Through him people respond and are called to serve in a particular location using their gifts, talents, natural abilities, and interests. Administration is ministry.

## Christian Administration

Much that has been written about Christian administration has been written about, for, and/or by pastors and from that perspective. The research and writings are not totally void of the needs and issues of other ministers, associates, or directors on a church staff, but they are not as well represented in the literature. This is not surprising since the majority of churches are single-staffed by a pastor, and, in some cases, this may be a bivocational pastor. Being a part of a multistaff experience is the exception, not the norm, for most pastors.

Robert D. Dale suggests an idea that is helpful at this juncture. "In the church and other Christian organizations, administration is growing people, not simply doing things. Administration is vital if a church is to reach its mission."[1] Growing people is also critical to the vibrancy and future of recreation and sports ministry within the local church setting in order to accomplish its unique purpose within the context of the overall mission of a local congregation.

According to Caldwell, administration is not only a gift but also people and organization.[2] Those who are called to lead are exercising their gifts in unique areas of ministry. This does not preclude the fact that continuing education is a must for the minister of the twenty-first century. Gifts need to be further developed and refined. (Professional development issues for the minister are discussed in chap. 4.)

At the heart of ministry and administration are the people the church is seeking to reach, teach, disciple, equip, and empower to do the ministry of the church: "The wise minister learns early on in vocational ministry that we are in the people business and sees the wisdom of getting things done with and through people. Some of these people will be paid to assist in doing church, but most of them will be volunteers in the sense that they are ordinary church members who will be challenged to discover and develop their gifts in ministry."[3]

The uniqueness of the church, since it is an organization, requires the minister to understand that uniqueness with respect to administration. For the minister the challenge is balancing the spiritual and the administrative. In that tension the recreation minister will practice his or her gifts within the local church.

## Administration of Recreation and Sports Ministry

Administration of the recreation and sports ministry requires the minister to recognize and embrace the concept that recreation and sports can be ministry. Not all who serve in this area of ministry within a local congregational setting will bear the title *minister*. In some settings and under other circumstances, the designation may be "pastor of" or "director of." Regardless of the title, the person called, empowered, and charged with the recreation and sports ministry is ministering in a unique manner to meet the needs of a postmodern culture.

The staff person guiding this ministry finds that administration is biblically based and seen in the New Testament as a gift (1 Cor. 12:28). This is not to suggest that everyone who ministers through recreation and sports has or must have the gift of administration. It is clear though that God values the ability to orchestrate resources for the life of the church and the accomplishment of its ministry here on earth.

Today the modern church seeks to balance corporate business savvy with the ministry of the church. For some the integration of business principles into the management of the church is bothersome. Others seek to understand the principles and apply concepts with Christian guidance. Individuals such as Ken Blanchard[4] and Peter Drucker[5] are revered and quoted as the church strives to be more relevant in today's world in order to reach people.

## Personal Administration

Each minister has strengths and weaknesses. Being able to identify each area responsibly and truthfully will allow the minister to understand how the task of administration will be executed under his or her leadership and what will be needed in order to be effective. Through professional development and/or other evaluation, the weaknesses will require the minister to find ways to grow in these areas to be effective.

The nature of ministry is self-directed. The mission of the church and the mission of the recreation and sports ministry give parameters as to what the minister should do. In most churches, if a staff member has the recreation/sports responsibilities, it will be in a multistaff church. Depending on the size of the church, other church staff and the recreation and sports staff (paid or volunteer) will require the recreation and sports minister to know how to manage personal time in order to accomplish many tasks that need attention at any given point in time.

### Time Management

How the recreation and sports minister uses time will reflect a lot about personal work habits and the ability to juggle responsibilities and at the same time keep focused on the tasks at hand. The challenge will be to see even the smallest task as a part of larger ministry. If the minister sees everything as having "a purpose under heaven" (Eccles. 3:1), the routine experiences will continue to bring meaning throughout the course of his or her ministry.

Many ministers use personal calendars to help manage their schedules. With the advent of technology and personal computers, some find electronics a quicker way to manage their time on a day-to-day basis. Possibly the use of a calendar on the computer to log appointments and tasks that must be done daily will be most satisfactory. The use of a PDA (personal data assistant) allows the minister to do many things as he or she travels from place to place. For many this is now the preferred method of organizing personal time. Many methods of time management are now available. Each minister must decide on a method that is the best fit.

Support staff, whether a secretary, an administrative assistant, or a corps of volunteers, must be kept apprised of daily schedules. Allowing someone to help manage time, tasks, and people can provide multiple benefits. This frees the minister up to do ministry.

It is important to communicate to what extent staff can be a part of scheduling appointments and meetings. This will depend on one's sense of security with those on the ministry team.

## Communication

The nature of the church as an organization denotes the need for communication. The body has many parts, and each part requires attention at some point from the minister. The nurturing and involvement that are necessary by the minister will be more intense and time consuming than others. Again this is a part of the ministry through administration.

The recreation minister has many audiences that must be nurtured and addressed at any given time within the context of ministry. The audiences include peer ministers, other church support staff, governing councils/board/committees that comprise the church leadership structure, church members at large, and community agencies or organizations that require a relationship with the church through the minister.

The minister's style of communication will either greatly enhance or detract from the overall effectiveness of ministry. Making sure that telephone calls, E-mail, letters, personal notes, and memos clearly reflect the genuine nature of the individual minister is a priority. Ministry is happening through these tools of communication, so it behooves the minister to use these wisely and carefully to maximize positive influence on all constituents.

In today's world the speed at which life is lived impacts the church as well in the way ministry is done and the way in which communication is delivered at all levels and in all settings. The key for the recreation minister is to keep in mind that everything he or she does must be personal. Why the church exists and the ministries that are used to accomplish that purpose will help guide the minister in making choices to keep all tasks person centered. "If a church is to deepen spiritual lives, it has to know its members."[6] When members are known as well as their needs, communication can be tailored to reach them.

Communication is about sending a message and making sure the message is received. The fact that it takes multiple impressions to get the information to the specified audience challenges the church staff to use all outlets possible. To inform church members about opportunities for growth, ministry, and outreach through recreation and sports requires creativity in making sure that opportunities are presented in a timely and professional manner. The church's message is life changing and eternal. How it is communicated is therefore important and not to be taken lightly.

## Conflict Resolution

Even with the best of intentions, communication that is not understood can lead to conflict. Some people can deal with conflict, while others avoid it at all costs. The minister of recreation will encounter conflict because the nature of the ministry is personal and directly impacts people's lives.

No organization is devoid of conflict, and this includes the church. Where there are people, there is conflict. Osborne suggests that in the church the three groups in which conflict will happen are: (1) the congregation, (2) the governing boards/councils/committees, and (3) the staff.[7] In recreation and sports ministry, conflicts may occur within program areas, volunteer management, sponsorship of an activity, or other areas. The real key is having a strategy to deal directly and openly with the conflict.

Jordan proposed a seven-phase model of managing difficulties. The seven phases are:

1. Define objectives.
2. Identify the problem.
3. Analyze and interpret data.
4. Facilitate solutions.
5. Select the best solution.
6. Generate and implement.
7. Evaluate results.[8]

Each phase moves ultimately toward conflict resolution, but resolution does not mean that the final solution will be satisfactory to all involved.

Jordan's steps toward resolution allow all involved to help move toward a sense of reconciliation, which should be the goal for the church even in matters of conflict. This approach allows everyone to participate in seeking solutions and having ownership in the process. A systematic approach to deal with conflicts, which will occur with all three groups at some point within the church, will allow the recreation minister thoughtfully and carefully to approach conflict resolution.

The manner in which a minister of recreation manages professional time, communication, and conflict will shape personal administration. These areas of professional life and leadership shape one's ministry. Making sure that these areas have been approached as influencers in ministry will make the difference in a minister's longevity and ministry.

## Strategic Planning

Strategic planning is not a destination but a process by which an organization gives direction and focus to what it is doing. Within the context of the church and more specifically recreation and sports ministry, it allows leaders and members to help guide and shape the ministry of the church to reach the world for Christ's kingdom. Strategic planning is only one of four types of planning that an organization, regardless of size, should do, and this includes the church and specifically the recreation and sports ministry. The other three are comprehensive planning, community planning, and internal systems planning.

Wegner and Jarvi suggest that "the strategic planning process provides a means for developing a shared vision of the organization's future and then determining the best way to make this vision a reality."⁹ The recreation/sports minister has the opportunity within the overall mission of the church to do strategic planning as it relates to a specific area of ministry.

Recreation and sports ministry is given impetus and life according to the church's mission as a whole. When church members recognize recreation and sports ministry as part of the church's mission to reach people with the gospel, they will commit to support the ministry and encourage those outside the church to join them in church-sponsored leisure activities. The strategic planning for a specific area of ministry such as recreation and sports finds support in the overall church mission statement and possibly the church's strategic plan—a product of the process.

The minister of sports and recreation plays a crucial role in developing the strategic planning process for recreation and sports ministry. Making sure that all three groups—the congregation, governing groups, and staff—are represented in the process is a must. Within recreation and sports ministry specifically, different areas of ministry as well as interest groups need to help define what the future should be and will be for the recreation and sports ministry.

Having this road map to assist in developing and decision making for recreation and sports ministry is a valuable tool for this minister on an ongoing basis. Strategic planning is not a one-time event but a function of a vibrant and effective ministry.

## Environmental Scan

Within today's marketplace of life, the church must constantly and continually anticipate what is happening within the context of ministry within a given setting as well as at a broader view. This is what is called environmental scan. Environmental scan is the ability to look broadly at the location from which a church recreation and sports ministry provides ministry and service. At this point the recreation minister is then able to lead interested groups and leaders in the church to gather the necessary information internally and externally to help give movement to the process.

## Analysis of Ministry Situation

An organized and systematic strategy to gather information is a SWOT analysis. This analysis allows the recreation and sports ministry to look at its Strengths, Weaknesses, ministry Opportunities, and Threats that could hamper or stop the ministry from being effective. This information will help guide the ministry in future decisions based on realistic and honest appraisals from many perspectives.

## Vision Statement

After the information has been gathered from the environmental scan and the SWOT analysis, attention will shift to a vision statement. Scriptural guidance helps at this point: "Where there is no vision, the people perish" (Prov. 29:18 KJV). This admonition also applies to the recreation and sports ministry. The question the planning committee needs to answer is, where do we want the ministry to be in the future? A vision statement can help answer this question and define the preferred future for a church. This is not to discredit or fail to acknowledge the Spirit's leadership in committee member selection and work that is done. This whole process is seeking divine leadership for the church to help the church focus on and understand better what good work God wants to do within and through a local congregation and its recreation and sports ministry.

The recreation and sports ministry must then clearly define its purpose within the context of the local church. Developing a mission statement is the next step in the process. For most recreation and sports ministries, the mission statement will center on strengthening the church fellowship and providing a vehicle for outreach and evangelism. Some churches may also find that an opportunity to provide ministry to the community. The intent and heart would be outreach through relationship, but also this expanded mission would be driven by the vision and the information collected from the strategic planning process.

## Goals and Objectives

Goals and objectives must be developed for the recreation and sports ministry broadly and for individual areas/programs of ministry that comprise the church's recreation and sports ministry. Rossman and Schlatter present insight on how goals and objectives are interrelated at all levels.[10] This concept of interrelated goals and objectives gives direction to recreation and sports ministry as it relates to strategic planning.

## Action Plans

Strategic planning allows the development of goals and objectives for many different aspects of the plan. Action plans track the goals and objectives and monitor them in relationship to accomplishment, deadlines, and persons responsible. Without this step the planning process will never reach its full potential.

## Evaluation

Evaluation will help complete the planning process and identify successes, failures, and decisions that need to happen to ensure the future of areas of ministry within the recreation and sports ministry. This part of the strategic planning process needs to be done regularly in different areas of recreation and sports ministry. This will assist in the annual review of the entire recreation and sports strategic planning process. Any adjustments and changes can be based on solid information and feedback from a variety of audiences.

The recreation minister must make this step a priority in order for the planning process to be effective and help move the ministry forward. It is easy to base everything solely on numbers as the indicator for evaluation. Such analysis is the business world's approach. If in fact the church is trying to deepen and influence lives for Christ, then other types of information from evaluation will prove useful and necessary at this point, so that both quantitative and qualitative analyses are used. Keep in mind that all areas/programs of recreation and sports ministry need an evaluation component in order to assist and give direction to the overall strategic planning process. If evaluation is not intentional and planned, then decision making will be made on unreliable and inaccurate information—all in the name of ministry!

## Personnel Management

Personnel management emerges as the next area needing attention after strategic planning is complete. The strategic plan will determine the staff needed to execute the actions within the plan. Regardless of whether staff members are paid or volunteer, full-time or part-time, the recreation minister will be required to work with at least one or more of the above personnel categories to carry out the vision and mission of the ministry.

Even a single-staff pastor must be able to guide and lead a staff of individuals to minister through recreation and sports.

Managing staff, whether paid or volunteer, requires more similar strategies than different. The word *staff* will refer to both paid and volunteers unless otherwise noted. Areas to be discussed will be staff relations, volunteer management, working with committees/councils/boards, and interns.

## Staff Relations

Individuals who choose to work with a particular minister desire to be more intimately involved in a particular area of ministry. Motivation may be the use of their spiritual gifts, skills, and interests from vocational or recreational experience(s), a deep desire to serve God in a unique way, or the charisma of the minister. The bottom line is that they want to be part of a winning team. Whatever the motivation, the minister must mold and shape the ministry team to be effective, and at the same time the experience must be satisfying and fulfilling for everyone involved.

The recreation and sports minister will quickly be involved in personnel matters in order to accomplish the ministry that God has called him or her to do through a particular church. Depending on the structure of personnel matters within a church, the recreation minister may have several options in personnel matters. One approach is to work with another staff minister who oversees personnel for the entire church with laypeople involved in the process. The second approach is to work directly with a church personnel committee in staff selection, particularly paid staff. A third approach is for the recreation minister to work directly with a church committee/council/board in staff selection. In a fourth approach the church empowers the minister to seek staff and be responsible for hiring as well as terminating on behalf of the church. Probably the fourth approach is the least preferred way since church layleaders' support of staff will make a difference for the minister in larger issues that may loom in the future. All ministry is a collective experience.

A recreation minister may have responsibilities in recruiting, interviewing, hiring, training, supervising, evaluating, and terminating. All of these tasks take time and energy. The minister must learn and adhere to procedures unique to the church. Knowing the expectations of the church regarding personnel will help the minister in staff selection and make the process more positive for everyone involved.

Staff development is an ongoing responsibility for the recreation minister. Bjorklund quotes Bobb Biehl's questions for getting better results from your staff:

1. What decisions do you need from me?
2. What problems are keeping you from reaching your goals?
3. What plans are you making that haven't been discussed?
4. What progress have you made?
5. On a scale of one to ten, how are you personally? Why?
6. How can I be praying for you?[11]

In this approach to staff development, the minister empowers the staff to move ahead without someone looking over their shoulders. A recreation minister must feel secure about the ministry team as well as his or her ability to share the ministry with others. Using business approaches with a person-centered focus helps define the nature of the work to be done within Christian ministry.

Tidwell gives some insight on the relationship between the pastor and other staff members. It applies at the next level for the recreation minister to consider the suggestions for the ministry team.

1. Acknowledge and respect one another's call of God.
2. Let all ministers be called by church action.
3. Extend trust and develop trust with one another.
4. Practice frequent, regular, and accurate communication.
5. Be close enough to one another that staff are confident of closeness, even when physical proximity is not close.[12]

A sensitive issue that the recreation minister may encounter is that of terminating a staff member. This may be an emotional issue and experience for the employee as well as the supervisor. Making sure that expectations are clearly articulated at the time of hiring is one key to avoiding this situation. Securing reliable references and using situational interview questions can assist in a positive hiring and placement of a person on the staff.

Another strategy to ensure success with hiring is to meet with your staff individually on a weekly or semiweekly basis. This allows them to have your undivided attention. It allows the minister to monitor the staff's projects and continuing areas of responsibility. They are able to seek guidance and insight from you that will assist in their success. A minister's ministry is with his or her staff. Even though time is spent with staff in one-on-ones and staff meetings, some individuals do not fit the position or the ministry team or are not able to perform. When this occurs, documentation over a period of time is needed to deal with this personnel matter.

The tedious job of documenting is necessary to build the information required to terminate or redirect the staff member either to fill another position within the organization (church) or to seek another avenue for ministry/employment. The recreation minister should view this as an opportunity for growth for the employee as well for the minister.

Having staff means a commitment of time, energy, and resources. The dividend is that the recreation and sports minister shares the joy and the sorrow of ministry and equipping the saints to go into the world.

## Volunteer Management

Working with volunteers has unique features that differ from paid staff. The management approach is more of a "coach" and not so much a "supervisor." The motivation is not extrinsic due to a reward (paycheck) but is intrinsic—personal satisfaction in making a difference to a cause. Volunteers are not forever. Life situations, personal and/or family life cycles, and/or personal interests and new experiences make volunteer management a fluid area. Stewart quotes Peter Drucker: "Volunteers need special handling—they can't be bossed like galley slaves."[13]

Volunteerism in the church is big business. As Stewart indicates, religion, when compared to corporate America, is fairly sizable: "Whatever else it is, religion is big business. America has more clergy than Ford and Chrysler together have employees. If U.S. religion were a company, it would be No. 5 on the Fortune 500, its $50 billion of revenues putting it behind IBM and just ahead of GE. Church land and buildings are worth uncounted billions. And God's business is really far bigger than mammon's numbers suggest: The figures don't include volunteer work, worth a jaw dropping $75 billion a year."[14]

Volunteers are agents of the church and act on its behalf. Therefore, churches and their ministries are liable for actions taken by volunteers. Recruiting and training volunteers needs to be approached in the same manner as for paid professional staff.

Volunteers need a task description. The nature of many jobs within the church does not demand a formal job description. On the other hand, if volunteers assume major leadership roles within recreation and sports ministry, a formal job description should be developed and approved by necessary structures within a church. Volunteers want to know who their supervisors are; the expectations for the task at hand; training that is provided; length of commitment; and what, if any, recognition can be expected.

Some of the volunteer literature suggests that organizations can offer benefits to a volunteer. Benefits can be both intangible and tangible. Intangible benefits include serving God through a particular ministry, using skills and talents in a specific manner or setting, or satisfaction from making a difference in the life of a child or teen. Tangible benefits include an annual recognition banquet; money for professional development for training needed for a specific ministry; or mileage reimbursement for travel required for a program area. Each church and recreation minister needs to determine the type of benefits the church can afford or provide based on resources and/or philosophy. Most important is a kind thank-you. Hearing, "You did a great job!" is meaningful for most volunteers.

## Committees/Boards/Councils

In most churches governing structures are comprised of volunteers. Depending on the unique organization and approach to governance within a local congregation, most churches use committees, boards, councils, or a combination of these.

Every group, such as committees, forms and reforms as people join and disassociate during the life of a group. Whenever a new person joins a committee, the group begins a new history. The recreation minister must constantly be aware of group dynamics and the vitality of the committees which help oversee this unique ministry within the church.

Many churches use committees in a variety of ways. Some committees are policy making in nature and oversee particular areas of ministry. In some instances committees function as "working committees" and actually make business decisions of ministry. In other situations committees are viewed as ministry teams. The role of committees varies based on the individual church and how governance is viewed and implemented to accomplish the mission of the church and what is perceived as acceptable practice with respect to fund-raising and sponsorships.

Just like individual volunteers, committees/boards/councils demand an investment in time, energy, resources, and recognition by the recreation minister. The purpose, task, and mission of the committee will dictate how much investment the minister will require. The dividends reaped by the minister from the commitment to committee development will be directly in proportion to the value placed on the role of committees in the life of the recreation and sports ministry.

Noyce suggests four areas of attention that committees need in order to be effective. Groups need: (1) cohesion, (2) task performance, (3) personal satisfaction, and (4) vision.[15] Committees need to feel connected. This could be done through a variety of ways, depending on how the group does its business. Possibly an annual retreat would help bring former and new committee members together to create a new history as they serve together. They need cohesiveness in order to understand the group's task and sense accomplishment when it is done. Individual members need to have a sense of satisfaction for their personal commitment in the life of a group. Their sense of making a difference is an important factor in people's willingness to continue to serve in the future.

Underneath all of this is the committee's ability to understand, know, and articulate the vision. When this occurs, all work and decision making can be filtered and evaluated according to the sense of vision outlined in the strategic plan. This is yet another way strategic planning supports the ministry of the church and specifically recreation and sports ministry.

## Interns

One last source of leadership and personnel is interns from a college, university, or seminary. Keep in mind that interns are not free labor. In fact, most institutions of higher learning would not likely place a student intern with a recreation and sports ministry if that was the perception or language used for enlisting an intern.

A minister should seek out an intern because of a commitment to the profession and ministry. Interns require time, energy, and some resources if they as well as the minister are going to benefit from this relationship. If the internship is positive, interns may be pursued to fill an opening on the staff. It is one way to groom a new staff member. The most important understanding is that an intern is a student learner and not a paid staff member.

Most interns participate for a semester or more, depending on the intern's institution. Many interns receive some type of academic credit. The minister-supervisor would work with the school's intern supervisor in some manner. The minister may be required to submit his or her credentials and professional involvement to qualify the church as a site for an intern placement. The recreation and sports ministry should be able to articulate the kinds of experiences possible in a given setting, the type of support (financial and housing) available, and any other features or benefits from this internship.

The intern will need supervision and time from the minister. It is a mentoring opportunity for the minister. Weekly meetings with the intern privately will help the intern learn from the recreation and sports minister. Full participation in the staff culture of the church provides another level of learning. This experience needs to be inclusive for the intern so that he or she can see the broadest perspective of ministry and understand as much of the daily ministry/work dynamics as possible.

## Budgeting

Budgeting can be complex or simple based on the process adopted by a given congregation. Simply put, a budget reflects the financial commitment of an organization to that which is deemed important and valuable. This statement of intent comes from planning and visioning and is a public declaration of what is going to happen if resources (financial, human, and physical) are available within the ministry of a church.

The five aspects of budgeting involve planning, authorization, management, control, and evaluation.[16] Each is needed for the budgeting process to be effective. The church may have different ways of implementing each aspect, but each aspect must be viewed as essential in order for the recreation and sports ministry to reach the goals that have been established.

Most churches use either a line-item budget or a ministry-based budget to reflect their commitment to ministry for the upcoming year.[17] Within the broader field of recreation and leisure services, other categories of budgets include zero-based, revenue, cash-flow, and performance.

A line-item budget indicates items for funding without regard for specific program areas or ministries. A ministry-based budget reflects planning and support for the mission and goals set forth by many individuals and groups within the recreation and sports ministry. Allocation of resources to specific areas of ministry allows the congregation and governing structures to understand and share in the vision for recreation and sports ministry.

Johnson indicates that there are eight steps in the ministry-based process of budgeting.

1. Analyze ministries.
2. Propose ministry actions.
3. Evaluate ministry actions.
4. Prepare the budget.
5. Present the budget.
6. Promote the budget.
7. Report ministry progress.
8. Review and evaluate.[18]

The recreation minister must understand the unique budgeting process within a local church. The process should involve staff and committees that relate to the recreation and sports ministry. This grassroots support and involvement will allow more individuals and groups ownership and promotion of the budget that supports the recreation and sports ministry.

## Risk Management

The church has the responsibility to deal with and manage for risk. Particularly in the areas of recreation and sports there are risks that must be acknowledged and addressed in some manner. The litigious society in which the church finds itself today requires the recreation minister to be current and knowledgeable in the area of risk management.

What then is risk management? "Risk management is a process with three phases: (a) risk identification and assessment, (b) risk response strategies, or what to do about the risks, and (c) management to reduce the frequency and severity of the risks through an operational plan."[19]

Risks come in many forms within recreation and sports ministry. Risks are not only present in activities conducted but also in equipment and facilities, staff that are leading activities, and financial choices that could cause damage to the overall budget and ministry of the church. The astute minister will analyze and evaluate all areas of ministry and make sure that a risk management plan is in place for the entire recreation and sports ministry.

Liability issues could be damaging to the church's ministries and staff. The minister should thoroughly understand state laws and whether they apply to the church. Documentation is vital for protection and to show prudence on the part of the provider of services, which in this case would be the church recreation and sports ministry. Types of forms used in recreation and sports settings include parental/guardian permission (appendix 9), participant information (appendix 10), accident/incident report (appendix 11), and abuse/neglect report (appendix 12).

The recreation minister has the responsibility and opportunity to influence people in the accomplishment of ministry. A biblically based understanding of administration as a call to serve others will guide the professional life of the minister. Personal administration through time management, communication, and conflict resolution allows the recreation minister to exhibit specific areas of leadership within the context of administration. Strategic planning, personnel management, risk management, budgeting, and partnerships are tools the recreation minister uses to accomplish ministry. The principles given provide a framework from which to begin to understand and apply in a ministry setting. The key point for the recreation minister to remember is that administration is done in order to better reach people with the gospel and to change lives for the kingdom. Ministry through recreation and sports is people centered.

---

**Notes**

1. Robert D. Dale, "Managing Christian Churches and Not-for-Profit Organizations," *Christian Administration Handbook,* Bruce Powers, ed. (Nashville: Broadman & Holman, 1997), 3.

2. William G. Caldwell, "A Theology of Administration," *Southwestern Journal of Theology* 37 (summer 1995).

3. Ibid., 33.

4. Ed Ernsting, "Turning Vision into Reality: The One-Minute Manager Clarifies the Real Issues," *Leadership* 17 (spring 1996).

5. Ed Ernsting, "Managing to Minister: An Interview with Peter Drucker," *Leadership* 10 (spring 1989).

6. Thomas A. Stewart, "Turning Around the Lord's Business: Marketing and Management Applied to Churches," *Fortune* (25 September 1989): 117.

7. Larry W. Osborne, "Stopping Conflict Before It Starts," *Leadership* 16 (winter 1995): 53.

8. Debra J. Jordan, *Leadership in Leisure Services: Making a Difference* (State College, Pa.: Venture Publishing, 2001), 151.

9. Dan Wegner and Christopher K. Jarvi, "Planning for Strategic Management," *Management of Park and Recreation Agencies,* Betty van der Smissen, Merry Moiseichik, Vern J. Hartenburg, and Louis F. Twardzik, eds. (Ashburn, Va.: National Recreation and Park Association, 1999), 104.

10. J. Robert Rossman and Barbara Elwood Schlatter, *Recreation Programming: Designing Leisure Experiences,* 3rd ed. (Champaign, Ill.: Sagamore Publishing, 2000), 91–94.

11. Kurt Bjorklund, "What Your Team Needs from You: Six Questions for Better Staff Development," *Leadership* 20 (spring 1999): 110.

12. Charles A. Tidwell, "The Church Staff as a Ministering Team," *Southwestern Journal of Theology* 29 (spring 1987): 33–34.

13. Stewart, 120.

14. Ibid., 116.

15. Gaylord Noyce, "How to Keep Committees Focused and Effective," *The Christian Ministry* 26 (January-February 1995): 19.

16. Andrew Holdnak II, Edward M. Mahoney, and James R. Garges, "Budgeting," *Management of Park and Recreation Agencies.*

17. Bob I. Johnson, "Planning and Budgeting," *Christian Administration Handbook,* 143–45.

18. Ibid.

19. Ronald Kaiser and Ken Robinson, "Risk Management," *Management of Park and Recreation Agencies,* 713.

# 7 Recreation and Sports Ministry Programming Process and Theory in a Church Setting

## Paul Stutz

The list of ingredients that comprise successful recreation and sports ministries often reaches to infinity with the vast amount of internal and external forces that affect ministerial outcomes. Geography, competition from within the community for leisure allegiances, and available resources can have a tremendous effect on ministry outcome. But what ingredient is key? What one thing is common to recreation and sports ministries that stands out regardless of the internal and external forces at work?

Answers can be as diverse as the thoughts such a question provokes. A leader sold out to God's will? Yes, of course. A charismatic personality that influences people to participate in ministry activities? Perhaps. Someone with a vast knowledge of and experience in leading and coaching in various types of recreation and sports venues? By all means. The list could go on and on, yet one thing emerges as a common thread. The ability to program, or function as a programmer of activities and facilities, is a paramount consideration for someone fulfilling his or her ministry calling within the confines of a recreation and sports ministry. Morlee Maynard suggests that in any recreation or sports ministry, creative programming will be the key to accomplishing its goals.[1] When considering the ministry of recreation and sports to be only a small slice of the total leisure-service delivery system, Robert Rossman addresses the entirety of all recreation and sports professionals, stating that "programming is the reason for the profession and for the existence of leisure service organizations."[2]

The ability to combine the ingredients of people, environment, and equipment into an event that effects positive change in the lives of those who participate might be considered a gift, and many ministers and leaders in the field of recreation and sports ministries are truly gifted people. On the other hand, it takes additional time and toil for most of us to muster what could be considered a successful recreation and sports event from a ministry perspective. A plan or format is needed to get the most out of ministry energies. The following pages address some areas of concern that assist in ensuring that programming efforts and resource use will result in ministry.

## Programming Foundations

As with other areas of leisure-service delivery, in ministry the recreation and sports program is the means to an end. Rossman states that the end result of recreation programming should be the leisure experience. Defined, a recreation or sports program is "a designed opportunity for a leisure experience to occur."[3] A program then is the track that guides the participant toward the leisure experience, not the experience itself. Like an order of worship for a church service, it guides the parishioner toward worship but is not worship in and of itself.

## Recreation and Sports Ministry Programming Model

All too often ministries are developed on the coattails of other successful ventures played out in other congregations or sports ministry environments. What works well in some ministry environments does, in fact, succeed elsewhere. However, a recreation and sports ministry that produces the most fruit seems to follow a plan and be guided by a mission or purpose that becomes a common thread that sews the entire ministry programming process together.

Multiple programming processes have been introduced, each having its own unique element that brings predicted success to the programmer of recreation activities and events.[4]

Adapting from the various models, ministry can be achieved. The eternal spiritual consequences and God's kingdom purposes are the differences experienced between programming for recreation and sports ministry and programming energies spent in other areas of recreation delivery services. Program planning might be considered the development of environments in which people might experience leisure, but program planning for ministry must create environments in which people might experience God.

An adapted programming model to guide energies and efforts toward ministry being accomplished can be seen in the following steps:

1. Assess needs.
2. Identify ministry objectives.
3. Design programs for ministry.
4. Implement ministries.
5. Evaluate ministries.
6. Determine disposition of ministries.

At each step within the model, intentional ministry efforts need to be assessed before continuing to the next phase. Modifications may need to be made in order to be the most effective steward where resource utilization is concerned. As a process, recreation and sports ministry programming has a dynamic inherent within it. Nothing ever stands still; the process always moves. Using a plan for ministry, successful recreation and sports programmers are action oriented while at the same time reacting to the changing needs of people and the ebb and flow of ministry direction.

## Assess Needs

Often in ministry environments leaders find themselves in anxious times. Events have been planned, publicity has been implemented, and yet people still do not respond to program offerings as leaders expect. Chances are that the target audience for the event was not consulted on what they would like to do. An event was planned, then the leaders had to recruit people who would fit the mold for participants in this event— a much more difficult scenario than to first determine what people want to do, then provide those activities.

Recreation and sports ministry programs are then designed as a response to the church's or organization's assessment of individual and group recreational needs. The attitudes and feelings expressed through a needs assessment should not be taken lightly. People recreate for a variety of reasons, but all reasons point to meeting needs. For this reason the recreation minister must be mindful of the many physical, emotional, social, psychological, and spiritual needs that are met through recreation participation.[5]

Carpenter and Howe state that "the needs assessment process is vitally important as it sets the tone for the rest of the programming process."[6] It is the element that sets the stage for the development and direction of the ministry plan.

Needs assessments provide the recreation and sports minister two things. First, they generate program possibilities. The data gathered tells the ministry programmer where to begin concerning program offerings as well as which activities and events to avoid because of lack of commitment to participate. Second, needs assessments allow for input from those the ministry desires to reach.[7] The opportunity to discover those activities that people want is provided from the most reputable source.

Probably the most widely used needs assessment instrument used in recreation and sports ministry venues is the survey. Surveys help the recreation minister feel the heartbeat of people concerning program offerings. These advantages are also inherent in surveys:

1.   Surveys can be comprehensive as needs assessment tools. Depending on the expenses of time and money, surveys can measure anything from pure demographics to complex items such as feelings and attitudes.

2.   Surveys can, and should, be customized. Information gathered to support a recreation and sports ministry in one location will not suffice as a basis for ministry in another church. Tailor-design the instrument to your own target populations—your congregation, your community.

3.   Surveys are versatile. The survey can be administered orally, in writing, by phone, or through E-mail or Web-page attachments.

4.   Surveys are flexible. The information one seeks can be designed specifically into the instrument without the survey becoming biased. Computers also allow for the acquisition of vast amounts of data.

5.   Surveys are efficient. It doesn't take a battalion of people to administer a survey. At most, a recreation and sports ministry team or committee can easily handle the job.[8]

Established as the standard for determining which recreation and sports ministry programs will best meet needs, the survey, however, is not without deficiencies. Weaknesses found in surveys include:

***Surveys are not the ultimate answer in determining programs.*** They are a great tool for determination purposes, but other means of assessment should be considered as well.

Simple observation may, at times, be the most helpful tool for the recreation minister. To all but the strongest Christians, church attendance is simply another leisure choice. Attending church on Sunday mornings lines up with other choices—golfing, camping, or spending a day at the lake. A wise leader in recreation and sports ministries is concerned with where people are and what they are doing when they are absent from church. For spiritual purposes, yes, but also to see if it is possible to harness the passion people have for other leisure pursuits that supercede their worship attendance from time to time and motivate them to be passionate about sharing in a corporate setting. To put it bluntly, the person who says he can worship God in his bass boat more effectively than in the pew may not just be making excuses. Recreation and sports ministers need to observe these pursuits not to be condemning but to be encouraging people to bring this passion for spending time with God into the rest of the body of Christ whenever it gathers.

Also observe what is happening within recreation and sports trends. Can some of these leisure activities be harnessed for ministry purposes? Can intentional evangelism and spiritual growth be the end result from using trendsetting sports and leisure pursuits? The answer to both questions is yes, provided the activities are wholesome and positive.

***Surveys can be misunderstood.*** Most survey instruments used in recreation and sports ministry settings involve the vague category of asking people whether they are interested in a certain activity. This does provide data from which ministry can be developed but only to a limited degree. Asking people if they are interested in certain activities becomes problematic because everyone is interested in everything to a certain degree. To some, an activity is their life's passion. To others, the same activity is only a passing thought, but still they have a level of interest.

The data received from a survey in recreation and sports ministry needs to have what could be called a "field of dreams" concept; that is, if we offer it, will they come? A programmer needs to know a person's intentions toward participation in a recreation and sports ministry function.

***Some people become exuberant on paper.*** A properly developed survey will keep people within the bounds of reality as they complete the form. A needs assessment instrument that returns with all activities highly affirmed gives the recreation and sports ministry programmer no better sense of ministry development than instruments that return blank. Here, again, simplicity and tailor-made design help to keep responses within the bounds of realistic program delivery for ministry purposes. Surveys should not include activities and events the ministry cannot deliver. Those activities that are resource prohibitive or do not meet the criteria for ministry purposes need not be included in a survey. Not only does this make good sense, but it keeps people limited to what can be done and keeps the exuberance found in survey completion to a minimum.

## Identify Ministry Objectives

For decades now, management systems have been driven by schematics and plans that guide their efforts based on mission/purpose statements and the development of a related set of goals and objectives that guide organizational efforts toward the mission. Churches and ministries have joined in the chase to become more efficient and effective in their physical and fiscal expenditures as they attempt to make their efforts significant for the kingdom of God, although some may perceive corporate structure in the church as unscriptural.[9] Of all managerial entities that need to be guided effectively through goals and objectives, ministries should lead the way. The end result of ministry is far more important than a product the public wants or needs. Ministry deals with the eternal souls of people, not the temporal desires that may be the end result of other management-oriented efforts.

Without purpose/mission, goals, and objectives to guide the efforts of a recreation and sports ministry, energy is often misdirected or wasted. Purpose answers the question, why does the ministry exist? Goals answer the question, what does the ministry hope to accomplish? Objectives answer the question, what results does the ministry expect to accomplish?[10]

The purpose or mission statement for a recreation and sports ministry should be directly related to, and supportive of, the overall mission of the church or governing entity. If the ministry is a stand-alone organization in and of itself, then its purpose or mission will be the foundation stone on which all ministry efforts will be placed.

A recreation and sports ministry cannot function without a clear statement describing its reason for existence, a mission or purpose statement. A mission statement allows the ministry to focus on awareness of direction, purpose, and a reason for being.[11]

In developing a dynamic purpose or mission statement to guide the efforts of a recreation and sports ministry, the church functions of worship, evangelism, missions, ministry, discipleship, and fellowship would serve well as a basis.[12] Ministry mission should be developed with the idea that mission accomplished will result in the fulfillment of such functions. Also, any activity or event sponsored by the recreation and sports ministry should have the intentional purpose of directly relating to at least one of the above church functions. Without such a target to shoot for in ministry, the delivery of recreation and sports activities will only be activity for activity's sake.

A statement of ministry mission cannot be accurately developed without first considering what Richard Ensman calls strategic strengths and weaknesses. Strategic strengths related to recreation and sports ministry would include ministry resources, both tangible and intangible, that allow the ministries to flow with efficiency and effectiveness. Strategic weaknesses involve staff, volunteers, facilities, equipment, or other resource limitations that would hinder or prevent a ministry from producing expected results.[13]

The pragmatics of forming a mission statement are delineated with such variety that determining which methods to use could cause anxiety to occur within the leadership of a recreation and sports ministry. This is not to say that mission or purpose formulation is all doom and gloom. On the contrary, it should be looked upon as an adventure of determining and "putting feet" to the will of God through recreation and sports.

A mission or purpose statement for ministry should define three things. First, the mission statement defines the target audience. Who should be affected by the recreation and sports ministry? Why should people come and invest their time and lives in this ministry? Second, the statement should define a value premise. This premise is based not on what the recreation and sports ministry does but in terms of the fundamental value it represents in meeting the ministry needs of the target group. Third, a statement of mission or purpose should delineate what makes the recreation and sports ministry special.

To put it all together, what is the ministry's special means for creating value in order to win and sustain the allegiance of the people it is trying to reach?[14]

Albrecht also delineates the characteristics inherent in a valid statement of mission or purpose. Effective statements should be:

1.  Definitive—It defines what the person needs, the organizational values offered (ministries), and means to get the two together.

2.  Identifying—It makes clear the ministry.

3.  Concise—A basic statement of mission should easily be written on the back of a business card.

4.  Actionable—It gives the reader some idea of what the statement looks like in action.

5.  Memorable—The statement should be something reachable (within the bounds of faith), yet spectacular![15]

Rossman states that there is a hierarchical structure or arrangement of using goals and objectives that begin with the mission or purpose statement. This statement delimits what the ministry will accomplish and is not measurable. Mission accomplished, however, is measured through a series of goal and objective statements that are increasingly more specific until an objective is born that is operationally clear, specific, and measurable.[16] V. Kerry Inman agrees that goals are general statements about expected results, yet objectives are concrete statements about measurable results that can be used to determine if the goals were met.[17]

Goals are broad in scope yet enduring in concept. Goals are usually formulated by recreation and sports ministry leadership, perhaps with the assistance of a board of directors or ministry team or committee. The efforts of such groups in the formulation process should include a glimpse at past ministry effectiveness, current ministries, and future ministry hopes and dreams. Examples of past information valuable for goal construction are successful ministries (and those not so successful), budget and resource history, and demographic changes, especially church membership. Types of current information include member involvement in ministry, what other churches or ministry organizations are doing in the community, and local image of the church or ministry organization. Data concerning the future includes socioeconomic trends and demographic forecasts.[18]

Goals are broad, enduring statements that express some desired result. Goals guide a recreation and sports ministry in determining what is important and what achievements are needed to accomplish ministry mission. Neil Dougherty and Diane Bonanno suggest that when writing goals, the statements should:

1.  Support the mission or purpose statement.

2.  Be acceptable to congregation members or ministry organization members.

3.  Be broad. Broad goals are flexible goals that endure with the changing times.

4.  Be clearly stated. Be written in a language that all can understand.

5.  Be within the realm of possibility. Goals in recreation and sports ministry should have a faith element but not be viewed as impossible.[19]

Rossman gives excellent insight applicable to goal formulation for recreation and sports ministries concerning the proper wording of statements. Goal and objective statements should include:

• An infinitive—Each statement should begin with the infinitive marker *to* followed by a verb indicative of the action to be taken.

• A subject—Each statement should contain a subject that conveys what is going to be accomplished.

• A measurement device—Each statement should make clear how the accomplishment of the goal is going to be measured and documented—a time frame. It should be noted, however, that some statements are simply declarations of an agency's (church's or ministry's) intention to accomplish something or to give direction in a specific way.[20]

Consider these examples of goals that would relate to a recreation and sports ministry:

• To maximize participation in the church recreation center on Friday evenings.

• To develop a sports ministry.

• To become more evangelistic in our leagues and tournaments.

Once goals have been established, the mission achievement focus becomes more specific with the development of objectives that are the operational channels through which goals are achieved. The objective element of achieving recreation and sports ministry mission becomes the track on which the mission train travels. Objectives are the movement of the mission by the people.

People become pragmatically involved in ministry through the fulfillment of ministry objectives. Dale McConkey states that using objectives properly in the church requires active involvement and participation by all members.[21] People orientation continues as Stoner and Freeman contend the "objectives clarify tasks and give people a better understanding of their role in the mission. Objectives also challenge individuals. They give them a sense of purpose and increase motivation."[22] Ministry is like another administrative task: it is most effective when accomplished through people. People want opportunities to share in ministry. Through people both the mission and the missionary are fulfilled.

When developing objectives, these characteristics should be considered. Objectives should:

1. Be clear and concise.
2. Be in written form.
3. Name specific results in key areas.
4. Be stated for a specific period of time.
5. Be stated in measurable terms.
6. Be consistent with the overall mission/purpose.
7. Be attainable, but with sufficient challenge.[23]

Examples of objectives that relate to previously expressed sample goals might read:

Goal: To develop a sports ministry.

Objectives: To develop a coed basketball league for children ages six to eleven years of age by December 1, 2004, with at least eight teams. To provide a soccer clinic for girls thirteen to fifteen years of age by November 1, 2004, with at least fifty girls attending.

To further develop the goal and objective hierarchy, leaders in recreation and sports ministries can tightly focus their energies to fulfill ministry purposes for their own unique settings. For the basketball league, additional objectives at the recreation and sports ministry program level could include the following:

Objective: To develop a coed basketball league for children six to ten years of age by December 1, 2004, with at least eight teams.

Program focused objectives for the basketball league include:

• Each player will hear a gospel presentation.
• Each player will play in every game.
• Each player will be recognized at an awards banquet at the conclusion of the league.
• Each player will have a uniform.

The use of mission/purpose statements, goals, and objectives allows leadership in a recreation and sports ministry to keep their focus on ministry with intentional purposes. The further a purpose or mission is developed through goals and objectives, the more likely that intentional ministry will be kept in focus.

These management principles are not solely for corporate systems. There is, and must be, a place in ministry for the development and implementation of a goal and objective system that keeps the energies expended through a recreation and sports ministry focused on what is primary, that is, ministry, changing the lives of people for the sake of God's kingdom.

## Design Programs for Ministry

After the formulation of ministry mission, goals, and objectives, decisions need to be made as to how what has already been developed becomes reality. Through what methods will the mission be achieved? What will be the intricacies involved in program development in order to ensure that ministry will be the end result?

With the vast array of possibilities for using recreation and sports as a ministry tool, decisions must be made on which methods would best suit one's unique, individual ministry setting. By nature, recreation has a social purpose; that is, it exists for the good of a society. This is why we see parks and recreation services and departments even in the smallest of municipal government systems. These "societies" determine which recreation and sports events would be beneficial within their boundaries of service. Where ministry is concerned, often the church stands as the society that dictates what is and what is not acceptable when considering recreation and sports as a ministry tool. When a parachurch ministry organization is responsible, they become the society that dictates what is acceptable for ministry. Geographical location must also be brought into consideration, for what works as ministry in one locale may not be acceptable in another; the societies are different.

Because of the differing external and internal influences affecting the outcomes of a recreation and sports ministry, care needs to be taken in developing those activities that will best deliver ministry as well as be inviting to the intended target population. Various activity formats are available through which a sports or recreational pursuit may be introduced. Carpenter and Howe consider the recreation activity format as being the most versatile.[24] From a ministry standpoint, their viewpoint is also apropos. Major recreation activity formats consist of:

- Outdoor recreation (camping, hiking, fishing, shooting sports, etc.)
- Sports (team and individual)
- Games (vigorous and passive, physical and mental)
- Fitness
- Arts (drama, music, crafts)
- Trips and outings
- Social recreation (parties, banquets, receptions, etc.)
- Voluntary service (missions, ministry projects, etc.)
- Special events

An individual activity can also be developed in more than one way in order to meet the diverse array of needs possible. For instance, basketball could be formatted as: a league, a clinic, a tournament, or an open facility/gym.

Carpenter and Howe suggest that there are four advantages to developing and using the recreation activity format.

First, the formats can be combined. This is especially important when ministry is the objective. A sports awards banquet (social recreation) could be held and the coaches (volunteer service) recognized for their excellent efforts. Also, a trip could be taken (trips and outings) to hold a soccer clinic (sports) for the purpose of evangelism (volunteer service).

Second, the recreation activity format allows for a participant to progress through different skill development levels. In recreation and sports ministries, people's main objective in participating is the development of skills, especially for those outside the congregation or organizational mainline participants. They commit to being involved with skill development in mind, and the spiritual aspects are "extras." Unless participants feel comfortable within the boundaries of the activity skillwise, they will cease to participate.

Third, the recreation activity format lends itself to an almost limitless array of possibilities programmatically as long as the offerings are conducive to ministry. It allows for a variety of ministry possibilities and fosters the participant's ability to make choices concerning their recreational pursuits.

A fourth advantage of the recreation activity format is that the activities allow themselves to be analyzed by recreation and sports ministry leaders to determine an activity's effectiveness toward reaching ministry goals.[25]

Designing programs that minister sometimes requires recreation and sports ministry leaders to "color outside the lines" in order to be effective. Rossman addresses the struggle to be creative with programming while focusing the results of recreation and sports on ministry. Creativity in programming involves the ability to overcome problems by using novel solutions. Innovation is the key. It involves taking a risk to facilitate ministry. This is often discomforting, but new horizons in reaching people for Christ are also rewarding.

At the same time, recreation ministers must avoid getting into a rut and staying too long with comfortable programs that have offered some success. The creative abilities are not active for one reason or another. Like any other ministry, sports and recreation programming can get stuck in habitual thinking, using the same solutions to the same problems resulting in the same outcomes.

Christ's ministry was definitely "outside the lines." Jesus was so far out of the box that those known for their religious fervor did not recognize or appreciate his message. In recreation and sports ministry programming, leaders should be limitless in their attitude to do whatever it takes to reach and grow people.

To avoid the appearance of a program that lacks substance, recreation ministers design, with great intentions and integrity, their ministry programs. Recreation and sports ministry programs are designed

- to meet real needs.
- to change lives for the better.
- to give people a positive recreation experience.
- to introduce Christ into people's leisure time.
- to succeed.

## Implement Ministry

In a recreation and sports ministry, activities are delivered to people, through people. Ministry implementation cannot be achieved without people to take the goals and objectives, relate them to the determined activity formats, and deliver a ministry that will make a difference in the lives of those who participate. As recreation and sports ministry philosophy moves through the programming cycle, more and more people become involved.

In the development stage, formats were introduced as a means by which activities are delivered for ministry purposes. In the ministry implementation stage, an activity has been categorized into a format (sports, games, social recreation, etc.) and now is delivered to a specific group of potential participants for the purpose of intentional ministry. The plans for ministry are set into motion through people. When programs are implemented, all of the initial surveying, goal and objective development, and organizing prove their worth.[26]

Since the foundation for involving people is the greatest at the ministry implementation stage, it is imperative that recreation and sports ministry leaders be adept at placing the best people in positions to ensure ministry. At this juncture of the ministry programming process, delegation is not an option; it is a must. It is an administrative function that must be exercised by leadership in a recreation and sports ministry, especially in the church setting, if ownership of the ministry is to be delegated to the people.

In a recreation and sports ministry, administration is defined as the process of planning, organizing, leading, controlling, and evaluating the work of ministry personnel with intentional purposes that include a steward's heart for human and fiscal resources. The functions of leading, staffing, and controlling are abounding with human resource orientation. Without people these functions have no purpose in the ministry process. This definition of administration, like most, is based on getting things done through people.

Which people, however, are best suited to be involved in the implementation of a recreation and sports ministry? Too often, ministry leadership is simply after someone with a pulse because time has run out and an event must be staffed. There is a process that assists recreation and sports ministry leaders in acquiring the right people for the right ministry tasks. This process is comprised of several elements:

*Prayer*—The beginning place for staffing a recreation and sports ministry event is at the throne of God. God's hand in the staff selection process is paramount if his will is to be done through the event. Pray for the right people. Pray that God will uncover them for service.

*Task analysis*—The leaders in a recreation and sports ministry must themselves be knowledgeable about what is involved in completing the various tasks that comprise an activity or event. A question that needs to be asked is, "Do we need someone to occupy a place on the ministry team to complete this task?"

*Job description*—Yes, even for volunteers! This summary of the duties and responsibilities of the job is paramount if credibility is going to be given to the task. People will feel that their position in ministry is important if there is a written description of what is expected of them.

*Recruitment*—The ideal is to have a pool of people who are willing to assist in ministry. Often in ministry circumstances, however, the luxury of choosing people from a pool is nonexistent. To develop a ministry pool, leadership assessments are often a good way to develop a base for involving people in ministry.

*Selection*—Match the right person to the right ministerial task. In order to do this, leaders must take the time to get to know those from whom they are choosing. Building relationships in ministry should not present a difficulty if leaders are actively ministering within their own circles of influence.[27]

Once the right people have been selected to assist the leaders in recreation and sports ministries, two additional important aspects of staffing must be considered.

First, people need to be properly trained in order to be most effective in ministry circumstances. Handing people job descriptions and pointing them in the right direction is not training. Training involves personal contact with the staff member in order to channel the skills and abilities of the person to the tasks of the job. Training is where ministry team members acquire the necessary tools they need to fulfill the responsibilities of their position.

Second, volunteers need to be properly oriented as to their role in the overall recreation and sports ministry scheme. During an orientation session, volunteers are made to feel that they play a vital role in fulfilling ministry purposes. This stage is the beginning of praise that must continue throughout the staff member's service. A clear picture of ministry purpose and direction is given along with definite areas of focus for various roles. Orientation involves making volunteers feel that the ministry cannot be completed without their valuable assistance. Orientation answers the questions:

1. Who are team members in this ministry endeavor?
2. What is the recreation and sports ministry trying to accomplish?

3.  What is the volunteer's role in assisting the recreation/sports ministry toward its mission?
4.  What impact does the recreation and sports ministry have on the total ministry of the church or organization?

Most recreation and sports ministry events and activities are staffed with volunteers. Although many of the larger churches and organizations have paid staffs, still the ministerial load is carried by volunteers. In some instances the total recreation and sports ministry is implemented on a volunteer basis. Volunteers bring their own needs to the recreation and sports ministry staff.

Gene Pomerance gives helpful insight to the recreation and sports minister as to the reasons people volunteer in a recreation setting.

First, some people volunteer because they are required to do so. Some people may be required to volunteer as part of a missions project. Oftentimes, for example, a recreation and sports ministry has student interns who are volunteering, in a sense, as part of their degree plan.

Second, people volunteer for what Pomerance calls "inner-directed" reasons. These people want to make a difference in their world. They are interested in the opportunity to have a positive impact on society. In a recreation and sports ministry, these people may be the majority as they are "called" to serve in a ministry environment.

Third, some people volunteer for personal growth or self-development reasons. They might be interested in learning a new skill. Some people need experience on a resume for future employment purposes.

Finally, some people volunteer for social reasons. They want to meet new people or be around a certain group of people. Like the inner-directed volunteer, social volunteers may be a majority found in recreation and sports ministries. Being with God's people or sharing with people outside one's faith should be a hallmark of those who volunteer in ministry environments.[28]

Volunteers need to be compensated in some way. Pomerance offers the thought of "psychic" compensation for volunteers. Psychic compensation is anything other than money that provides a reward for their efforts.[29] In a recreation and sports ministry setting, this may be recognition at a banquet, a certificate of appreciation, or tickets to some sort of amusement or attraction.

Volunteers also need an appraisal process. Appraisal makes them feel their service to the ministry is as important as that of those who get paid to do it. The appraisal format for volunteers needs to affirm their efforts and assure them that they are not taken for granted by the recreation and sports ministry leaders.

One of the most common ways to implement a recreation and sports ministry program is by a seasonal format. From a pure sports ministry perspective, people are extremely seasonal. They want to play football during football season, basketball during basketball season, and so on. Also, seasons allow for the recreation and sports ministry programmer to use thematic interpretations to promote activities and events.

Of special interest to contemporary ministry programmers is the "time deepening" format. Recent research has determined that people will more likely participate in an activity that is complete yet compact in duration. In a recreation ministry that offers an arts and crafts program, for instance, people are more likely to come to a one-time flower-arranging class than to a six-week painting class. The precious element of time becomes a barrier to participation in recreation and sports ministries if activities become too time-consuming.

The fast pace of Western culture combined with "time-saving" technological advances have made time a valuable commodity. Geoffrey Godbey states that while people used to speak of passing the time, today people "spend, lose, save, or even make time."[30] To make the most of their time, says Tom Goodale, people do more in less time, different things at the same time, and measure time in smaller, more precise amounts.[31] Factors that stress the time people have to give toward active participation in recreation and sports ministries must be considered by those who implement ministry programs. To become too big of a restraint on people's time will cause the program to become too big a constraint in the lives of those the ministry is trying to reach.

## Evaluate Ministries

The evaluation process in recreation and sports ministries, as in other recreation delivery systems, is vital to the fulfillment of ministry mission. Evaluation is necessary to determine if ministry goals and objectives were achieved. To neglect this stage of any programming arrangement would be failing to be interested in delivering the best possible recreation and sports ministry offerings.

Program evaluation is one of the most important aspects of any leisure-service delivery system.[32] Ruth Russell agrees about evaluation's importance but adds that it is also one of the least understood and most confusing aspects in program planning.[33] As part of such a delivery system, the recreation and sports ministry is not exempt from such scrutiny. Those involved in ministry ventures are called to rise above the rest when it comes to being effective at what they do. Recreation and sports ministries differ from other agencies delivering the same programs in that ministries are involved with the eternal. The end result is not only a satisfying recreation experience but a closer glimpse of God. To be most effective at doing this, evaluation of ministry programs is a mandate not an option.

Like most organizations that employ evaluation techniques, recreation and sports ministries also view the need for evaluation from a dual perspective, formative and summative.

Formative evaluation monitors the ongoing progress of a program; it is flexible and dynamic. Formative evaluation keeps the ministry on track while the programs are in progress; that is, it forms and improves what is being evaluated while it is being developed. Formative evaluation is process oriented. Summative evaluation makes decisions that "sum up" the overall quality or worth of a program. This type of evaluation is product oriented. It is performed at the conclusion of a program or activity and judges the overall impact that a program had on the intended target audience.[34] Both types of evaluation are necessary if a recreation and sports ministry is to bear the fruit desired by those planning and designing the ministry.

Evaluation of programs in a recreation and sports ministry also needs to consider both the objective and subjective natures of people being involved in an activity based on intentional ministry purposes. From an objective standpoint, evaluation needs to provide data concerning the number of participants involved in ministry programs, costs involved in delivering a particular ministry, and stewardship of facilities. Objective evaluation assists leaders in a recreation and sports ministry in guiding and taking inventory of all resources used to produce a program.

The subjective nature of recreation evaluation is especially important in recreation and sports ministry settings. Subjectivity is involved because different programs, or various aspects within the same program, have different meanings to different people. With this in mind, the spiritual dimensions involved in ministry programming must be considered. Some method of determining spiritual effectiveness must be inherent in the evaluation process.

From an overall perspective, evaluation serves many purposes. Knutson offers these as roles fulfilled through evaluation:

1.  To show others that the program is worthwhile.
2.  To determine whether a program is moving in the right direction.
3.  To determine whether the needs for which the program is designed are being satisfied.
4.  To determine the costs of a program in terms of money and human effort.
5.  To obtain evidence that may demonstrate to others what is already believed to be true regarding the effectiveness of the program.
6.  To support program expansion or reduction.
7.  To assist in comparing different types of programs in terms of their effectiveness.[35]

Before an evaluation process can be properly implemented to assist in ministry, Murphy and others suggest that the following questions be considered in order to direct evaluation energies in a manner that will be most productive:

1.  What will be the purpose of evaluation?
2.  For whom will the result be intended?
3.  Who will use the results?
4.  What resources for conducting the evaluation are available? (human, fiscal, and physical)
5.  What are the constraints? What would hinder the effective implementation of the evaluation process?
6.  Exactly when would formative and summative evaluation processes begin?
7.  Are there any deadlines?
8.  Who will conduct the evaluation?[36]

Concerning the last question above, many commercial firms conduct evaluation research from a nonbiased perspective. In the corporate and business world, these services are extremely helpful. In ministry, however, the reminder of the subjective nature of the spiritual element would lean toward those responsible for the ministry also being responsible for the evaluation process. In a recreation and sports ministry, with the intentional purpose being the common thread that sews the entire programming process together, those involved in the planning and design aspects are most familiar with the desired outcome where ministry results are concerned. Those outside the ministry circle, though competent to do evaluation research, may not have the ministerial perspective needed to disseminate ministry results.

Evaluation instruments can literally "run the gamut" when it comes to which method for gathering information is best. Like needs assessment, the recreation and sports ministry needs to tailor-design the instrument that will give them the information needed to make disposition decisions at the conclusion of a program. Also, techniques for formative evaluation need to be considered carefully in order for the ministry program to keep on track toward its ultimate destination.

In recreation and sports ministries, evaluation tools that are summative in nature usually attempt to determine two things—one objective in nature, the other subjective. Evaluation of programs of this nature will not be foolproof as respondents are reacting to their perception of how things went. What went well for one respondent might be viewed as disaster by another.

First, an instrument for recreation and sports ministries needs to discover how people felt about the pragmatics of the program. The satisfaction of the participants toward a particular program is essential if leaders in a recreation and sports ministry are interested in programs that meet ministry objectives.[37] Examples of information needed include:

- Was the time of the activity convenient?
- Did the leader communicate adequately?
- Was the activity's duration adequate? too long? too short?

Some open-ended questions would also be appropriate in this stage of evaluation. Examples of such questions are:

- If you could change the times, what time would be more convenient for you?
- What additional incentives would make participation more attractive?

In recreation and sports ministries, however, the subjective nature of spiritual change within the lives of participants also needs to be somehow considered. This type of questioning would fall into the category of information that Susan Hudson describes as attitudes and beliefs. Attitudes essentially describe how a person feels about something; however, various influences cause people's attitudes to change.[38]

Attitudes are always focused on an object, either physical, social, or abstract. In this case the abstract is a spiritual element purposefully integrated within the confines of recreation program delivery.

Attitudes also have a "feeling" component.[39] Of special importance for ministry purposes is a participant's intensity of feelings toward a particular spiritual focus or program element. Questions that allow for discovery in this area include:

- What spiritual growth have you experienced as the result of spending time in this class?
- What spiritual truth have you gained insight toward as a result of your participation in this activity?
- What teachable moments related to spiritual insight were most memorable?

The important thing to remember about evaluation techniques is that information is being collected for three definite areas of concern to the recreation and sports ministry:

1. Were ministry goals and objectives met?
2. Were the lives of participants changed in a positive spiritual manner?
3. What changes, if any, need to be made to the program in order to make it a more effective ministry tool?

## Determine Disposition of Ministry

In a recreation and sports ministry, or any ministry for that matter, it is difficult to justify and determine the future of various programs. Especially in local church ministry, the status quo often becomes a standard that everything is doing fine. Those in charge of ministry environments often go to great extremes and are involved in great energy expenditures in order to keep up with the latest ministry trends. It becomes easy simply to "turn our backs" on those programs that are not effective as ministry tools, hoping that they will just go away, but not so. Robert Rossman reminds the recreation and sports ministry leader that program disposition is also an option for this area of recreation program delivery. In fact, in ministry circumstances, program disposition becomes a matter of stewardship above and beyond the other entities that are also involved in delivering recreation and sports programs. Rossman states that final disposition of a recreation program should be determined on information gathered during the evaluation process.

Only three choices are made during the disposition process:

1. Continue the program as is with no changes.
2. Continue the program but with modifications.
3. Terminate the program.[40]

The disposition of programs has to be addressed in what Rossman describes as the "decline" stage of the recreation program life cycle. This life cycle includes the stages of program birth (or introduction), program growth, program maturation, program saturation (where the newness wears off, number of participants levels off; in ministry, "tradition" takes over), program decline, and program death.[41] (See fig. 7-1.) To avoid program death, programmers in recreation and sports ministries must make one of the available disposition choices.

In ministry environments the first two alternatives are easy. The termination of ministries, however, is another issue. What constitutes ministry termination? When tradition has carried a ministry offering for so long, what characteristics must be evident in order to terminate services?

- Budgetary issues may or may not allow for certain recreation and sports ministries to continue. It simply costs too much.
- Recreation trends change. When people become more interested in other leisure outlets and facilities are limited, certain ministries may need to end.
- The minister thinks the time has come to end the activity. When certain programs are not bearing fruit and resources are limited, certain ministries may need to be terminated.

Ministry termination is often the most difficult of disposition choices because usually something good can be found within any program. A question always worthy of consideration in recreation and sports ministry operations is stewardship: Are we doing the most (providing the best ministries) with what we have (all available resources) to reach and grow people for the kingdom of God? To answer this question, sometimes program termination is not just a vital choice; it is the only choice.

Ministry termination is not the end. It is the making available of resources for the recreation and sports ministry to do something else, to

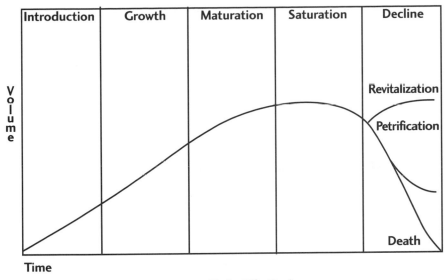

*Figure 7-1: Life Cycle*

reach new horizons in ministry, to develop and implement new programs with greater kingdom impact.

The disposition choices of continuation and continuation with modifications may be easier to administer than program termination, but the same seriousness of intentional mission must be followed. All disposition alternatives are about being the best stewards of the resources God has given us. To do anything less would misuse the greatest opportunity—to reach the most people possible in ministry.

The greatest plan for developing recreation and sports ministry programs is invalid without the hand of God being present from the beginning. Often one can get caught up in administration and fail to fulfill the duty to minister. Although program planning and implementation is in itself ministry, care must be taken not to get so wrapped up in a system that a minister fails to relate to the everyday needs of people. A delicate balance must be achieved and sustained in order for the recreation and sports minister to be most effective. On the one hand, there should be a system of operation that guides the ministry toward its fulfillment or mission, through the provision of leisure pursuits that have positive physical and spiritual results in the lives of people. On the other hand, the efficiency of such a system should allow the minister the freedom to move among the people, becoming personally involved in their lives and growth.

A system for planning and providing recreation and sports activities that consumes leadership is of little use in ministry environments.

Full and active recreation and sports ministry facilities are not necessarily the marks of a great ministry, although the more people present, the more ministry opportunities possibly exist. Many programs will run themselves because of recreational trends, the current interests of people, and facilities. What must happen within a ministry context is that those offerings that provide the programmer with the most intentional ministry possibilities must be sought. Today these activities may not represent the traditional sports and activities that once comprised most ministries. Whatever the activity, there must be a system that guides efforts toward mission accomplishment. Ministry is the mission, and its accomplishment is not only found in great programs but etched into eternity on behalf of those whose lives are touched and grown through participation.

---

**Notes**

1. Morlee H. Maynard, *We're Here for the Churches: Southern Baptist Entities Working Together* (Nashville: LifeWay Press, 2001), 66.

2. J. Robert Rossman, *Recreation Programming: Designing Leisure Experiences* (Champaign: Sagamore Publishing, 1991), x.

3. Ibid., 3.

4. Patricia Farrell and Herberta Lundgren, *Recreation Programming: Theory and Technique,* 3rd ed. (State College, Pa.: Venture Publishing, Inc., 1991), 25; Rossman, 72; Ruth V. Russell, *Planning Programs in Recreation* (St. Louis: C. V. Mosby, 1982), 25.

5. H. Dan Corbin and Ellen Williams, *Recreation Programming and Leadership,* 4th ed. (Englewood Cliffs: Prentice-Hall, 1987), 59.

6. Gaylene M. Carpenter and Christine Z. Howe, *Programming Leisure Experiences: A Cyclical Approach* (Englewood Cliffs: Prentice-Hall, 1985), 77.

7. Ibid.

8. Susan D. Hudson, *How to Conduct Community Needs Assessment Surveys in Public Parks and Recreation* (Columbus: Publishing Horizons, 1988), 2.

9. R. Henry Migliore, Robert Stevens, and Dave Loudon, *Church Ministry Strategic Planning: From Concept to Success* (New York: The Haworth Press, 1994), 9.

10. V. Kerry Inman, *Planning Church Events with Ease* (Grand Rapids: Zondervan Publishing House, 1988), 31.

11. Tim J. Holcomb, *Church Administration from A to Z: Support for Church Growth* (Nashville: Convention Press, 1994), 10.

12. Great Commission Council of the Southern Baptist Convention, *We're Here for the Churches: The Southern Baptist Entities Working Together* (Nashville: LifeWay Christian Resources, 1999), 21–27.

13. Richard Ensman, "Preparing the Annual Program Plan," *The Clergy Journal* 69.6 (1993): 46.

14. Karl Albrecht, *The Northbound Train: Finding Purpose, Setting the Direction, Shaping the Destiny of Your Organization* (New York: American Management Association, 1994), 153.

15. Ibid., 157.

16. Rossman, 61.

17. Inman, 30.

18. Sharon Hunt and Kenneth Brooks. "A Planning Model for Public Recreation Agencies," *Journal of Parks and Recreation Administration* 1.2 (1989), 8.

19. Neil Dougherty and Diane Bonanno, *Management Principles for Sport and Leisure Services* (Minneapolis: Burgess Publishing Company, 1985), 46–47.

20. Rossman, 59.

21. Dale McConkey, *MBO for Non-Profit Organizations* (New York: American Management Association, 1975), 173.

22. James Stoner and R. Edward Freeman. *Management,* 4th ed. (Englewood Cliffs: Prentice Hall, 1989), 253.

23. Migliore, Stevens, and Loudon, 60–61.

24. Carpenter and Howe, 111.

25. Ibid., 111–12.

26. Corbin and Williams, 94.

27. Rossman, 298–300.

28. Gene Pomerance, "The Care and Feeding of Volunteers," *Parks and Recreation Magazine* (November 1994): 54–55.

29. Ibid., 54.

30. Geoffrey Godbey, *Leisure in Your Life: An Exploration,* 3rd ed. (State College, Pa.: Venture Publishing, 1990), 46.

31. Thomas L. Goodale, "Is There Enough Time?" in Thomas L. Goodale and Peter Witt, *Recreation and Leisure: Issues in an Era of Change* (State College, Pa.: Venture Publishing, 1991), 38.

32. Peter J. Graham and Lawrence R. Klar Jr., *Planning and Delivering Leisure Services* (Dubuque, Iowa: William C. Brown, 1979), 45; James Murphy, E. William Niepoth, Lynn M. Jamison, and John G. Williams, *Leisure Systems: Critical Concepts and Applications* (Champaign, Ill.: Sagamore Publishing Company, Inc., 1991), 365.

33. Russell, 283.

34. L. R. Gay and Peter Airasian, *Educational Research: Competencies for Analysis and Application,* 6th ed. (Upper Saddle River, N.J.: Merrill, 2000), 8; Farrell and Lundgren, 235; Murphy et al., 365; William F. Theobald, *Evaluation of Recreation and Parks Programs* (New York: John Wiley & Sons, 1979), 58.

35. Andre L. Knutson, "Evaluation for What?" in William F. Theobald, *Proceedings of the Regional Institute on Neurologically Handicapping Conditions in Children in Evaluation of Recreation and Park Programs* (New York: John Wiley & Sons, 1979), 57–58.

36. Murphy et al., 365–66.

37. Ibid., 379.

38. Hudson, 11.

39. Ibid., 14.

40. Rossman, 467.

41. Ibid., 468–71.

# 8

# Recreation and Sports Ministry: An Evangelistic Approach

## Greg Linville

During the 1970s, Francis Schaeffer urged Christians to change their method of evangelizing because Western civilization had entered a post-Christian era. The Western world no longer believed in the existence of God, much less that Jesus Christ was the way to salvation. He predicted that ensuing generations would no longer have a working knowledge of Christianity, faith, or the Bible. Consequently, Christians should not expect a friend or family member to pray to receive Christ simply because a follower of Christ asked them to do so. Schaeffer realized, and taught, that those wishing to be effective in sharing the gospel of Christ needed to establish long-term relationships with secularized associates and be prepared for a lengthy process of helping these people come to faith in Christ.[1] His words proved true in the 1970s, and they are even more valid for people of faith in the new millennium. Schaeffer's exhortations serve as a foundation for this chapter on sharing faith in a postmodern new millennium. It is designed to aid the evangelistic efforts of two groups of people: recreation and sports ministers as well as pastors and church leaders.

In addition, this chapter is designed to enlighten anyone interested in winning the world to Christ as to how and why a sports and recreation ministry is an effective way to reach people for Christ and, subsequently, is a vehicle for church growth.

# Identifying Secular, Churched, Never-Churched, Dechurched and Other-Churched Persons

If churches and ministries are to reach people for Christ, they must first understand them. A few definitions will help. This chapter describes four distinct groups of people who share the need of a personal relationship with Jesus Christ.

People in need of a personal relationship with Christ are defined in two ways: in relationship to their association with religion and in relationship to their worldview. It is assumed that all are nonbelievers (having never responded to God's love and having no personal relationship with him). These groups can be identified in two ways. First, by their worldview, which can be *secularized*—having no formal association or affiliation with any faith or religion and no worldview based on any religious creed—or *religious*—having a formal association with a religious group or at least a worldview based on a religious creed.

They can also be identified in relationship to their involvement with a specific church:

*Churched*—people who are at least somewhat active in a church with regular or sporadic attendance but their church is not evangelical or they are newly involved or have never taken the church seriously. Regardless, they have no personal relationship with Christ. They may be seekers or just involved for social reasons. These people may hold to some moral code but are likely influenced by secular society. Most churches have at least a few people like this and for the most part reach them effectively. While much could be said about reaching this group of people, the thrust of this chapter will focus only on the next three categories.

*Never-Churched*—most likely also secularized but at least having never been influenced by any church, faith, or religion.

*Dechurched*—having had some interaction with a particular church or faith (possibly even a cult) but not having a positive association or relevant experience with it and in their present situation not involved with any church. Most are of a secular mind-set, but some may hold to some religious creed or worldview.

*Other-Churched*—people who are adherents or at least associated with a faith or religion other than Christianity. They may be of a secular mind-set but are generally religious to some degree.

Collectively, the latter three groups will be referred to as "nonchurched" except where a distinction is needed to identify a specific group. Each group is distinct, and knowing these distinctions will help identify how to reach them. These distinctives become apparent when combining the faith group association with being conditioned by secular or religious philosophies. For example, a person described as secularized, never-churched, nonbelievers are different from those who have repudiated the faith they were raised in yet who still adhere to its basic moral tenants. This second group is described as moral, dechurched nonbelievers.[2] Figures 8-1 through 8-5 provide a visualization of these various groupings.

## Charting the Four Groups of People

These graphs show two different polls. The vertical continuum charts the worldview gradient—Christian or secular—of a person. The horizontal axis charts the religious or nonreligious level of an individual. Those above the east-west axis are Christians, while those below the line have not yet responded to the love of Christ. The closer to the top of the graph, the deeper their faith; and, conversely, the closer to the bottom of the graph, the further they have to travel on their spiritual journey to come to full maturity in Christ.

Those on the left side of the north-south axis of the graph live a life with little or no involvement in any religious ritual. If they are on the right side of the graph, they do partake in religious activity, with those on the far right attending services and partaking in religious activity at least on a daily basis.

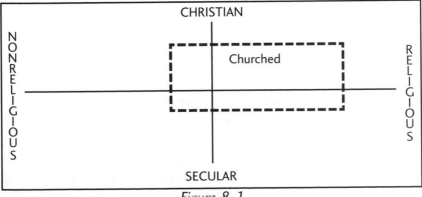

*Figure 8-1*

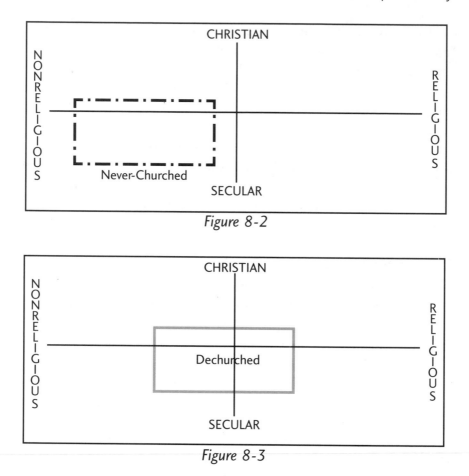

Figure 8-2

Figure 8-3

Figures 8-1 through 8-4 indicate that each of the four groups primarily lies in one of the quadrants. For example, most of the churched people reside in the upper-right quadrant, whereas the never-churched would almost exclusively be identified as being in the lower-left quadrant. Figure 5 shows that corporately most would fall in the secular half of the graph and that, other than the churched group, most people are identified in the nonreligious, secularized quadrant.

## Demythologizing the Common Stereotypes of Secularized, Nonchurched People

In his book *How to Reach Secular People,* George Hunter identifies three myths concerning secularized people.

1.  Secularized people have no spiritual hunger or aptitude.

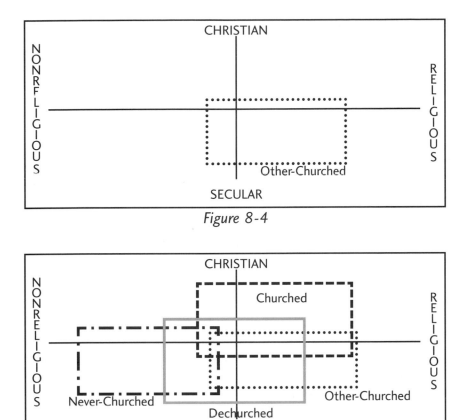

*Figure 8-4*

*Figure 8-5*

2. Secularized people have no sense of morality.

3. Secularized people have no significant beliefs.[3]

Because most Christians believe these stereotypes, they miss golden opportunities to reach secularized, nonchurched people.

Polling data verify that secularized people maintain a spiritual hunger. The vast majority of Americans say they believe in God and identify themselves as Christians. Recent Barna polls reveal that more than 80 percent of Americans say faith is "very important in their life today," and 60 percent say they are "deeply spiritual."[4] More enlightening is another Barna poll that indicates that 64 percent of nonchurched people describe religion as being "either very important or somewhat important."[5] It remains true that many Americans are totally secular and others have only nominal belief in God, yet secularism has not, and in fact cannot, eliminate the spiritual nature of people. Each person is created in God's image and has a God-shaped vacuum that only God can completely fill. The church can tap into this spiritual vacuum and offer hope to those who are searching.

A second myth often assumed by Christians is that secularism eliminates a person's innate sense of morality. C. S. Lewis illustrates this point in *Mere Christianity* by describing a scene on an English bus. Two secular people encounter each other, and each wants the last available seat. The one left standing makes a moral judgment about the other person who has just taken the last seat.[6] Lewis's point is well stated. Secular people make moral judgments, even over something as innocuous and insignificant as a seat on the bus. This demonstrates that humans have an innate sense of right and wrong—a moral sense.

This sense of morality provides a door of opportunity for the church to reach secular people. For example, churches can take advantage of the knowledge that even spiritually noncommitted parents want their children to receive moral training and to establish positive values.[7] The church that offers an athletics program for children, which includes character development, provides the needed beachhead with which to begin the process of reaching whole families for Christ.

The third misconception is that secularized people hold no significant beliefs. While secular people may not believe in the Judeo-Christian code, it is illogical to assume they don't believe in anything. Their beliefs might even include much that is antithetical to followers of Christ, but they are beliefs nonetheless and need to be understood. These beliefs include at least some aspects of the following tenets.

1. Human beings are the center of the universe.
2. Existence is caused by matter, plus time, plus chance.
3. Science is the final authority.
4. Science and technology will solve all problems.
5. Life after death is not guaranteed, nor is it knowable.[8]

Followers of Christ would do well to realize that secularized people are innately spiritual and moral beings who hold beliefs important to them. Rather than condemning secularized people for holding wrong beliefs, and thus alienating them, churches should affirm the personhood of anyone who holds to a set of beliefs and, through the vehicle of relationships, share why belief in Christ is preferable to all others.

## Reaching Secularized, Nonchurched People

The first kind of secularized person is the one who has never had any relationship with the church—the never-churched (see fig. 8-2). Many throughout the world, including Westerners, have never come in contact with a Christian church, nor have they experienced any positive Christian influence. People in these situations are like a blank sheet of paper, waiting to be written on, and are often receptive to a loving relationship with an attractive Christian. Reaching them entails establishing personal relationships, free of religious activity and language, and engaging in social activity—possibly church programs that meet their perceived needs—which enables the friendship to grow. If the never-churched observe Christians to be vibrant and attractive, they will eventually be open to the gospel.

The second group of people may be the hardest segment of the nonchurched community to reach. This is the dechurched group (fig. 8-3), people who have had a negative personal experience with a Christian or with the Christian church. The so-called dechurched are often harder to reach than those living in cultures devoid of Christianity. Far too often, individual Christians and local churches have made their first contact with a never-churched person in the form of a condemnation or a rejection. Initial communications that "condemn a nonbeliever to hell" typically force nonbelievers further from Christ. They become dechurched by negative Christian outreaches.

The other kind of dechurched person is one who was raised in the church or became part of a church or ministry and had a bad experience. This group may take longer to reach than any other group. For the dechurched, trust in Christianity has been destroyed, and regaining that trust is the first order of business. Once that trust has been reestablished, the Christian can begin to invite the dechurched person back into religious activity or programming that will eventually lead to restoring their faith in Christ. The dechurched have been innoculated over the years by small doses of negative Christianity, and it may take some time to win them back!

Surprisingly, the third group—the other-churched (fig. 8-4)—are sometimes the easiest people to reach for Christ. They already believe in the concept of God, final authority, and the importance of faith. They are accustomed to religious activity, which may provide an easier pathway to faith in Christ than someone who has never had any religious experiences. This is especially true for those who are more secularized and less entrenched in their religion. The less religious they are, the easier they are able to embrace Christianity. There are also many times in which they have had a troubling experience with their own religion or even have come to realize their religion is shallow or doesn't provide answers or fulfillment. Into this void the distinctive significance and truth of Christianity breaks through with such attractiveness that the other-churched person accepts it gladly. But for other-churched people who are deeply committed to their religion and have not yet encountered its inherent shortcomings, embracing the gospel message will prove more difficult and will take much longer. Timing, continued activity, and deepening of the relationship are crucial in reaching them.

Recreation and sports ministry is a natural nonthreatening avenue to building relationships with these groups. People will attend an event where they think they will be comfortable. They know what basketball is

---

### Tips for Reaching Those "Below the Line"

1. Go to them; don't expect them to come to you or the church.
2. Learn to speak secular. Eliminate Christian jargon and language.
3. Accept them as they are, but love them enough to challenge them to grow.
4. Use nonreligious methods. They don't want Bible study or worship.
5. Don't assume they believe the Bible to be of any value.
6. Never criticize another religion; someone they love may belong to it.
7. Affirm rather than condemn. Assume they desire spiritual peace.
8. Invite them to your home, rather than inviting them to church.
9. Identify their perceived need and then meet it.
10. Help your church to begin programming to meet these needs.

---

or what they can expect from an aerobics class. These types of activities, done intentionally, will attract and open doors for relationships to the church.

Relationships and attractive programming/ministry are the keys to reaching the nonchurched. They provide winsome reasons for the nonchurched to consider a personal relationship with Christ as well as removing the obstacles and roadblocks to accepting Christ.

## Understanding Roadblocks to Reaching the Nonchurched

Though the nonchurched may never have had any contact with a church, they may have received negative information about Christianity in general. Many nonchurched people living in Western society are either generally misinformed about, or have had a negative experience with, Christianity. Misinformation may have come from a biased mass media, or they may simply have no information. Many nonchurched people believe Christians to be:

- Uneducated
- Uninformed
- Unintelligent
- Unloving
- Condemning/critical
- Hypocritical
- Narrow-minded
- Intolerant

In addition many believe that churches are:

- Corrupt
- Constantly seeking financial contributions
- Not warmly open and accommodating
- Legalistic

Some Christians blame the secular press for negatively influencing the public against Christianity, but regardless of why Christianity is viewed in a negative light, it is imperative for Christians to get into the secular world lovingly to clear up these misconceptions. Recreation and sports ministry is a natural way to encounter skeptics.

Churches are seeing the need to instruct their members on how to be positive witnesses rather than conducting themselves in self-righteous, harsh, condemning ways. Parishioners need encouragement to enter into long-term, loving relationships with nonchurched associates, coworkers, and others. In addition, churches should also provide attendees with attractive programmatic ministries to invite the nonchurched community. These and other actions could begin to reverse and overcome the negative stereotypes many non-Christians have of Christians. In summary, the recreation and sports ministry program that has Christ as its center will go a long way to help demythologize negative stereotypes about the church and Christianity as it affords familiar, nonthreatening events and activities to the community.

## Identifying Characteristics of Churches That Effectively Reach Nonchurched People

Churches that effectively reach secularized, nonchurched nonbelievers can be identified by a common set of characteristics, which are manifested in their philosophies and methodologies for outreach.

### Philosophies of Recreation and Sports Ministry That Effectively Reach the Nonchurched

*The first philosophy is that relational styles of evangelism, which are enhanced and aided by attractive activities and events, are the best for reaching the nonchurched, whereas traditional church activities have little or no appeal.*[9] George Barna's research indicates two approaches that have a positive effect in getting nonchurched people to attend church. The first is a personal invitation by a trusted friend or family member. The second is an invitation to an interesting and "top-quality" event.[10] These two items must work in tandem, to be more than occasionally effective.

In the early 1840s a young man by the name of George joined a firm in London as an apprentice. When he arrived, he could find no other believer in Christ among the scores of employees. He began to pray that God would bring specific coworkers into a personal relationship with himself. Through George's influence a number of the young men began a personal relationship with Christ and joined in a daily time of group prayer and Bible study. This gathering annoyed one of their coworkers, who began to antagonize the group.

George encouraged the new believers to reach out lovingly to their nemesis and find how they might connect with him. They did and discovered the young man had a special affinity for oysters. An oyster bake was planned and the coworker invited. George carefully instructed that the purpose of the evening was not to proselytize but rather to engage in a fun evening. The man accepted the invitation and later wrote in his memoirs that he was most impressed by the group's "frivolity." So impressed was he that he accepted their invitation to attend the Bible study and prayer time. Within a few months he, too, responded to the love of God and accepted Jesus as his Lord and Savior. A few months later he joined with George Williams and ten others in that firm to form the YMCA! In fact, the man who liked oysters is the only one of the twelve whose original YMCA membership is still in existence!

George Williams's philosophy of building relationships with non-believers and then inviting them to attractive activities became the mainstay of the YMCA ministry. Some Ys still use this simple methodology today in their efforts to win people to Christ. Every church has done fellowships or sponsored a sports team; this concept is not foreign to most churches. Barna's modern-day research verifies that this age-old methodology is by far still one of the best ways for churches and other ministries to reach secular, nonchurched people.

***The second philosophy is that becoming a Christian is a process, not an event.*** Social science recognizes that change does not happen overnight. Political parties understand this same principle. It is also true in spiritual concerns. A person moves through a process: first becoming aware there is another belief system, then admitting it has some validity, and eventually acknowledging the new system to be the most valid. In the decision-making phase, a change from the old system is made, followed by a period of incorporating the new belief into one's life.

While normally a long-term proposition, this process can be shortened by extreme conditions. Just as a valley is normally formed over many years by a gently flowing river, it can be totally changed in just a few hours by a raging torrent. When this process is hastened, there is still the need for the person to go through a stabilization period. Premature babies need to be carefully monitored and attended to so they can "catch up" a bit before entering into a normal infant life. Similarly, anyone who has a dramatic conversion needs to "catch up" by being shepherded through some of those missed points of processing their faith in Christ. It is not unusual for this process to take five to seven years or even longer for a totally secularized adult, two or three years for a secularized teen, and two to three years for an adult who has been raised in the church or in another faith.[11] Involvement in a quality recreation and sports ministry is a way to help move someone through the Christian growth and multiplying process.

***Outreach is the job of every believer.*** These churches believe that reaching the nonchurched person is not just the responsibility of the pastor or the church staff, but it is also the responsibility of each member. In fact, evidence suggests nonclergy types are often more effective in reaching people for Christ.[12] Recreation and sports ministry gives members a place to live out their gifts, talents, and abilities for the sake of the gospel.

*Outreach is best done by individuals who are part of a larger outreach community.* It's one thing to encounter one positive Christian. It's dramatically different to see positive Christianity being lived out by a whole community. This concept is found in John 10:10, where Jesus says, "I have come that they may have life and have it in abundance." The abundant life lived on a higher plane is an attractive life.

*The church's primary mission is reaching nonbelievers rather than to serve as a fellowship for believers.* Programs and ministries to and for believers must be designed to empower church members for service and outreach, as opposed to merely providing the believer a spiritual country club. All recreation and sports programs/ministries of the church must have the ultimate goal of outreach. We must not settle anymore for activity for activity's sake. Keeping the Christ distinctive is imperative if the church is to stay true to the Scriptures. The presence of Christ must be made openly known and testified to at each recreation and sports ministry event, class, or workshop.

*God is a God of redemption, and nonbelievers matter to him (Luke 19:10).* Unless churches see this as their primary task, they will continue to offend the secular person and lose their ability to fulfill the mission of Christ to seek and save the lost. Caring for people by meeting the felt and real needs of life can be provided in a comprehensive recreation and sports ministry setting. (See appendix 13 for ideas.)

*Secularized, nonchurched nonbelievers must be accepted as they are.* Too often churches require regenerate behavior from unregenerate people. In the 1860s a young street worker and his wife began to have real success in reaching the urban poor and disenfranchised—so much so that many of their new friends began to attend Lord's Day services with them at their church. The church people were offended by the way the newcomers looked, behaved, and even smelled. They asked William and Catherine to stop bringing the heathens to church. The Booths never looked back and went on to found the Salvation Army, an organization designed to care enough to accept unregenerate people as they are and yet love them enough to challenge them to grow in their faith.

*In order to be effective, outreach programs must be attractive to nonbelievers.* Because time is so highly valued in our culture, when it comes to reaching the secular person, it does not matter how beautiful the church building is or how great a preacher, choir, or music ministry is. What matters is the quality of programmatic ministries. Not providing quality programs is one of the biggest shortcomings of churches attempting to reach the nonchurched. Recreation and sports ministries that are effective in their outreach efforts know they must meet what George Williams identified as the perceived need of the secularized person. Only then will they ever hope to meet their spiritual need. This includes:

- Providing creative and innovative recreation and sports ministry events.
- Creating "bridging" programs that will move nonchurched people from outreach programs into the mainstream of the church body.
- Initiating recreation and sports ministry events and other church activities that are attractive to the nonchurched.[13]
- Being willing to stop doing "what has been done before" so that "what needs to be done" can be done.

## Methodology for Reaching the Nonchurched

1. Each recreation and sports ministry team responsibility area must define their target group geographically and/or demographically. Unless the ministry team identifies who they wish to reach, they will not effectively design appropriate ministries to attract their target group.[14]

2. After identifying whom they are to reach, the ministry team must do the necessary research to determine what the perceived needs of this group are. This research will form the foundation of all future plans for ministry.

3. From this research the recreation and sports ministry leadership team can select activities, services, and involvements that will be attractive to the unchurched, even if it means changing what has always been done.

4. The overall vision for outreach should evolve from the vision statement of the church leadership, but the specific plans of the outreach must evolve from the members. Church leaders ought not dictate how this ministry should happen but rather let the mission statement serve as a guide and catalyst for formulating specific ministry action plans.

5. Church leaders need to provide the members with the ministry skills and training they need to carry out the plan successfully.

6. Perhaps a single church may not have enough critical mass to carry out a particular vision. At this point they should engage in dialogue with other churches and ministries and join other cooperative efforts in reaching the nonchurched. While most churches would find it impossible to form an entire softball league, they could easily collaborate with other churches and together gather the amount of people, resources, equipment, and facilities needed to accomplish the task.

## Recognizing the Importance of the Individual in Reaching the Secularized, Nonchurched Nonbeliever

Churches can have the greatest plans in the world, but unless they have solid individuals to carry out those plans, the preparation will be in vain. In order for individuals to reach their friends, family members, and associates, they must embody seven basic principles.

*1. Have a personal, growing relationship with Christ.* This includes living a life that proclaims Christ by its basic integrity, warmth, peace, and joy. A solid attractive Christian life speaks loudly and encourages others to consider Christ. In addition it means living a life that encounters secular society on a regular basis. While at first this might appear too basic even to mention, it may well be the biggest hindrance in reaching secular people for Christ.

The Christian community demands purity of character in its members and condemns living a secular lifestyle. Therefore, most believers are put in an untenable position: either reach out to the secular world and risk the condemnation of the Christian community for associating with questionable activity and people, or stay in a safe Christian environment but develop no relationships with nonbelievers.

Recreation and sports ministry offers a way to get outside the church walls to encounter the real world of the secular culture using tools that are palatable to the world. This is the concept of being "in the world but not of the world" as the Scriptures admonish us to do. Believers will find many doors acceptable and open as they seek to impact culture using recreation and sports as a personal evangelism tool.

*2. Have a desire for reaching the nonbeliever.* In the use of recreation and sports, unless evangelism is intentional, it will be accidental at best. There is nothing religious and nothing inherently good or bad about softball; how it is used makes the difference. The desire for reaching the nonbelieving individual must be accompanied by a plan to use recreation and sports ministry events intentionally to share the gospel.

*3. Have a basic working knowledge of the Bible so as to be able to share various passages with others.* The Word of God is what opens blind eyes and closed hearts. Recreation and sports ministry is a natural for sharing the love of Christ using analogies from sports, crafts, camping, nature, and games.

*4. Be committed to prayer, including maintaining an "Andrew prayer list."* Coaches, instructors, and workshop leaders must see their contact with participants the way a Sunday school teacher sees the class— as an opportunity to minister and mentor the students. This is what George Williams did when he first arrived at his firm in London. He listed apprentices who needed Jesus as Savior. He prayed he would have the opportunity to introduce them to the Messiah, just as Andrew, one of the twelve disciples, did when he brought his brother, the apostle Peter, to Christ. R. A. Torrey suggests that we ask God to:

- Lead us to those for whom we should pray.
- Lead us to what to say to those for whom we are praying.
- Empower us to reach those for whom we are praying.[15]

*5. Know your optimal target group.* Answering the following questions will help to define and understand the group of people one is best positioned to reach. The questions to ask are:

- What are your age, ethnic or cultural background, life experience, educational background, geographic location, personal interests, and personal gifts (both spiritual and natural)?
- Where do people most often affirm you?
- Where do you feel most comfortable and at peace?
- Where do you feel most uncomfortable and tense?

The answers to these questions will provide an understanding of the persons one is most likely to reach. While teenagers might occasionally impact a senior adult, they most likely will best relate to other teens. Similarly, mothers are best suited to reach moms, athletes have a better chance of relating to athletes than do nonathletes, and people can more easily influence those with whom they share a common cultural or ethnic background.

**6. Learn how to "speak secular."** Once believers have established a relationship with a secular person, they often are unable to communicate verbally their faith because they only know Christian language. They need to learn "secular." Just as international missionaries must learn the language of the people they are going to reach, so must "local missionaries" learn to speak the language of the culture they wish to reach. A few examples will serve to encapsulate this concept.

- Eliminate all Christian jargon such as "washed in the blood," "saved," "repent," "born again," and "sanctified."
- Never initiate the relationship by being critical of any other faith or denomination. Even if the person is a never-churched person, he or she may not approve of condemning others and often may have had some association with the particular faith or denomination being condemned.
- Learn which terminology is acceptable and understandable by the secularized person and yet can still communicate an evangelical faith in Christ. Phrases like "spiritual development," "coming to faith," "faith journey," or "encountering the Eternal Being" have an easier path to recognition for the secular person.
- Affirm rather than condemn. Assuming the person does want to be spiritually right is vital to the development of the evangelism process. No one appreciates being condemned; everyone appreciates affirmation.

**7. Maximize the "perceived need" concept.** If the individual follower of Christ is a member of a congregation having programs designed to reach the nonchurched, his or her job will be made easier by having attractive activities or facilities to invite the nonbeliever to attend. However, it is still imperative for anyone who attempts to reach out to friends or neighbors to be able to identify what these people perceive as being their needs.

Recognizing the neighbor's desire for quality child care opens the door to recommend the church's preschool program. Suggesting the various youth activities at the church to a friend who is experiencing difficulties with a teenager will generally be well received. Inviting a coworker to join the church's softball team or basketball league will provide a first step toward a deeper relationship with the church. Individuals who are effective in reaching out to nonbelievers understand the principle of first meeting the perceived need of their friend so they can eventually meet the spiritual need.

## Evangelism Is a Process, Not an Event

Understanding that coming to Christ and then growing in him as a process is the foundation upon which sports and recreational evangelism is based. Coming to faith in Christ and maturing in that faith is a process, not a one-time event. There is most certainly a specific time in which the Holy Spirit does his regenerating work in the heart of a person, but that regenerating work is the result of a much longer period of cultivation and preparation. It is not unusual for the secularized nonbeliever to experience a six- to ten-year process before coming to the point of regeneration. This is followed by a lifetime of continual, perpetual maturing in one's faith.

## Biblical Teaching on Coming to Christ

The Book of Acts is a repository of stories about people coming to personal faith in Christ. The majority of these narratives demonstrate the aforementioned process. The Ethiopian eunuch spent time reading the Scriptures prior to Philip's appearance. Cornelius was reported to be a man diligent in seeking out spiritual matters, which eventually led him to send for Peter. Peter was able to explain to Cornelius who Christ was and his need to receive him as Lord and Savior. These and other passages verify that the normal course of coming to Christ is, in fact, a process.

The human body has been designed by God with an ability to heal itself. When the body receives a flesh wound such as a cut, burn, or scrape, it has the capability to heal itself. Proper cleansing and medicinal ointments can aid or hasten the healing, but normally the body follows the natural process of healing without external aids. Every person who has ever lived will experience this natural, healing process, but some, in unique situations, will experience a much more dramatic and instantaneous healing as the result of God's supernatural and miraculous grace. While each person experiences the normal process of healing on a regular basis, a few people will experience an instantaneous healing. The same is true for evangelism using recreation and sports ministry as a vehicle. While most will go through a process in coming to Christ, God miraculously moves in others instantaneously.

Consequently it is important for churches, ministries, and evangelistic organizations to alter their endeavors to become more process oriented and less event driven. Training members in lifestyle evangelism is a great way to start. Adding programmatic ministries such as aerobics, child care, and adult sports leagues increases the impact as these enable a positive, relational atmosphere for conversion to occur.

Evangelistic efforts need to focus more on true conversion as opposed to a decision. Zacchaeus, Luke, Peter, and James the half brother of Jesus are representatives of conversion. The rich young ruler and Simon the sorcerer are portrayals of a decision. The latter two made a temporary decision to follow Christ but never truly converted, whereas Peter and James were truly converted, following Christ even though it caused their deaths.

This process orientation fits perfectly with sports leagues and recreational activities for many reasons, but it will not make much sense until one understands that evangelism is a process. Just as a farmer cannot reap a harvest without first planning, acquiring tools and seed, preparing soil, planting, cultivating, and pruning, a spiritual harvester cannot reap a spiritual harvest without taking much the same approach and philosophy.

---

### *Postmoderns: Secularized, Nonchurched Nonbelievers . . .*

1. Have an innate hunger for spirituality.
2. Need positive associations with Christians to counter negative, preconceived notions and may also need help in overcoming any personal negative encounters with Christians.
3. Are often more effectively reached by the laity than by clergy.
4. Are most effectively reached in a relational manner.
5. Can most effectively be reached having their perceived needs recognized and met.
6. Normally come to a personal faith in Christ by a process that can take many years.
7. Recreation and sports ministry is a relational, nonthreatening evangelistic approach.

---

"The harvest is ripe." It is also important to realize a farmer can reap prematurely and ruin the harvest in the haste of wanting to harvest the crops. A good harvest takes time and effort.

With this accumulation of data, it becomes clear why and how a sports, recreation, or activity-based ministry is so effective in reaching the secularized, never-churched, dechurched, or other-churched nonbeliever. Not only are sports and recreation ministries a natural way to reach out to the secular community, but they also serve as a catalyst to enrich the lives of members and engage them in outreach activities.

## Understanding How Sports and Recreation Ministries Work in Reaching Secularized, Nonchurched Nonbelievers

The following elucidates six reasons why a sports and recreation ministry is effective:

1. It reaches the largest cross section of people.
2. It specifically reaches secularized, never-churched, dechurched, and other-churched nonbelievers.
3. It specifically reaches the two missing groups of people in most traditional churches.
4. It fulfills church growth principles by empowering and focusing the laity.
5. People are most easily influenced by having fun.
6. Athletic and recreational facilities attract people.

*1. It reaches the largest cross section of people.* Longtime sports ministry pioneer and apologist Rodger Oswald has often made the claim that if the apostle Paul were alive today he would either be a musical athlete or an athletic musician. As such he would embody the 1 Corinthians 9:19–23 admonition to use all means "that I might save some."[16] Oswald's point simply is that the top two universal languages are sports and music. In Western societies, music and sports are used consistently and effectively to promote and advertise products, messages, and businesses. Bill Shirley in his article "Mad About Sports" mentions that in 1983 a beer company tried to determine how to reach the greatest number of people with one advertisement. Their research discovered that 75 percent of all Americans watch sports once a week. In addition, 70 percent discuss, read about, or participate in sports daily, and thirty-five million people identify themselves as being avid sports fans.[17]

Sports and recreation are activities that most people understand and participate in. For many they are a passion. Billions of dollars are spent each year purchasing sporting goods. Recreational vehicle sales are at an unprecedented high. Linear parks are the latest rage and afford millions of people the ability to cover thousands of miles on their bikes, skates, cross-country skis, or simply on foot without ever having to travel on a road.

This postmodern generation has taken the "extreme" in sports to new levels. Bungee jumping and snowboarding are now even seen as a bit tame by those who "mountain board" or jump out of planes onto virgin snow so they can ski slopes that are inaccessible by conventional means. This new generation is "doing the dew," and those who wish to reach them with the love of Christ must create new avenues of contact.

Hardly any athletic event is held without a sponsor. Why? Because marketing research demonstrates people are interested in sports, and sports sell products. Why should the church not use sports and recreation to get the Word out? Even the apostle Paul used sports words, analogies, and metaphors to communicate the gospel message.

Churches must recognize they are not in competition with one another as much as they are in competition with the leisure culture of the day. Secular Western society has traded the Lord's Day for the Leisure Day. The primary Sunday activity for secular society is sports and recreation, not church attendance. Leisure has become the goal.

*2. It reaches the secularized, never-churched, dechurched, and other-churched nonbeliever.* When you are out of your cultural comfort zone, you can feel your temperature rise, and the risk of embarrassment can be painful. Similarly, people who are not familiar with a church culture feel embarrassed and out of place in church settings. They don't know what to wear, say, do, or think. They don't know if they're to kneel, stand, or sit. They have quite a difficult time deciphering the language of "sanctified, redeemed, repent, sacrament" and hope they never experience being "washed in the blood"! Yet, if they come to a church gym, they immediately know what to wear, say, and how to act. They never have to worry about kneeling; they stand to cheer and sit the rest of the time. They know that *technical* and *flagrant* refer to rule infractions and that *zebra* is the nicer of the two horse names shouted at the people who constantly blow whistles and know a funny kind of sign language.

One of the common reasons people don't come to church is they simply aren't comfortable attending functions where they feel out of place. The Lord's Supper is unfamiliar for many. An activity that is a common occurrence in the secular world is much more likely to be attended by people not familiar with the church. The key is to find activities that enable an initial comfort so relationships can begin and then allow those relationships to serve as the security blanket during more unfamiliar and uncomfortable services or functions of the church.

In addition, providing a step-by-step entry to the church is wise. A brief "thought for the day" (rather than "meditation") before or after a ball game will start to introduce the concept of spirituality. Holding a "team huddle" at the end of the game (rather than "devotional") continues the progression by enabling people to hear a biblical message in an informal and relevant setting. Inviting someone to a "couples' group" or a "men's gathering" (rather than a "Bible study") takes the next step in building the bridge to the church. An invitation to a "banquet" (rather than a "revival") can get someone into a church building. After all this, an invitation to a worship service might actually receive a positive response!

Sports and recreation ministry enables the relationship to begin by being a "safe haven" for the nonchurched person. It also provides a touch point with a person each week, season after season, year after year, enabling some of the discomfort to fade away. The importance of this cannot be overlooked. The profound truth is that if a true conversion is desired, rather than just a decision, a sports ministry that keeps a person engaged over the years may be better than a one-time evangelistic event and should be pursued by any church desiring long-term substantial growth. Events can and should be used but only in conjunction with an overall plan and must be recognized as one step in the overall process, not the only step.

**3. It reaches the two missing groups of people in most traditional churches.** The two groups most often missing from typical churches are youth and men. Many traditional American churches lose their youth shortly before or during high school years. Churches often see teenagers lose interest.

Generally speaking, the socialization patterns are much different for men and women. Women are much more verbally gifted, and men relate much more to activity. This is not to say that women never participate in any activity or that men never talk, but generally speaking, women are more comfortable with conversation, whereas men are more desirous of activity.

Once a church begins to add activity-based ministries, men get involved and become engaged in church. The man who won't teach a class relishes coaching a youth league team or organizing a biking club. Once word is out about a "happening" youth center or activity, youth will come out in droves. A java house with a small laundry located next door brings single people flocking to church.

None of this should be misunderstood as an argument for doing away with Bible study or worship. It is not intended to disparage teaching, fellowship, or the music ministry of a church. Rather, it asks churches to consider adding more activity-based ministry to the overall program, particularly with an eye toward being relevant and inclusive of men and adolescents. It is not always necessary to replace traditional, tried-and-true efforts of the church but rather add to them in order to attract nonchurched youth and men and to motivate the youth and men already in the church to become more involved

**4. It affirms the priesthood of the believer by empowering and focusing the laity.** McGavran and Arn, in their book *The Ten Steps for Church Growth,* demonstrate that evangelism must be a priority if church growth is to take place—and much more so for valid recreation and sports ministry. In addition, they state that church members must be encouraged to discover their spiritual gifts in order to find a niche where they can use them. Members must be provided opportunities if they are expected to serve effectively.[18] These church-growth principles are beautifully found within a sports and recreation ministry.

As has already been demonstrated, sports and recreation ministry is considered to be the most strategic tool for evangelism the church has today. If a church wants to grow, the experts say to focus on evangelism and outreach. Since sports and recreation are proven evangelistic tools, it makes sense for churches to tap into this great resource.

Sports and recreation can also aid a church by helping parishioners discover their gifts and to find a place to use them. While only so many classes need teachers, a church can facilitate large numbers of activities that need a coach, league director, referee, clinician, or boat driver. While not everyone has musical gifts, many have gifts in dramatic arts, athletics, dance, and recreation or resources like a ski boat. By providing a place for laypeople to use their skills, gifts, experiences, resources, and training, a church empowers its members to exercise ownership in the overall outreach ministry. It gives them opportunities to serve in the way God has ordained them.

   ***5. People are most easily influenced while having fun.*** Plato is quoted as saying, "Students are at their learning best while having fun." Churches and ministries today are still experiencing the wisdom of this old proverb. People are more easily influenced and guided when enjoying themselves. Churches that engage a nonchurched person with exciting, fun programming find participants much more open to the good news of Jesus Christ. One little girl once remarked to her father, "Daddy, I like our recreation minister; he makes it fun to go to church!" It is OK to have fun at church.

   Churches that have winsome, attractive programs for youth find many of those youth either joining the youth group or returning later in life when they get serious about faith and look for a church to join. Churches that provide relevant recreational opportunities for men witness many of these men bringing whole families to church services. Many women who are attending churches today began in an aerobics or exercise class. What each experienced was a winsome open door that met a felt need of recreation, competition, or fitness. During involvement in the felt-need activity, they began to have fun, were inspired by the prayers and spiritual thoughts communicated during the activities, established relationships with church members, and eventually entered into the overall body life of the church. The church's ability to influence these nonchurched people was all made possible because of the element of fun, of creating a positive, attractive, and winsome activity.

   ***6. Athletic and recreational facilities attract people.*** A recreation minister's testimony is all about the education minister visiting his home after his family had just moved to a new community. The minister knew how to capture this young teenager's imagination when he asked him, "Do you like to play basketball?" The boy answered yes, he loved to play basketball. The wise minister began to explain how the boy could be involved in the life of the church and play basketball and take part in a myriad of other recreational activities. The teenager made up his mind that that was the church for him. Through this ministry he became a Christian. Over the years he became involved in leading recreation activities. He found that God could use his gifts, talents, and interests in leading recreation events, thus he found the call of God to recreation and sports ministry. The facility was an attraction, but the programming and intentional sharing of the gospel were the keys to his becoming involved in a lifelong ministry.

The memorable line from the classic movie *Field of Dreams* is "build it and they will come." Voices out of cornfields are myths to be sure, yet the truth of buildings attracting people is reality. More than one hundred years ago, Robert McBurney saw the membership and participation numbers skyrocket when he led the New York City YMCA through a ten-year building program. Building a new stadium propelled the Cleveland Indians from last to first in attendance as they tripled the amount of paid spectators in one year while fielding the same team! Buildings do make a difference.

Churches in the know realize that the nonchurched, dechurched, and other-churched person won't come to a church just because it is architecturally appealing. (In fact, if it is built to look like a church, it might even be an obstacle to their attending.) Yet these same churches know that properly programmed athletic facilities will be an attractive entry point for people to get involved in church. Strategically placing ball fields and walking tracks in full view of passersby is a way of attracting people to a church. Facilities and proper programming are tools to attract this leisure-oriented, competition-driven unseeded culture to the abundant life in Christ.

Sports and recreation ministry is one of the most strategic tools for reaching the world for Christ. It can attract a secular nonchurched population. It provides a vehicle to keep the nonchurched involved over a long period of time, allowing relationships to grow and the evangelism process to occur while creating opportunities for one-on-one, small- and large-group evangelism to take place. If churches are serious about reaching the never-churched, dechurched, and other-churched population, they will not find a better methodology than sports and recreation ministries.

---

### Notes

1. These concepts can be found in Schaeffer's writings. One particular aspect of Schaeffer's genius was that he practiced George Hunter's "Celtic style of evangelism." He established a haven where anyone, including atheists, agnostics, and people of other spiritual persuasions, could come and enter into the daily life of an ongoing Christian community and through their involvements experience and learn the distinctive difference and significance of Christ and Christianity. Through Schaeffer's ministry and community, some responded to the love of Christ, while many others became convinced of their faith in Christ. For more infor-

mation on the Celtic way of evangelism, read George Hunter's wonderful book by that title (Nashville: Abingdon, 2000).

2. George Barna helps distinguish between the unchurched and the dechurched in *Evangelism That Works* (Ventura, Ca.: Regal Books, 1996).

3. George Hunter, *How to Reach Secular People* (Nashville: Abingdon, 1992).

4. Barna, 2.

5. Ibid., 52.

6. C. S. Lewis, *Mere Christianity* (San Francisco: Harper, 2001).

7. Barna reports that 75 percent of all parents indicated they would be interested in a church that provides religious teaching or training (*Evangelism That Works,* 58).

8. Even this is changing for many people in the new millennium. The shift is moving toward the idea that the natural world—the earth, animals, trees, the universe—is the center of existence, and each of these things is to be more highly valued than people. An example of this would be to compare the outrage that occurs when animals are mistreated to the acceptance of abortion.

9. Barna has found that less than 1 percent of the nonchurched people he polled identified any issue of spiritual nature to be their core concern (*Evangelism That Works,* 54).

10. Ibid., 64, 70.

11. These differences can be explained by understanding that teens have much less baggage to unpack and in general just move through things more quickly than do adults. In addition, those adults who were raised in and/or experienced a faith community have already taken the initial steps in the process. They may already believe in a god and assume there is a final authority such as Scripture.

12. Some research indicates that the laity is twice as effective in bringing people to faith as are paid clergy. This research comes from the National Evangelistic Association and is reported by George Hunter (*How to Reach Secular People,* 115).

13. Many churches use some type of signal to alert their members as to the nature of a particular program or service. One popular device is the "red light, yellow light, green light" approach. Red is designed strictly for believers. Yellow is for people who are comfortable with things like prayer, Scripture, and spiritual discussion but may not yet have a personal faith in Christ. Green light is designed strictly for nonbelievers. I am indebted to my good friend from England, John Bussell, who described how his church uses this system to reach the nonchurched. Through John's leadership his church has one of the most progressive recreational outreaches in Great Britain.

14. Robert McBurney—the premier general secretary of the first 50 years of the YMCA and certainly the one who established much of the YMCA philosophy—recruited a local businessman, Cephas Brainerd, to help him take a survey. They first determined their demographic group (young men under 30) and their geographic boundaries (New York City). After determining their target group of people, McBurney and Brainerd surveyed the social, spiritual, and relational needs of young men in NYC. This survey became the driving force behind what services and ministries the YMCA provided in New York City for the next few decades. The survey of McBurney and Brainerd indicated young men needed a positive environment for socialization and recreation. Thus, facilities to accommodate these activities were bought, rented, or built.

15. R. A. Torrey, *Winning Men to Christ* (1910).

16. Rodger has made this or similar statements at many CSRM conferences and confirmed it with me in a phone interview on 23 January 2002.

17. Bill Shirley, "Mad About Sports," *The Plain Dealer* (18 January 1987): G–3.

18. Donald A. McGavran and Winfield C. Arn, *Ten Steps for Church Growth* (San Francisco: Harper & Row, 1977).

# 9 Ethic of Competition in a Church Setting

## Greg Linville

In the final analysis most competitors hold to the "win at all costs" philosophy of sports. Yet at some point during their career, many amateur and professional athletes pause to reflect on the meaning of sports and their involvement in them.

## Sportsmanship, Gamesmanship, or Christmanship

Church leagues are notorious for unruliness and out-of-control competitiveness. Church leagues and programs have been shut down because some "Christian athletes" let the emotions of competition get out of hand.

The decade of the 1980s saw Nike skyrocket as a major supplier of sporting goods in America. The company chose its name well: *Nike* means "conqueror," and all athletes desire to be conquerors. The mythological Greek goddess of victory was named Nike. Although we know that just wearing a pair of shoes advertised by professional athletes won't help us perform like them, we feel more confident when we are wearing quality shoes and uniforms.

Americans want to win; we adhere to the motto of the late Vince Lombardi: "Winning isn't everything; it is the only thing." Athletes, coaches, and all who follow athletic teams love to be associated with winners, even if it's nothing more than a sporting goods company whose name suggests victory. The problem is, there are always more losers than winners, and even the best athletes fail. What began for most athletes as a joy ends up being the source of frustration and bitterness.

Is it possible actually to enjoy sports and competition? Do athletics have any redeeming value for the individual and the church? Absolutely! Not only can churches have teams enjoy competing, but they can use competition for building Christian character, evangelism, and discipleship. It is possible not only to attain a victory but to experience overwhelming victory as we allow God to use our abilities and interests in sports.

Modern-day philosophic foundations for competition ethics stem from the concept of sportsmanship. As one contemplates modern-day sports, it is imperative to heed the advice of Dr. Arnold Beisser: "In sports, unless more than the surface is explored, men become slaves, instead of exercising free will."[1] Sportsmanship needs to be reviewed "below the surface," particularly in light of what continues to happen in the sports arenas around the world.

Sportsmanship is an admirable goal; however, it is seldom adhered to. Sportsmanship is usually overruled by a desire to win; it is seldom rewarded. The acceptance at face value of the prevailing views on winning enslaves many to the ethic of "win at all costs." Winning is exalted as the ultimate accomplishment. To subdue and conquer an opponent is the pinnacle of success and fulfillment in sports. Conversely, losers are worth nothing, totally useless, inept, and are taunted and trampled by opponents. These attitudes and actions are hardly congruent with the essence of sportsmanship and yet are a direct result of the faulty philosophical premise upon which sportsmanship is based.

A common understanding of certain words is important to understand any further discussion of competitive ethics. The word *ship* means "to send, bear, or transport." When used in the English language as a suffix, it denotes "the bearing of a condition, character, office, or skill." The word *man* is the generic word used to describe the human race. Therefore, *man-ship* has the connotation of humankind bearing certain conditions, characteristics, offices, or skills. When *sports* is added to *man-ship,* it becomes *sportsmanship,* the definitive word to describe the characteristics, skills, and ethics that sports people bear upon themselves as they compete.

But the definition of *sportsmanship* continues to evolve depending on who defines it. Generally it represents acceptable ethics and morals—such as having fun, playing fair, using skills, maximizing abilities, and being a gracious winner or loser—all positive and useful within a church context.

However, these ethics are determined by the popular opinion of a society, which has no permanent mooring.

Morality changes according to culture, country, religion, or popular opinion. Sportsmanship has no final authority. It fluctuates with places, times, players, and coaches. One thing does not change—the desire to win. Thus, the final authority or ethic of sports is to win, and the ethic of sports is not determined by the philosophy of sportsmanship but rather by the pragmatism of gamesmanship. Although sportsmanship espouses such things as fairness and fun, only winners are rewarded.

So out of sportsmanship a new ethic evolves—gamesmanship. Gamesmanship maintains that the highest ethic of sports is to win. Fun is no longer the foundation of competitive ethics; winning is.

Because gamesmanship has replaced sportsmanship as the basis for determining competitive ethics in secular as well as church sports, athletes have received mixed messages as to what their attitudes and actions should be. What they hear and see communicated by parents, coaches, and athletic administrators even in a church league is to win regardless of the cost or means. What players are told and what they observe are contradictory. Athletes are told to have fun, be coachable, and respect authority. Then they observe coaches, school administrators, and booster club members yelling obscenities at umpires, referees, and opposing teams. Their coach says, "All that matters is to give your best effort," yet the coach only plays the best athletes on the team. Kids receive the verbal communication to have fun, but what they observe are adults concerned only about winning.

Athletes are also confused about what is really fair. One coach accuses another of cheating while also being guilty of cheating. Coaches believe their actions are justifiable because they do not consider what they do to be cheating. They believe they are only "bending a rule" to benefit their own players or program. In essence they base morality on humanistic pragmatism. They do whatever it takes to win, communicating by their actions that winning is more important than any standard of morality. These coaches believe they are concerned about their players, but in reality their priority is to win.

One of the saddest accounts of what pressure to win can do to a man is found in the autobiography of coach Taylor Locke. Locke was head basketball coach at four major universities. He began to cheat in earnest after losing time and again to other universities who had, in his opinion, won because they had cheated. In his book *Caught in the Net,* he relates his experience while coaching at Clemson University.

> At Clemson I lost touch with my values. Stuff was just laying there. Money came easy and so did the women. There were alumni wives who were quite open about their personal need for affection. . . . I had never been a part of anything like this before. After I married Nancy and all through my years at West Point and Miami, I wouldn't even consider looking at another woman. It was the way I was brought up.
>
> But, my values changed almost overnight at Clemson. The pressures from losing in my first two or three years made me an easy target, I guess. I was drinking too much Scotch, popping too many pills. Life was moving too fast for this small town guy to handle. My values slipped and slipped and slipped, and the people who got hurt were my family. We had some family problems . . . but those problems could be attributed to basketball, not booze, pills and women. I was . . . married to my job. . . . Everybody says there is God, your family and your job. I loved my job first. . . . If I can offer one bit of advice to a young coach today . . . it is that the individual must be willing to accept the unwritten code which already exists. . . . Just go out and get the job done. If it is recruiting, then go out and recruit. Play the game by the same rules of the street. It is like in sales or anything else—somewhere down the line you are going to have to give out green stamps. You are going to have to cheat somewhere down the line but do it and don't talk about it. Take it from someone who cheated and got caught.[2]

By his own admission, Taylor Locke relates that he lost his moral basis for life, but this is not the saddest part of his story. It is not that his family suffered or his mental or physical health failed—all as direct results of his conscious decisions to cheat and turn his back on what he knew to be right. Even after being caught, fired, ridiculed, and causing everyone great agony, he still does not admit that cheating, lying, and breaking the rules are wrong.

This is the epitome of "gamesmanship." Some coaches and athletes believe it is acceptable not only to lose your soul but also your marriage, health, and integrity just to win a few more games. This belief system, based upon humanistic relativism, is not a new one, as demonstrated by the following quote:

> The emphasis upon winning and the absence of a body of established amateur traditions permitted large outlays of money for football, the open recruitment of player talent, fierce training schedules, and clear cases of premeditated brutality. The eligibility problem, professionalism, deaths and serious injuries from football, and a lack of gentlemanly behavior, and the issue of whether to make football even more financially rewarding and respectable all contributed to a virtual state of anarchy among the nation's colleges. Consequently football became the subject of a vigorous nationwide debate which eventually involved college presidents, faculties, the press, and even the president of the United States. . . . The spirit of American youth, as of the American man, is to, "get there" by fair means or foul, and the lack of moral scruple which pervades the struggles of the business world meets with temptations equally irresistible in the miniature contest of the football field.[3]

This quote is not from the 2002 *New York Times* or *Chicago Tribune*. It was written in 1890. No, the problem is not a new one. The pressures to win at all costs have been negatively affecting those involved with athletics for years. These problems occur because of the aforementioned fluctuation of morals and values, which even in a church setting have their root in the philosophy of humanistic relativism. The major tenant of relativism is that there is no ultimate or final authority and, therefore, everything is relative. People are free to establish their own morality and do whatever they wish. They decide for themselves what is moral and right. How this affects sports and athletes is easily observed.

Since only winners are rewarded, athletes believe it is right to cheat if cheating helps attain a win. Moralistic platitudes are forgotten. Victory is the priority. The result of relativism is ethical chaos. Teams, leagues, and

institutions able to exert necessary influence of power, money, prestige, or favors increase chances of winning and fend off being penalized for cheating even when caught. Those that cannot or will not cheat or exert unprincipled influences compete at a great disadvantage. The best athlete or team doesn't always win. Sadly, those with the lowest set of morals are too often the victors.

Tragically, as a result of this cheating, the essence of competition is compromised, and victory becomes a hollow shell, lacking meaning and accomplishment. Competitors who cheat to win, cheat themselves because in the end their victory is meaningless.

What began innocently enough as a code of ethics to rule unscrupulous competition among athletes has degenerated into immorality. Sportsmanship always devolves into gamesmanship.

For Christian athletes and churches desiring to use sports, to compete with the proper code of ethics, neither sportsmanship nor gamesmanship is totally satisfying. Total fulfillment and satisfaction can only be found in "Christmanship." Christmanship encourages athletes to live out the characteristics, attitudes, and skills that emulate Christ and conform to his image in the arena of competition.

Christmanship embodies the best of sportsmanship (fun, fairness, being a good loser, etc.) and the best of gamesmanship (giving one's best effort within the rules to win), but it transcends and surpasses them both. It challenges the Christian athlete to compete as Christ would compete. For most athletes, however, this concept of Christmanship may be nothing more than a nebulous idea.

Since there are no known accounts of Jesus' having competed in leagues or competitions of his day, we must look at different Scriptures that reveal the foundations and parameters from which this ethic must be constructed. Nevertheless, Christmanship will prescribe specific actions and attitudes and enable athletes to experience a total fulfillment and satisfaction in their competitions. Their actions will not be based on relativistic morals that change with the winds, nor will they find their root in the quagmire of pragmatism, but rather their actions will be rooted in the authority of God's will as revealed through his Scriptures. Only through these scriptural concepts and principles will athletes experience overwhelming victory.

# Remolding Our Minds

Before exploring specific actions and attitudes required in a Christian ethic of competition, an attitude adjustment must take place. Jesus Christ must be allowed to remold one's mind. The apostle Paul mandates in Romans 12:2 to let God remold our minds. This is never more true than in the realm of competition. Athletes must put aside all previously held beliefs concerning sports and allow God to begin afresh with their minds. Most athletes have been coached and have competed in ethics prevalent in a relativistic society. As previously explained, these ethics are based on the pragmatism of winning at all costs.

Thoughtful and prayerful consideration is necessary before considering the following six areas. At first glance these actions and attitudes may not fit into a previously held belief. But upon further contemplation even the most fiercely competitive of all athletes will understand true fulfillment comes only by allowing Jesus Christ to shape one's thinking. The seven areas are teammates, coaches, officials, opponents, competition, winning and losing, and success.

## Teammates

At first athletes might not believe they have a problem with teammates. Commitment to the team is assumed. However, a closer look at why athletes compete reveals self-centered motivations, which have nothing to do with concern for one's team.

Athletes are rarely bold enough to admit they compete not for the team's sake but rather for their own glory and for their own personal gratification. Athletes do not play for a team, school, or club solely for the benefit of that group. They play for their own glory and for their own particular satisfaction, fulfillment, thrill, and excitement. This is a subtle yet profound difference. If an individual is participating for his or her own gratification and is unwilling to submit to the team's needs, problems arise. Athletes must clarify their own motivations for competing by asking themselves the following questions:

- Why do I feel bad when I make a mistake? Is it because it reflects poorly on me (embarrassment) or because it hurts the team?
- When I'm caught stealing in baseball, miss a shot in basketball or soccer, bowl out in cricket, or miss a tackle in football, is my first

thought of how I hurt the team's chances to win or about my own batting average or shooting percentage?

•  Do I willingly sacrifice personal gain to enhance the team's chance to succeed?

•  When I don't play to my fullest potential (don't run out a pop fly on the baseball field or give all I have to score a try on the rugby pitch) or don't come to a game properly rested and prepared, do I consider that I have let my teammates down?

•  Why do I feel excited and good after having played a great game and yet the team lost?

Athletes would do well to understand the relevance of Philippians 2:3–4: "Do nothing out of rivalry or conceit, but in humility consider others as more important than yourselves. Everyone should look out not only for his own interests, but also for the interests of others." The apostle Paul indicates that we must "live together in harmony, live together in love."

As important as this biblical principle is, it must be balanced by another concept as described in John's Gospel. Athletes should be concerned about teammates and the team's best interest, and they should never feel guilty about their own enjoyment and enthusiasm of competing. In John 10:10, the apostle communicates that Christ came so we might have a fulfilled life. Therefore, we can be assured God rejoices when we compete to our fullest ability and thoroughly enjoy our participation in sports. After all, Christ is the one who created us and knows us in the most intimate sense possible. As a loving Father, he is happy when we experience exhilaration while competing.

The early Greek athletes probably understood this concept better than do present-day competitors. They believed the gods had created them with certain abilities and gave them opportunities to use their gifts. They viewed their competition as an act of worship. In the movie *Chariots of Fire,* Eric Liddell provides the best articulation of this in Hollywood history when he describes how he felt about running and how it fit with his call to the mission field. "I believe God made me for a purpose; for China, but he also made me fast, and when I run, I feel his pleasure and to give it up would be to hold him in contempt. To win is to honor him."

Therefore, Christian athletes and church-based sports ministries should promote the joy of competing and know that their competition pleases Christ, but they must always keep personal gains, goals, and personal preferences in balance with the goals and needs of their team and teammates.

## Coaches

Players often resent their coaches. They even resent the coaches' demands for hustle, conditioning, and discipline. Most athletes do not understand what discipline really is. They believe that discipline is punishment. However, discipline is not necessarily what athletes deserve when they do something wrong.

A dictionary definition of *discipline* is "training to act in accordance with rules or actions." Discipline connotes much more the idea of training than it does of punishment. It refers to the constraints that it takes to train athletes in appropriate ways of conducting themselves. Wise athletes will submit themselves fully to knowledgeable coaches who care enough about their athletes to push them to excellence. Athletes should never resent rigorous training and discipline designed to push them to excel. Rather, athletes should resent the coach who never pushes them to excel. Discipline coming from a caring, educated, and wise coach will be a positive force propelling athletes to attain their greatest potential. This potential will only be reached, however, if the athletes willingly submit and fully apply themselves to it.

It is appropriate for athletes to desire and for churches to seek to provide the best possible coaching available. Rather than blindly enrolling in the local church league and/or school athletic program, athletes should research the satisfaction levels and successes of the teams and leagues they are considering joining. Particular questions that need to be asked of a league, school, and coach are:

- What is the statement of purpose for your league, school, and/or coach?
- What is your philosophy of competition and coaching?
- What policies do you have about team membership and/or cutting players?
- What added expenses and/or fees are there to participate in sports?

- Are the coaches in the leagues trained in the psychological, emotional, and physiological aspects of coaching?
- What is the philosophy of playing time?
- What is the methodology of teaching styles?

There are times when athletes have no choice in who their coach is and will have to play for a coach who is intolerable for one reason or another. At this point Christian athletes have a unique opportunity to give evidence of their faith. Of course, Christian players should never obey a coach's demands to cheat or purposely injure an opposing player, but for the most part they should go beyond what their coach requires in terms of conscientious training and effort. Regardless of how a coach treats players, those players must always demonstrate respect for their coach. Moreover, in relating to a coach, Christian players must keep the goal of emulating Christ as their top priority. Christ will be glorified if church leaders and coaches help athletes keep their priorities straight and seek Christmanship as opposed to personal gain.

## Officials

The third area in which church leaders and athletes must remold their minds is the way they view and interact with the officials who are involved in sports. Nowhere in athletics is there more verbal abuse or more frustration vented than from athletes and coaches toward referees and umpires. Everyone knows at least one horror story of a Christian athlete or team loosing their Christian witness by behaving inappropriately toward an official. Officials, athletes, and church teams must learn to get along as partners in competition.

Athletes must understand that officials are facilitators of competitions, not enemies. An official's role is to facilitate leagues, games, competitions, and tournaments. Officials include league directors and commissioners, referees, umpires, scorekeepers, tournament directors, and others. These people are needed to ensure that competitions proceed in the fairest way possible, while in a church ministry setting, keeping the Christ distinctive central to the competition. Athletes must understand that without officials there would be no games, no competitions.

Not only should officials be regarded as facilitators, but Christian competitors must also view them as people created in the image of God. Since God created these people and furthermore since Christ died for them, it is imperative that Christian athletes go out of their way to love them. Moreover, Christian athletes must explore how they can enhance officials' ability to do their jobs.

This attitude is diametrically opposed to the most common ethic of most people who are involved in athletics today. Most competitors operate under the "win at all costs" concept concerning officials. They believe they are entitled to "work officials" to gain an advantage over an opponent. Most athletes have been trained to "work an official." Coaches and trainers have taught their athletes how to gain an unfair advantage by using what they consider "techniques" to get an official to call things their way. Because of this, coaches of most athletes believe they have the right to yell, scream, threaten, intimidate, or even physically abuse an official in order to get a call changed or an event run to one's benefit.

Christian athletes who operate under the Christmanship concept need to relate the command of Romans in regards to their interactions with officials. Rather than "work" an official, Christians must "live at peace with everyone" (Rom. 12:18). Romans 12, therefore, mandates that even if players are persecuted by officials, their response must be to bless them and to strive to live at peace with them. The apostle Paul did not ask us to get along with others as long as the other persons are willing, rather he said we are to live at peace with them as much as it depends upon us. Christian athletes cannot assume responsibility for an official's actions towards them. They can only be responsible for their own actions toward the official.

Caz McCaslin, founder and president of Upward Unlimited, has developed the Circle of Praise and the Circle of Criticism to illustrate this phenomenon. The Circle of Praise states that the coach sets the standard for the players and the spectators. If the coach speaks kindly to the officials, encouraging them and calling attention to the good calls, then the team and the spectators will do likewise. The coach's positive actions and positive comments elicit positive actions and reaction from players and spectators alike. The opposite is also true for the Circle of Criticism. As a coach talks negatively to officials, finding fault with calls and verbalizing his displeasure, players and spectators alike take on the negative tones of the coach. These escalate until an "us against them" attitude is fostered, causing dissention and tension between coaches, players, and spectators, all directed at the officials. Thus, the vicious Circle of Criticism is born, bringing dishonor to the cause of Christ and limiting, if not destroying, the opportunity for any Christian witness to be effective.

Players in youth leagues, junior and senior high school, college, and even pros must realize that they should rarely, if ever, have any confrontations with game officials. This is not their job or role. Those confrontations must be left up to coaches and athletic directors. Most coaches and athletic directors have avenues available to them through which they can explain their grievances. It is imperative that they go through their given systems to address unfair practices. Athletes should either remain silent in their interactions with officials or seek ways to compliment and encourage them.

The typical interaction with officials proceeds as follows. Coaches or players start the process with officials rather low-key. When they perceive that the official is not listening to their complaints, their intensity, volume, and/or profaneness increases. If their verbal attacks are regular and consistent, they are most often tuned out by the official, or even worse, the official is distracted from calling the game. Thus, the coach must become even more demonstrative. Coaches may even intimidate and physically assault an official. Sometimes these actions get immediate results. However, the results are always short-term gains. The long-term result is a lost relationship and most likely an official who may spite a coach or athlete who has previously intimidated him. Then the cycle begins again. To experience overwhelming victory, athletes must seek to understand and appreciate officials.

## Opponents

Most amateur church league athletes have known the frustration of rushing out of work, jumping into their trusty automobile, speeding down the highway while simultaneously putting on their uniform and eating a fast-food burger and fries. They arrive at a dusty softball field or a sweat-filled gymnasium only to find that their opponent did not show up. What was excited anticipation of a game that had captured the mind of that athlete now is nothing more than a frustration because there is no one to play. This illustration points out that opponents are important, and athletes need to reconsider how they view these opponents.

Actually the word *opponent* is an inappropriate term to describe the players on the other team. *Opponent* conveys the idea that competitors have enemies. There are no enemies when it comes to sports, only other competitors. Athletes must realize the people with whom they compete must be seen as "co-competitors." Without them there would be no game or competition. Co-competitors must be viewed as people created by God and for whom Christ came and died. They must be treated with utmost dignity and respect. They must never be cheated, purposely injured, intimidated, discouraged, or forced to compete in a manner that is damaging to them or that hinders any opportunity to bear a witness. Winning by anything other than one's own ability is not fulfilling. If athletes must cheat or harm their co-competitors to win, the win is not due to their being superior athletes or team. Rather, it is due to that athlete's having lower morals. Jesus admonishes us to be the light that drives out darkness or salt that brings flavor. Cheating to win extinguishes the light and contaminates the salt, thus bringing reprehension to the cause of Christ.

Co-competitors must also be encouraged to excel. Not only are they to be treated fairly and given an equal opportunity to win a contest, but they also must be encouraged to compete to their fullest. A scene in the movie *Chariots of Fire* exemplifies this concept. The sprinter known as the "Flying Scot," Eric Liddell, was just about to compete in the four-hundred-meter race in the Olympics when he was given a note by Jackson Schultz, an opponent from the American team. It read: "It says in the old book, 'He that honors me I will honor.'" Witnesses remember that Liddell crossed the finish line, having won with that note clutched in his hand. The movie version is not quite reality in that the note actually was written by the British team's trainer and signed by the entire British team, but the movie director used Schultz to personify all the notes and words of encouragement Liddell did receive from his opponents, and thus the basic truth of the event was portrayed. Liddell was one of the most respected athletes of that generation and was greatly encouraged by all the encouragement he received from his co-competitors because he suffered much ridicule from others for not participating in a race on Sunday, which he believed would be breaking the commandment to keep the Sabbath holy.

Encouraging one's opponents sounds ludicrous until church leaders, athletes, and coaches examine their premise for competing. If winning is the only goal, then, of course, athletes can do anything to win—including cheating, injuring, intimidating, and discouraging their opponents.

However, if the goal is to compete against the best there is and to measure oneself against that competition, as well as to win, then true competitors wish for their co-competitors to push them to their full potential. Furthermore, for those who are believers in Christ, the goal is to conform to the image of Christ—Christmanship. In the ethic of Christmanship, cheating, maiming, intimidating, and even discouraging is not appropriate, and winning is only important when it is the measuring device used by both competitors.

Beyond the attempts to encourage co-competitors, athletes must also strive to compete at their fullest potential, regardless of the score. If athletes do not compete to their fullest potential, they are making a statement that their co-competitors are not worthy of their best effort. Furthermore, it does not challenge the co-competitor to improve. A true competitor never insults a co-competitor by not giving his or her best effort. There is a difference between competing with full intensity and humiliating an opponent however. Ideally, once athletes have an understanding of the full implication of competing in the image of Christ, they will place less emphasis on the score and outcome, and they will place more emphasis on their own efforts. However, there are still some times when the score differential is so huge that an opponent feels humiliated. At times like this, Christian athletes have to ask what Christ would do.

Bob Briner in *Roaring Lambs* put the purpose of competition this way:

> Many well-known stars as well as movers and shakers in sports make their commitment to Christ very public. Such Hall of Fame caliber names as Tom Landry and Roger Staubach in football, Julius Irving in basketball, Orel Hershiser and radio announcer Ernie Harwell in baseball, and Stan Smith in tennis are only a representative few who openly and avidly proclaim Christ. . . . It is clear that the call to be salt calls for both competence and commitment—we must be at our best in order to win the kind of hearing Christ deserves. . . . Our responsibility is to do our best and to leave the results with Him in the knowledge that the ultimate victory is ours through Christ.[4]

The purpose of competing is to worship God with and through our athletic abilities. We see in Briner's quote that his stated purpose of competing to be the best is to gain a platform. Our culture holds winners up on a pedestal. Once there they have a platform from which to speak, and people of all ages and all walks of life listen. Christian athletes must strive to be the best at what they do in order to gain a hearing in the world. Competition can thus be considered the fulfillment of one's duty to God. For when you are the best, people will listen, and your biblical worldview will get a hearing.

We do not compete to harm or humiliate an opponent. We compete to first of all glorify God, then to be best, to hone our skills, to win the game. However, striving for excellence should never give license to willingly humiliate an opponent.

Although some of the issues surrounding one's co-competitors are rather complex, they are best dealt with by asking the question, "What would Christ do in this situation, and how would he compete?"

The issues become more clear when athletes contemplate the meaning of competition itself. Competition is a measuring stick. Just as I want my car's oil to be measured by an accurate stick, I, as a competitor, want to measure myself against proper and accurate competition.

## Competition

There are people who wish to dispose of all competition. They believe that competition is harmful, wrong, and even repugnant to God! They also believe competition to be innately evil, but is it? Can competition be acceptable within a Christian ethic or in a church ministry context? The answer is unequivocal. Not only is competition compatible with the Christian ethic; it is also part of God's design for the world. Competition is part and parcel of the universe that God created.

In God's natural revelation to us we see that nature is full of competition. Trees stretch to the sky, competing for sunlight; roots extend deep into the ground, competing for the moisture and nutrients needed to survive. Church leaders need to understand that competition is an amoral force. In and of itself it is neither good nor bad. Competition may bring out either the best or the worst in all who compete. However, we cannot blame competition if athletes fail morally, emotionally, or psychologically.

It is how athletes choose to react to competition that determines whether competition is positive or negative. God's design for competition is to help mold athletes into the men and women he desires them to be. Any attempt to remove competition from our lives will only hamper our spiritual development, not enhance it.

Therefore, competition needs to be redefined. The word *competition* comes from the Latin verb that means "to seek together." Rainer Martens in his book *Joy and Sadness in Children's Sports* has described competition as "activities directed toward attaining a standard or goal in which a person's or group's performance is evaluated relative to selected other individuals or groups."[5] Competition assumes cooperation. It demands that co-competitors challenge one another to excel. Challenging one another to excel completes the concept of competing *against* someone. When competitors view competition in its proper sense, they will be able to minimize the negatives that are associated with it and enhance the possibilities of competition being truly a cooperative effort to help develop them into the people they need to become. Therefore, competitors do not compete *against* one another in the classic sense of that word.

To help understand this, a closer look at the word *against* is necessary. The word *against* has as its root word *again,* which means "once more, additionally, or furthermore." From this connotation the following definitions of the word *against* are derived: "close beside or in front of; in anticipation of; or as contrasted with." Therefore, playing against someone in this sense assumes that something is done once more—or again— and in contrast. Competitors contrast their skills *against* other competitors. Thus, competition becomes a gauge or a measuring stick that competitors use to judge themselves. One does not compete *against* an enemy but rather competes *against* a standard that may sometimes be embodied in another individual or team but may also be embodied by oneself, a clock, or a challenge.

## Winning and Losing

Athletes desiring to gain a proper perspective concerning winning, losing, and competition will be aided by answering the following questions:

- Is it fulfilling to win by forfeit?

- Is it fulfilling to win every competition by large margins?
- Is it fulfilling to win a game only by cheating, taking performance enhancing drugs, or any other unfair action?
- Is it fulfilling to have my team win a game without my participating?

As evidenced by the answers to these questions, athletes should recognize that winning by forfeit or by having far superior talent is unfulfilling. It is also unfulfilling to achieve victory by cheating, for cheating does not accurately gauge abilities, only morals. Moreover, athletes are rarely satisfied if they do not play in a game, even if their team wins. Furthermore, whenever players become so wrapped up in winning and losing, they never truly enjoy the ecstasy and thrill of simply competing. They never find fulfillment in meeting the challenge of competing against a standard. It is sad to see so many competitors never experience true exhilaration and excitement in competition because they are so concerned with winning.

Winning is important, but only when it is a result of one's dedicated and determined effort. Winning is never as important as competing. Trophies pale beside the memory of the game in which the trophy was won. Only when competitors "remold their minds" can they experience the fulfillment. Talent is unfulfilling. This understanding of competition provides the foundation from which to talk about what success is. In the case of children, they just want to participate, to play the game. As they get older, participation can get overshadowed by winning. Just playing a sport, just participating, will always be a primary motivator for people of all ages. This participation concept has great implications for the church. For as we provide avenues of participation, we provide open doors to the church to the nonbelieving world.

## Success

Success is not the gift, but rather what one does with the gift (Matt. 25:14–30). All gifts are of equal value, but all uses are not. The gift of music is no more important than the gift of parenting. The gift of drama is no more important than the gift of athletic prowess. All gifts are necessary to human life. All gifts are important. The question becomes, how do athletes use their gifts? Success then becomes not which gift one has, but rather, what one does with the gift.

Success is not only being number one but also being a consistent winner. The professional basketball team, the Los Angeles Clippers, finished its 1987 season with a record of 12 and 70. Does this losing record make them unsuccessful? The team consisted of a dozen or so of the top 250 basketball players in the world. They were highly successful athletes. Their team may not have been successful as a unit; however, this does not mean as individuals they were not successful. They were not number one, but they could still be considered successful if they adhered to the true spirit of the word *competition* and thus cooperatively pushed teams they played to greater heights. One must be careful in establishing criteria for success. Christmanship rejoices with the team or individual that finishes number one but never maintains that athletes can only be successful by being number one.

Success is not money, prestige, trophies, or any other earthly treasure. For the Christian, success is one thing only: competing in such a way as to maximize one's gifts to the fullest and always in the image of Jesus Christ. What makes this so significant is that this concept of success actually gives athletics and recreation validity and worth. Because of the intrinsic worth of sports, athletes understand that competition is a force that can mold them into the image of Christ in such a way that they will feel free to compete when they realize that they can worship God in and through their competing. Then they learn lessons from competing. Competition does have worth when athletes conform themselves to Christ while competing. If athletes can be judged by God as being successful by simply using the gifts given to them by God, sports must not be condemned as being of less importance than any other endeavor.

Some may argue that sports in and of themselves have no redemptive value, but by using that criteria what does? The world of finance? Teaching? Medicine? The only endeavor that could possibly claim for itself any eternal significance would be some sort of religious activity. The logical conclusion, therefore, would be for everyone to become full-time religious workers, and that is totally illogical because the world could not survive without doctors, farmers, and teachers. Athletes and church leaders who use athletics for the gospel's sake must realize their efforts are meaningful. They must be set free to use their gifts fully and alongside every other gift given. Success is conforming to the image of Christ in whatever he has given us the ability to do (Phil. 3:7–14). This view of success will not be easy to accept by a mind-set that has believed winning is everything. Neither should it be used as an excuse for losing consistently. However, for the Christian competitor it will bring fulfillment like nothing else can. Churches wishing to impact culture realize the value of sports and competition as reaching and teaching tools. As these tools are properly used and administered by church leaders, they will be used by God to touch and mold the hearts and minds of those who wish to participate in athletics.

In order for athletes to have their minds remolded, one essential question must be answered. Have you said yes to Jesus Christ? Do you have a personal relationship with him?

He cannot remold your mind unless you give it to him. You will not experience an overwhelming victory unless you decide to compete Christ's way. Are you frustrated by athletic experiences? Has the fun disappeared? Is your life lacking peace and fulfillment? Please consider giving your life, including your sporting life, to Christ. It is as simple as praying: "Dear Jesus, please forgive me for trying to live my life on my own. I want you to come into my life. I want a personal relationship with you. Please give me your guidance. Amen." That's all there is to it. If you prayed that prayer, you now have a new coach. His name is Jesus, and he is overjoyed to be in right relationship to you.

Christian athletes must emulate Jesus Christ in everything they do, including how they compete. They must step out of the humanistically based ethic of sportsmanship and the pragmatically based ethic of gamesmanship and follow the principles of Christmanship. The practical aspects of Christmanship are attained by competing in the image of Jesus Christ. These precepts include interacting with teammates, coaches, co-competitors, and officials as Christ would interact. These precepts also demand that players not miss the exhilaration of competing by being so caught up in winning and losing a game. Athletes must compete with a zeal that is infectious. They must also have a proper view of success and seek to give their ultimate effort to using and maximizing their gifts. Christian athletes must compete in the image of Christ and allow their experiences in competition to further mold them into the image of Christ. In the words of Brother Lawrence, competitors must "practice the presence of Christ" in everything they do, including their competition!

## Notes

1. Bill Shirley, "Mad About Sports," *The Plain Dealer* (18 January 1987): G–3. Quoting from Arnold R. Beisser, *Madness in Sports* (Bowie, Md.: Charles Press, 1977).

2. Taylor Locke, *Caught in the Net* (West Point, N.Y.: Leisure Press, 1982), 139, 172, 174.

3. Benjamin Rader, *American Sports* (Englewood Cliffs, N.J.: Prentice-Hall, 1983) 134–35.

4. Bob Briner, *Roaring Lambs* (Grand Rapids, Mich.: Zondervan Publishing House, 1993), 44, 46.

5. Rainer Martens, *Joy and Sadness in Children's Sports* (Champaign, Ill.: Human Kinetics Press, 1978).

# 10 Introduction to Recreation and Sports Ministry for All Ages

## Judi Jackson

As we consider recreation through a lifetime, we need to explore the interests, abilities, and developmental issues typically associated with the different ages and stages of life. What we want to understand are the norms, or the standards, so we may plan recreation programs to suit the age group with which we are working.

Life is separated by stages into general age divisions. Infancy usually is regarded as the period of childhood between birth and eighteen months (those who are, for the most part, prespeech). Early childhood (referring to toddlers and preschoolers) generally includes those from eighteen months to five years of age. The category of middle childhood spans the years between five and twelve. The youth, or adolescent, years cover those from thirteen to eighteen (but can be lowered to age ten and raised to age twenty, depending on individual development). Young adults include anyone from age twenty to approximately thirty-five to thirty-nine years old. Median adulthood typically begins at age forty and continues through age sixty. Finally, senior adults are grouped together as anyone sixty years of age and older.

## Exploring Infants and Preschoolers

One misconception regarding infants and preschoolers is that there is a particular age at which specific motor skills should be mastered and, if they are not, the child is considered developmentally delayed. On the

contrary the concept of *maturation* allows for age variation in the unfold-
ing of a child's potential. Granted, the variation is usually subtle in the
first year, but no parent should be alarmed, for example, if their child is
not walking by ten months of age. On the contrary, a more normal progression involves a child learning to walk after the one-year mark and
sometimes even closer to two years.[1]

Considering recreational options for newborns is a new phenomenon
and focuses on providing infants the appropriate opportunity to progress
in a natural, unforced manner. Natural instincts as well as imitation and
gentle stimulation guide the development of both gross and fine motor
skills. An infant is limited in the amount of motor activity in which he can
engage, but his senses are active. When a cylindrical toy or rattle is placed
in a baby's palm, the general response is for the fingers to attempt to wrap
around the object. A simple game of pat-a-cake helps teach an infant the
basics of coordination and relationship with others. Reading a book aloud,
even to the youngest of infants, stimulates the child's sense of hearing and
may even help to develop the sense of sight as colored pictures are shown
throughout the storytelling process. Through these types of trial-and-error
motor activities, infants experiment with their bodies and begin to master
the skills necessary for the next developmental levels. Parents and other
child-care providers should see their main responsibility as providing a safe
environment in which infants can move freely and are protected.[2]

The Playorena program, designed in 1974 by Michael and Susan
Astor in Marion County, California, was structured to take toddlers step-
by-step through the stages of early motor development while educating
parents in the process. Parental awareness of the sequential and individually differing nature of the developmental process is crucial in reducing the
negative effects that result from unrealistic expectations. "Young children
have a strong innate need for all different kinds of movement and motion.
We know that a parent's confidence in their child, and in their own parenting skills, provides the basis for the child's own self-confidence."[3]

In the last twenty-five years, another toddler-oriented program,
Gymboree, has used the Play with a Purpose philosophy to emphasize the
importance of play, movement, and exploration in the early years. This
has led to a lifestyle concept that respects and encourages the natural
activity necessary for health, growth, and learning in kids. For example,
children need opportunities to experience and practice balance, whether

lifting up a tiny head as a six-month-old or sitting erect when sliding as an eighteen-month-old. They also need to grow in body awareness, knowing body parts and how to use them in movement, as well as encounter a variety of visual sensations, sounds, and touch experiences. All of this is done as the parent plays alongside the child, helping to build the foundation for social skills, cognitive development, physical ability, and self-esteem. So whether done in a structured play group environment or one-on-one in the home, this parent-child interaction becomes a valuable foundation for future stages of play and recreation.[4]

The key to playing games with babies is remembering to keep it simple. With so many infant toys and programs available, it may be hard to believe that the parent or caregiver is the child's favorite toy. In their 1997 work *Becoming the Parent You Want to Be,* Davis and Keyser offered suggestions on how parents can facilitate constructive time for and with their infants:

***Give babies plenty of "floor time."*** While putting babies on the floor is contrary to many of our previous customs, it is one of the best ways to support both physical skills and the development of a baby's sense of competence. Babies who spend time on open, clean, safe, flat surfaces, free of infant seats or other restrictive carriers, have the opportunity to learn about their bodies in space. They get to learn what positions they can get themselves into and out of. They develop the muscles they need for the next developmental challenge. Babies who are playing on the floor are strengthening all of the muscles they will later need to roll over, sit up, and crawl. Babies who are crawling on their own are exercising the muscles they will later need for walking. Limiting the amount of time babies spend in car seats, infant carriers, swings, chairs, and other restrictive containers allows babies to have lots of chances to develop their muscles, skills, and body awareness during "floor time."

***Get down on the floor with your baby.*** In spending floor time with your baby, you can watch and see what your baby does, where she looks, how she moves. You can see the world from her perspective. You could sing with her or just talk with her. Just being on her level allows her to communicate with you using all the subtleties of her nonverbal, as well as verbal, communication.

***Support your infant's achievements.*** All parents want to do the best job they can to support their baby's growth. Rather than buying lots of expensive equipment, what babies really need is parents' attention, observation, and responsiveness. In the first year of life, babies are learning trust. They are figuring out that the world is a place where they will get their needs met, where they can make things happen, and where they can explore safely. Our job is not to "teach" them these things as much as it is to get to know them, to enjoy them, to provide safe and interesting learning spaces, to learn their unique communication systems, and to be responsive to them.[5]

Once children enter the world of crawling, and later walking, new realms of possibilities open up to them. Mobility is now independent of someone else's whim to move them from here to there. Instead, the child is free to explore—within reason—his environment, whether that be a small travel playpen or a wide open backyard. In either situation, supervision and attention continue to be warranted because of the age and relative immaturity of the child. But the key now is that the child can test his level of independence. Lefrançois described the process of learning to walk as the child's "most significant motor achievement, with extremely important social and cognitive implications. . . . Self-locomotion facilitates the process of becoming familiar with the world."[6]

Because healthy toddlers are notoriously busy creatures, it is imperative for parents and caregivers to plan proactively, rather than *react* in a panic. While it would be easier to plop a child into a playpen or stroller to keep him from wandering away, it's really best for a freewheeling toddler to use his body as much as possible. As he walks, runs, jumps, and climbs, he is strengthening important muscles as well as developing a healthy sense of independence.

Using movement games such as Mother, May I?; Red Light, Green Light; and Hokeypokey is a wonderful way to help a young child be active while, at the same time, focusing on specific skills such as stopping and starting on command and learning her body parts. Even purpose-filled quiet times can be useful in training a child in the value of relaxing and unwinding with a favorite song tape or a colorful picture book. (See fig. 10-1 for a summary of some physical and motor achievements of early childhood.)

In addition to developing motor skills, most children are growing in their use of language to express feelings, needs, and preferences. Before now, parents and caregivers had to learn the unique dialect of babies. They had to differentiate between the cry of the tired, the cry of the hungry, and even the cry of the lonely. But when words are introduced, a

| At 2 years begins to | At 3 years begins to | At 4 years begins to | At 5 years begins to |
|---|---|---|---|
| Walk | Jump and hop on one foot | Run, jump, and climb with close supervision | Gain good body control |
| Run | Climb stairs by alternating feet on each stair | Dress self using buttons, zippers, laces, and so on | Throw and catch ball, climb, jump, skip with good coordination |
| Actively explore environment | Dress and undress self somewhat | Use more sophisti-cated eating utensils such as knives to cut meat or spread butter | Coordinate move-ments to music |
| Sit in a chair with-out support | Walk a reasonably straight path on floor | Walk balance beam with ease | Put on snowpants, boots, and tie shoes |
| Climb stairs with help (two feet on each stair) | Walk on balance beam | Walk down stairs alone | Skip |
| Build block towers | Ride a tricycle | Bounce and catch ball | Jump rope, walk in a straight line |
| Feed self with fork and spoon | Stand on one foot for a long time | Push/pull wagon | Ride a two-wheel bike |
| Stand on balance beam | Catch large balls | Cut, following lines | Roller-skate |
| Throw ball | Hop | Copy figure X | Fold paper |
| Catch | Gallop | Print first name | Reproduce alpha-bet and numbers |
| Jump | Kick ball | | Trace |
| Push and pull | Hit ball | | |
| Hang on bar | Paste | | |
| Slide | String beads | | |
| | Cut paper with scissors | | |
| | Copy figures 0 and + | | |

*Figure 10-1:*
*Physical Characteristics of the Child Age 2 to 5\**

*G. W. Maxim, The Very Young, 4th ed. (Columbus, Ohio: Merrill), 80.
©1993 by Macmillan College Publishing Company.
Reprinted in Lefrançois's textbook (p. 189) by permission of Prentice Hall, Inc.

child—even with single-syllable grunts—can relate much more of his deeper concerns. He wants to play with *that* toy; he needs *this* shoe tied; he asks for something to eat *now*. This rapid development of verbal skills can be nurtured in a number of play settings as simple directions are given, repetitive rhymes are chanted, and engaging songs are sung. Even reading to the youngster can contribute to this task in a young child's life, offering a wide variety of sounds and words to help grow his vocabulary and ability to communicate.

One writer went so far as to suggest that reading books to a child— whether infant, toddler, or preschooler—is as vital to his development as a healthy diet and good night's sleep.[7] Orr cited a recommendation from the American Academy of Pediatrics that, during well-baby visits, pediatricians should *prescribe* reading activities in an effort to stimulate brain and language development as well as begin to develop literacy skills.[8]

In addition to reading to a child to fuel her imagination, it is also important to provide her with plenty of unstructured time to play. "Play is activity that has no long-range goal, although it might have intermediate objectives (to hop from here to there, to make a sand hill, to fly a kite, to pour a cup of pretend tea). Play is what children, and grown-ups, do for the fun of it. But that play has no ultimate purpose does not mean it is unimportant and useless. In fact, it is extremely important for all aspects of the child's development: social, physical, and intellectual."[9]

Today's children—even preschoolers—are busy doing lots of good and important things. Ballet lessons, T-ball team practices, and even children's choir at church are admirable activities in which to involve a child, but care must be taken to give this same child time to play. Yes, there is an element of play in each of the above activities, but the required structure forces the child to fit a mold rather than allowing her creative juices to take over and find the fun for herself. Countless studies reveal the danger of too much television viewing and computer programming in regard to their effect on a children's creative development. But more and more studies are being conducted to determine whether the push for overactive, overtrained children is taking its toll on their ability to participate in freelance play.

## Exploring Middle Childhood

This need for unstructured play continues into a child's middle childhood years (ages five through twelve), but unfortunately the addition of a demanding school schedule and a myriad of extracurricular activities cuts into this need greatly. One child psychologist warns parents and professionals to remember that play is a child's way of learning and, through free play, a child learns to function within his peer group, make rules, test the limits of acceptable behavior, and role-play future occupations.[10]

Just because research can prove the importance of unstructured free time for children doesn't ensure that children will always know what to do with the time. They are used to someone else planning their time, and when free time is allotted, they sometimes whine that there's nothing to do. Pellegrini points out that this transition from busy to bored may be "a blessing in disguise. Downtime challenges a child to focus on the present and find something constructive to do. Resist turning this into TV or computer time. These activities don't require any imaginative thinking and do little to help your child's development. When programmed stimulation shuts down, a child's mind opens up."[11]

One key developmental issue of children this age is the need to set and attain personal goals.[12] While some of this will be accomplished through academic pursuits, much of it will be addressed as each child explores his interest in particular hobbies and/or tests his ability in different activities like sports or music. Cooper expresses concern that children are not being allowed to develop at their own pace but, instead, are expected to achieve a certain level of ability at certain ages despite physical, cognitive, or social diversity. "Various studies have confirmed what many coaches and parents have known all along: some children are simply slower than others to develop basic physical skills like catching or hitting balls, or executing movements that require agility. In a few instances, the boys and girls who learn these skills earlier, say at ages 4 to 5, may have a natural ability that others lack. In many cases, though, certain children merely grow and develop faster than the rest, or their parents do more to train them at a young age. The others can still catch up—if they are just given a chance."[13] Cooper calls this the Rule of Rhythm and stresses that the child's personal developmental pace should dictate appropriate recreational challenges, not predetermined age-graded programs.

While recreation for children in this middle developmental stage should not be limited to competitive sports, it is during this time that much team-oriented activity is introduced. Children are given the opportunity to play in Biddy Basketball, Dixie Youth Softball, and an abundance of other kid-oriented leagues. One church-centered program designed for children in the first through sixth grades is exploding around the country. Upward Basketball, founded in 1986 by Caz McCaslin in Spartanburg, South Carolina, focuses on developing the self-esteem of each participant while teaching respect for authority, sportsmanship, character, and basketball skills. In addition, because of the involvement of countless volunteers and supportive parents, the evangelistic potential of this ministry is far-reaching. In 2001, Upward Basketball expected to involve more than 130,000 children in more than 750 leagues across the United States.

One reason Upward Basketball and similar programs are so successful is that they are designed to address a child's basic needs and seek to help him successfully work through the encounter. Hartzell identified several specific needs of children ages five through twelve:[14]

***Children need love and acceptance.*** In the competitiveness of today's athletic climate, a sports program that is designed to allow every child to play equal amounts of time is an anomaly. But no matter how unusual it is, this type of program is vital in responding to a child's need for love and acceptance. Instead of being penalized for not running the fastest or shooting the best, the novice can play hard and develop his abilities alongside others who are hoping to do the same. There's nothing like a "great catch," "good defense," or even a simple pat on the back to get a child pumped for his next opportunity to play. In this atmosphere of unconditional love and acceptance, replete with verbal and nonverbal strokes of affirmation, a child can grow in his ability to play a particular sport or realize that this sport is not really something he enjoys.

***Children need strong moral development.*** While children have a lot of good innate qualities, they also have a lot of questionable influences. In a society that thrives on personal rights rather than universal truths, being intentional about teaching biblically based morality is a must. Children must learn to respect authority, and what better place to do this than on a basketball court with the assumed fairness of trained referees and established rules? Children also must be taught to play by these established rules or suffer the consequences. Penalty kicks are awarded in soccer when a player on the opposing team breaks a rule. In football, penalty flags are thrown, resulting in lost yardage, while baseball players may be subjected to automatic outs due to stealing bases before the appropriate time or batting out of turn. An emphasis on the positive outcome of respecting authority, playing by the rules, and other issues pertinent to the life lessons of sports can ensure a child's exposure to the right type of influence on his moral development.

***Children need to develop motor skills.*** Just because a child has learned to walk and run doesn't mean he is through developing motor skills. Some children will lean toward a natural propensity to run faster and jump higher but, in a general sense, even these motor skills can be learned and improved. Children need direction to progress at developmentally appropriate levels. My ten-year-old has participated in loosely organized basketball programs in the past few years. She has attempted to dribble the ball, pass to teammates, and even throw a shot toward the goal occasionally. But it wasn't until her current physical education teacher took the time this year to demonstrate and drill the girls on the proper mechanics that she began to enjoy the sport. While her age may play a vital part in her ability to understand and play the game better, the intentionality of this teacher's instructional strategy factors in heavily for future success.

***Children need to learn cooperation.*** What name has been most prominent in professional basketball through the past decade? Michael Jordan, of course. But even a player as successful as Michael Jordan cannot do what he has done without a team to play with him. Children need to know that, while each individual effort is important, teamwork accomplishes the most.

When only five years old, Sarah was introduced to the public library by her wise paternal grandmother. This same wise grandmother allowed Sarah to check out approximately twenty books to keep her occupied over an extended visit. But even twenty kiddie books can add up in weight, so Grandma Peggy suggested that she and Sarah work together to carry the books to the car. "Let's cooperate" soon became the catchphrase for sharing the load, whether books, groceries, or other weighty issues around the house.

***Children need to develop their decision-making skills.*** Experience has taught me that people—even children—like to have choices. Vanilla or chocolate? Paper or plastic? Friday or Saturday? Basketball or soccer? Choir or drama? The list is virtually endless of the choices children can be given as they develop their ability to make decisions and then live with the results. To be able to practice making choices in the safety of childhood builds a strong foundation for the future when decisions can have bigger and longer-lasting consequences.

The women's ministry committee at First Baptist Church hosts a mother-daughter tea that involves first- through sixth-grade girls, their mothers, and their guests. The first tea was planned entirely by the committee members, several of whom had daughters in the target group. Even though the event was well attended and well liked, the committee members took a different approach the next year and asked the fifth and sixth graders what they would do differently if they were planning the tea. The most significant suggestion was that they wanted to be involved in the program: they wanted to do a skit, sing a song, or play an instrument. Basically, they wanted to have a sense of ownership in the event.

As children are acquainted with the benefits of love and acceptance, strong moral development, improved motor skills, cooperation, and even decision-making opportunities in recreational settings, they will progress toward the socialization goals that are so important to this time of their lives. Middle childhood is not necessarily the period to specialize in a particular sport or hobby; instead, it should be a laboratory of wide-open opportunity during which individuals are exposed to diverse recreational pursuits, ranging from physical activities (games, sports, and dance), outdoor and nature pursuits, creative pastimes (arts and crafts, music, and drama), individual hobbies and club associations, and many other forms of play.[15] While Kraus acknowledges that these opportunities will differ according to socio-economic status, physical condition, educational level, and even previous recreational experience, he stresses the value of presenting a variety of encounters, noting that what is learned in childhood is not for childhood alone. Instead, Kraus emphasizes that childhood experiences prepare a person for adolescence which, in turn, prepares a person for the different stages of adulthood. He calls this the "continuous developmental process."[16]

Also factoring into this continuous developmental process are the issues related to gender differentiation. At the beginning of the middle childhood span, children are not as gender exclusive as they tend to be toward the junior high school years. Granted, gender typing has been present throughout their lives as others—particularly adults—have reacted to them in terms of their sex (i.e., dressing girls in pink; giving boys trucks to play with). However, most six-year-olds seem to be more concerned with *who* can run the fastest rather than *which* of the seventh-grade boys is the best athlete. As children age, they compare themselves more readily with children of the same sex and age and not with the whole grade in general.

Another gender-related issue deals with which activities are most appropriate for which sex. While the majority of politically correct people may lean toward girls being allowed to play boys' sports (and visa versa), practically speaking, it is usually better in competitive activities to allow the girls to compete against girls and the boys to compete against boys. The physical differences are not as evident in the early grade school years, but as both sexes move closer to the start of puberty, it is not unusual for a twelve-year-old girl to tower over her male counterpart in height. But neither is it unusual for the same age boy to outrun, outjump, and out-throw his female counterpart.[17] While this discrepancy may send some preteen girls to the couch to watch television or even noncompetitive boys to the world of video games, discerning parents and other caring adults need to step in at this point so that "the growing minds and bodies of these preteens [don't] miss out on the physical activity they so desperately need in this phase of development, thus setting them up for a lifetime of inactivity."[18]

Because physical inactivity has been acknowledged by the American Heart Association (AHA) as one of the main risk factors in developing coronary artery disease, much emphasis has been placed on encouraging children to get out and play. While some might eagerly apply this principle to sedentary adults, the AHA recommends that children age five and older participate in a total of thirty minutes of enjoyable, moderate-intensity activities on most days of the week, and a minimum of thirty minutes of vigorous physical activity at least three to four days each week to achieve cardiovascular (heart and lung) fitness. If a thirty-minute block of time is not possible in the child's busy schedule, then two fifteen-minute sessions or even three ten-minute sessions spread out through a day also will reap positive results. In addition to the physical benefits such as weight control, reduced blood pressure, increased HDL ("good") cholesterol, and lowering the risk of diabetes and some kinds of cancer, an active child should also see an improvement in her psychological well-being, including more self-confidence and higher self-esteem.[19]

One clinical dietician, who heads a weight reduction program at Children's Hospital in New Orleans, Louisiana, points out that it is not the threat of disease that will motivate a child to eat better or get more active. "What tends to work is telling them that they'll have nicer skin and better muscle tone, that they'll have more fun shopping because they'll fit in a smaller size."[20] Schumacher cited the example of a twelve-year-old who recently had lost eighteen pounds on the way to his thirty-five-pound weight-loss goal. His success thus far has resulted in being teased less for his larger size as well as an ability to participate in a variety of sports. "It used to be just baseball," he said. "Now I play football, soccer, and basketball. I feel much lighter. I'm quicker."[21]

## Exploring Adolescence

The challenge of involving adolescents in recreational pursuits is greatly influenced by what has been the norm in their lives up to this point. If they have been active children, they will more than likely transition into active teenagers. If they have been inactive, it will take motivations such as those just discussed to get them to buy into the benefits of a physically active lifestyle. Either way, it is crucial for the church to be prepared to offer recreational options to those in the thirteen to eighteen age range. The Carnegie Council on Adolescent Development pointed out that "the nation cannot afford to raise another generation of young adolescents without the supervision, guidance, and preparation for life that caring adults and strong organizations once provided in communities."[22] Reasons for the church to answer this imperative, as summarized from *Successful Biblical Youth Work,* include:[23]

*Recreation satisfies a normal need in teenagers.* Their bodies demand that they have movement, activity, and life. Christian leaders would do better to spend less time prohibiting youth from participating in certain activities by, instead, providing positive alternatives to the all-too-popular options offered by secular society. The apostle Paul understood that it is not enough to tell young believers what they *can't* do; we need to instruct them in the things that they *can* and *should* do (Eph. 4:25ff). True recreation involves more than entertainment; it includes participation.

In 1996, the *Frontline* news show broke the shocking story of a large number of teenagers—even as young as junior high—in Rockdale County, Georgia, involved in sexual promiscuity. As the story line developed, one of the more disturbing sidebars was the adolescents' explanation that they were involved in this sexual activity because "there was nothing for them to do."[24] In a wrap-up article on this tragic situation, Blum suggested that young people be given opportunities, with adult supervision, for active recreation so that they can have fun and enjoy themselves. It's not a matter of locking them away; it's about offering them "good, clean fun."

***Recreation builds values in the teenager.*** Young people are taught some kind of values almost everywhere they go. In school, teachers instruct through value-based education. In Bible study, many leaders break down the Scripture through a value-oriented approach. However, in recreational opportunities, values are more than taught; they are challenged. Does a young person believe it's appropriate to respect authority? Then watch his struggle when a referee makes a call that goes against him or his team. Does a young person believe that rules are a consistent way to ensure fair play? Then watch his reaction to elbows in his face during a particularly tight basketball game. In the heat of competition, values are not just taught to adolescents; they are built into their personality and decision-making process. A wise coach or recreation minister will be intentional in his use of value development in the lives of the teenagers with whom he has been entrusted.

***Recreation builds strong personalities.*** According to Towns, "personality is the sum total of all of our personal attributes—mental, emotional, social, spiritual, and psychological. It is the total impression or effect that we make upon others—or simply 'you.'"[25] Recreation can reveal personality strengths like loyalty and cooperation during a team-building activity. But it can also reveal weaknesses like disrespect and a bitter spirit after a disappointing loss. The positive aspect is that personality can be cultivated and developed.

The recreational leader who models good habits and strong personality will be a positive influence on those with whom she comes in contact. Something as simple as starting practice on time speaks volumes to teenagers about respecting their time. And something as crucial as being fair and honest shows them how they can treat their teammates in a like manner.

***Recreation relieves the pressures of life for the teenager.*** Youth need a safety valve through which to relieve the pressures of their lives. Recreation, when designed for "re-creation" rather than "wreck-creation," allows a young person to blow off some of the steam of a hard day in school, a tough relationship situation, or even conflict with a parent. It doesn't make the problem go away, but it does give the teenager a healthy outlet for some of the associated stress and hopefully a significant adult contact to help him work through the process. Because egocentrism is a natural construct of the adolescent thought process, young people need to be challenged to see beyond the imaginary audience that they perceive as always judging them into a world of personal acceptance and growth.

*Recreation trains teenagers in creativity.* "Entertainment alone cannot satisfy and bring out the best from youth. Young people learn creativity as they express themselves."[26] Motion Potion is a fun game in which a group of teenagers can get to know one another better by going around the circle, telling his or her name, and then demonstrating an action that can be associated with him or her. For example, Aaron, a baseball enthusiast, would tell his name and then position his body in a batting stance, maybe even pantomiming a home-run swing. Then everyone would say his name in unison and do the same. Each person in the group follows this pattern until everyone has created a motion that will help people remember one another better. By giving young people opportunities to work through solutions as individuals and/or as groups, a focused recreation leader is better preparing these teenagers for a productive and meaningful future.

*Recreation provides a sense of belonging for the teenager.* It is not news: teenagers *want* and *need* to belong. Having friends is important to them. They want to feel included so much that if they don't feel this way, they may never be able to tune into what is being said about the importance of spiritual growth. In the security of a sense of community many young people can finally open their ears *and* their hearts to the gospel message. This may take place on a sports team, during a summer camp, or even at a weekly recreation event. The key ingredient is a recreation facilitator who understands the value of teenagers working together and feeling that their contribution to the big picture really matters.

*Recreation gives teenagers an opportunity to meet the opposite sex.* Again, this is no news flash: teenagers are curious—maybe it's more accurate to say, very interested—about the opposite sex. And because of this curiosity and interest, most will search out ways to be together. While the church doesn't need to get into the matchmaking business, leaders can be proactive in offering wholesome activities that allow young people to be together in healthy ways. Even back in 1973, Towns pulled no punches when he pointed out that "the sex drive is strong and, if steadily pushed, it generates more emotion and tension than can be safely handled." His suggestion was to use recreation to sublimate and redirect sex drives into socially acceptable expression. For example, he noted that, in the recreational setting, "the bashful youth can meet, be on the same team, and share with the opposite sex. Those who are overly motivated can be sublimated and held in check."[27] When one boy heard the statistic that teenage guys think of sex every seventeen seconds, he corrected the presenter and said, "Not when I'm playing basketball." Then let's keep them playing basketball!

***Recreation attracts and holds young people.*** Some people complain that it is a shallow church that uses recreation to attract teenagers to their building and programs. Perhaps these same people have forgotten what it took to attract them to a personal relationship with Jesus Christ in the first place. Most Christians will testify of a "hook" that grabbed their interest in some way at some point in time.

John Garner tells of a smart minister who visited John's family after they moved to a new town and told them of the church's pool tables, Ping-Pong tables, and basketball courts. John was hooked. He didn't become a Christian because of the church's recreation facility, but he *was* initially attracted because of what they had to offer. If a church can develop a reputation for having a quality recreation program or a fun youth group, they won't be able to keep people away. Remember that one characteristic of adolescence is that young people do little in moderation. They like too much of a good thing or, unfortunately, too much of a bad thing. So, if they like something that your church is offering, they will come, and there's a good chance that they'll bring their friends.

Recreation is not a cure-all for the inevitable challenges of the youth years. Recreation does not ensure perfect, problem-free kids. But it does guarantee a step in the right direction because it advances the concept of total wellness. Youth are spiritual, social, mental, emotional, *and* physical beings, and recreation done right helps to advance all of these dimensions in the life of a young person. As Black pointed out, "Youth ministry is more than fun and games. However, youth ministry without fun and games is like eating cold pizza and a month-old soda. The basic ingredients are there, but the warmth and fizz are gone. Too little recreation in youth ministry leads to a lack of spark and vitality."[28]

## Exploring Young Adults

The transition to adulthood is as varied as the people who have to accomplish it. While many include an educational experience (college or vo-tech) in the transitional period, others jump right into full-time employment or even military training. Whatever path is chosen for the journey, the common denominator for those between the ages of twenty and forty is a change in focus from growing up to settling down. "Success in this stage of adulthood requires an understanding of new rules and standards, flexibility to adjust and change, and the ability to develop new personal styles and self-concepts."[29]

Accompanying this array of maturity issues is the decision—whether conscious or subconscious—of whether to pursue a lifestyle of wellness. The busyness of this life period tends to crowd out the importance of a healthy diet or active lifestyle because, for many, the focus is on the present, and right now most everything seems to be in working order. However, a flashing neon sign should be placed in the front yard of every twenty- and thirty-something who forgets that health choices made in these years have a tremendous effect on how well these same folks will age and how long they can maintain a high quality of life.

Because early adulthood is potentially the peak of one's physical development in terms of speed, strength, coordination, and endurance, it is also usually considered a period of high achievement for professional athletes as well as other recreationally oriented individuals. But it doesn't take an Olympics-style training program for someone to reap significant benefits from an ongoing effort to be active. The American College of Sports Medicine recommends a minimum of three or four thirty-minute periods of moderate-intensity exercise a week (or ten- to fifteen-minute sessions that accumulate to thirty to forty minutes per day) to reap cardiorespiratory benefits as well as help in the area of muscular endurance and even increased flexibility. Lifestyle activities may be a promising alternative to organized exercise, but further research is necessary to examine specific forms that can be helpful. The basic premise is that it is necessary to increase daily activity, whether through intentional or incidental exercise, in order to enhance energy production and expenditure.[30]

When asked what types of needs tend to dominate the lives of young adults, one group of Christian graduate students specifically addressed the importance of social contact as it relates to the need to belong. This bumps up against this generation's history as latchkey children who grew up with a strong sense of independence and self-sufficiency. However, this need fits closely with Erikson's psychosocial development construct for this age group: that they achieve a sense of personal identity and self-worth by successfully negotiating their relationships, whether with friends, parents, employers, or potential mates.

Recreational outlets allow young adults relatively safe environments through which to express creativity and productivity in an effort to grow in their ability to cooperate and work together. For example, a hearty game of Catch Phrase® will challenge one's ability to think quickly, work as a team, and laugh at both one's successes and failures. It is not meant to destroy a player's self-esteem; instead, it is a game best played in the context of friends and family to encourage personal growth and not individual domination.

Also important to this group of Christian young adults is the need to fill their lives with pursuits full of purpose and meaning. While the spectrum of ages and life directions included in the description of young adults is wide and diverse, there is still concern in most of them that what they invest their time and interests in really matters. Some may interpret this purposefulness as "tunnel vision," and yet in the big picture, this mind-set allows the young adult to pour him- or herself into activities, jobs, and relationships as an investment toward the future.

Caz McCaslin, mentioned earlier in this chapter, had served at First Baptist Church of Spartanburg, South Carolina, for ten years. In his early thirties, he was running a successful recreation ministry and could even boast of a children's basketball league that had kids on a waiting list after only three days of registration. But he didn't want a waiting list; he wanted a program that could accommodate as many children as wanted to play ball at the church. A wise mentor encouraged him to take his league design and write it as a sports program that could be marketed to churches all over the country. Several years and many churches later, the Upward Basketball program continues to minister to countless children around the country. McCaslin's interest in basketball combined with a passion for outreach translated to a powerful and effective sports ministry.

## Exploring Middle Adults

As individuals inch toward their forties, a number of curious things begin to occur both mentally and physically. For starters, the phrase "middle-aged" gets thrown their way more and more. While seemingly a statement of ridicule, the practicality of the phrase indicates that these persons have reached a life marker where, should they live to today's normal life expectancy of seventy-five years, then they are already more than halfway there.

Another interesting aspect of entering the middle adult years is the physical change that seems to creep up almost overnight. Although, from scientific research, we know that the slowdown of one's metabolism and the speed-up of one's weight gain is usually a gradual process (and not necessarily inevitable), that's not how it feels at the onset of the decade birthdays like forty, fifty, and sixty. With the looming threat of osteoporosis, adult-onset diabetes, high blood pressure, and a host of other lifestyle illnesses, the middle adult faces a daily challenge of how she will beat the odds and maintain (or improve to) a certain level of health so that she can age gracefully.

Beverly entered her forties with two teenage children and a busy husband. She was an elementary school teacher, working primarily because her family needed the extra income as they anticipated college and other financial obligations. She enjoyed her fourth-grade students but felt trapped, at times, by the restrictions of a daily school schedule. She wanted to exercise regularly, but finding the time was hard. She loved needlework and scrapbooking, but who had time for hobbies anymore? Plus there were her church commitments that already kept her away from home two or three nights a week.

It wasn't until her husband accepted a new job opportunity in a different state that Beverly saw significant changes in her hectic schedule. As one child finished college and the other began, she felt the freedom to stop teaching and begin pursuing other interests. One of those interests was long-distance running. Beverly recently celebrated her fiftieth birthday and, in the last several years, has run at least five half marathons (13.1 miles each). For folks who have been running all of their adult lives, this may not seem like a big deal, but for Beverly—and other middle adults like her—this represents a huge milestone that says chronological age does not have to be the determining factor for physical decline. It's a matter of what you do with the time and body you've been given.

Couey and Yessick stress the value of Christians taking care of their bodies—inside and out—so that they can serve God longer and better. "God created for every individual a uniquely different and highly complicated body in which to live during his or her limited existence. He expects us to care for His temple (our bodies) from our first to our last breath. He expects us to protect and feed our bodies properly and exercise regularly. Christians must grow not only spiritually, mentally, socially, and emotionally, but also physically."[31] Cooper addresses the fact that this stewardship of care is not limited to those under forty; instead, he boldly states:

> It's evident to me from the more than one hundred thousand people we have tested on treadmills at the Aerobics Center in Dallas that it's *not* necessary for a significant decline in endurance or aerobic capacity to occur after age forty. . . . I'm not saying that every older person can become a world-class athlete. But I am saying that there's a good chance that, with serious training, your performance as a middle-aged athlete can approach that of your earlier years. For that matter, even if you weren't in good shape in your teens or twenties, you can still get into great shape today. Many of my patients have reached their highest levels of lifetime fitness well after forty years of age.[32]

In addition to the mental and physical demands of middle adulthood, there is also the challenge of leaving behind the illusions of youth and focusing on a fuller, more balanced life. I love the saying, "It's never to late to change what you want to be when you grow up." In one's youth, the search for significance tends to focus on that "one thing" (one career, one person, one you-fill-in-the-blank) that will make you happy. As one matures, the understanding of this broadens so that, after settling the issue of eternal salvation found only in a relationship with Jesus Christ, each individual begins to see that it takes more than "one thing" to define fulfillment in life. Satisfaction is seen as multidimensional, achieved through involvement with family, work, church, friends, and so on. In addition, these dimensions are in a constant state of flux. Children grow up. Job descriptions change. Friends move away. Church needs vary. And so we grow, change, move, and vary with them, hopefully moving closer to becoming all that we were created to be.

Leisure pursuits during this life stage are as varied as the people partaking in them. More important than a grocery list of what middle-age adults like to do—such as learning new skills, volunteering, enjoying nature, engaging in exercise and social interaction, and so on—is the understanding that commitment to leisure activities is closely associated with personal happiness.[33]

Remember Beverly? With each finish line she crosses comes a satisfaction that she has stretched herself beyond limitations of earlier years and proven that she is still capable of growth and improvement. She is not denying the long-instilled work ethic that requires that she be a productive person; instead, she is learning the benefits of a balanced life and spreading that happiness to her family, her friends, and even her church commitments.

## Exploring Senior Adults

This pursuit of productivity and happiness is not sequestered to one's early and middle adult years. On the contrary, as the baby boomers (those born between 1946 and 1964) inch toward senior adulthood, there is no longer a sense of succumbing to the inevitability of old age. Instead, we see the field of gerontology exploding with research and scientific study in an attempt to capitalize on the experience as well as the potential of those who are sixty years old and above.

Because of the likelihood of lengthened longevity, descriptors of senior adults are also being subdivided to define the various stages of these advanced years. This becomes increasingly important as not all senior adults fall in line with the old-school paradigm that "to be old is to be sick and, after a certain age, to be sick is to be old."[34] More and more, Satchel Paige's famous age-related quotes come into play: "How old would you be if you didn't know how old you are?" and "Age is a question of mind over matter; if you don't mind, it don't matter."[35]

Health status, physical mobility, and mental acuity factor strongly into the definition distinctives. Neugarten used the terms "young-old," "middle-old," and "old-old" to differentiate between those over age sixty.[36] Garner prefers to use their activity choices, dividing the age span into "the challengers," "the goers-and-doers," and "the stay-at-homers."

Challengers are those who will take a challenge, try new things, desire to experience new places, friends, foods, and so forth. Goers-and-doers like day trips, in-town mission projects, and ongoing recreation opportunities at church or a community center. But the stay-at-homers are just that: those who prefer to do life from the comfort of their living room or their own backyard. They don't want to be ignored, but they are not the ones that most senior adult recreation programs address.

But no matter where senior adults fall on the descriptive spectrum, all are dealing with changes in physical health and ability. But even the gradual decreases can be unexpected, as seen in this classic gerontological story of how difficult it is to know what constitutes normal aging:

> An elderly square dancer went to his doctor because of pain in his left knee. It was causing him so much discomfort that it was keeping him from his favorite weekly dance group. The doctor smiled at the very old man and went into a long discourse on the process of aging. He explained that cells break down, muscles lose elasticity, resistance to movement in the connective tissues around joints and muscles increases, and joints become tender because of changes in the synovial fluid and weakened cartilage; "you see," he added, "it's all part of normal aging." "But, doctor," exclaimed the patient, "my right knee is as old as my left knee, and it doesn't hurt at all."[37]

## Older Adults Today Are Active

They don't have a rocking chair mentality. They have more energy and longer life expectancies than previous generations. Older adults today want to use their considerable experience to contribute to something worthwhile and be a part of something meaningful. Their lifestyle is a continuum of what they have been involved with earlier in life—traveling, giving, spending, seeking new experiences, and being concerned with their quality of life. In short, the older adult population in America is just now coming into its own. At the North American Congress on the Church and the Age Wave, several factors emerged as trends seen on the horizon:

1. Ageism in the church will diminish. This form of discrimination will see a decline.

2. New age classifications will emerge. Senior or mature adults will be those over seventy; middle maturity will range from fifty to seventy.

3. Church programs and staffing will reflect age-related concerns. The number of ministers to older adults will increase.

4. Aging will be viewed developmentally as opposed to chronologically.

5. Ministry to older adults will focus on the middle adults (fifty to seventy years).

6. Outreach to and by mature adults will receive priority.

7. The unique contributions of mature adults will be increasingly valued.

8. New churches for mature adults will be established.[38]

These eight factors alone show that a new age is approaching. New ways of engaging and involving this new generation of older adults are emerging. Churches will either prepare for this new "Age Wave" or be swept away by it. Those who are prepared will see the benefits of offering new and innovative ministry to older Americans.

***Differing Senior Adult Populations***—The above listing is not applicable to all senior adults. Older adults can basically be placed into three distinct categories. While the younger and middle senior adults fit the above criteria, the oldest adults are cut from a different mold.

***Older Senior Adults***—Our oldest adults view life differently. They are more conservative in all areas of life. Their thinking has been shaped by what they grew up with, primarily a strong work ethic that kept an eye on the basics of life. Nothing was certain for this age group, and nothing was taken for granted. The Great Depression and two world wars left their mark on how they view leisure. A more utilitarian approach to life is characteristic. They often do not want to be gone from home too long at a time and will be careful about spending money. Many are on fixed incomes because they did not have jobs that had good pension plans, or they were self-employed and did not put back enough, or they rely heavily on social security. They lived for their family and worked to provide the necessities of life. Leisure came at a price that some were not able to afford, so they did not plan on it in retirement. Neither leisure education nor leisure planning for retirement was given much thought.

The result is that the older (seventy and above) senior adult population is unprepared to cope with a leisure-oriented culture. They view the younger generation as wasteful and pleasure-seeking spenders. Churches will do well to note the differences in thought patterns between the older and younger senior adults. Two or three groups may be formed within a church to meet the perceived leisure needs of each group. Some churches have several groups that meet at times convenient to them and plan activities that appeal to that particular age grouping. Their activities and outings are tailored to meet the differing needs of the various groups' membership.

## Recreation Helps to Lead a Balanced Abundant Life

Leading a balanced life is biblical and essential to well-being. A balanced life includes taking part in recreation/leisure activities. Recreation helps people re-create themselves. Often, because of the strong work ethic of older adults, they have a hard time taking advantage of their leisure. Many have not learned to say yes to fun and re-creative activity that can enrich their lives. Scripture tells us that "Jesus increased in wisdom and stature, and in favor with God and with people" (Luke 2:52). This indicates that he was a whole person and that he needed what we all need, to grow in various areas of life. Breaking the routine and taking some time off are essential to well-being, growth, and living a balanced life. Jesus said, "I have come that they may have life and have it in abundance" (John 10:10). Recreation brings an element of joy and abundance to life; experiencing all that life has for us is good. God created us to live the abundant life. He wants us to "redeem the time" and use it to glorify him as we live. He has provided us with the capacity to play, sing, learn, converse, and to grow mentally, physically, spiritually, and emotionally throughout life. We don't stop growing just because we get older. In fact, we feel older when we stop taking advantage of the opportunities God gives us to grow in these areas.

Older adults need to have the opportunities to keep growing. Recreation provides a wonderful platform to allow the whole person's growth needs to be met. This in turn will help the person have the opportunity to lead a balanced abundant life.

## Meet Needs Using Recreation Programming

Churches have unique and growing opportunities to offer leisure services that can meet the needs of all ages of senior adults. Some of these needs are: (1) to be accepted by others; (2) to feel that they belong to a group; (3) to be recognized as individuals of worth; (4) to feel that they are contributing from their life experiences; (5) to have opportunities of growth in mind, body, emotion, and spirit. Perhaps nowhere in the life of the church can the senior adult as a whole person minister and receive ministry more than through recreation and fellowship. This ministry tool offers a fun, relaxed way to interact with peers in a nonthreatening way that is comfortable to members and nonmembers alike. Garner in *Forward Together, A New Vision for Senior Adult Ministry* states that recreation and fellowship programming should have the following characteristics:

*Programming must have meaning and purpose.* What is done should meet a need. To find out what is needed, a survey (see appendix 3) is taken of the widest cross-section of the senior adult population, including the homebound.

*Programming should be inclusive.* No one should be left out. Leaders should seek to provide ways that all can participate. Those with disabilities, those with little discretionary money, those with transportation problems should never be left out of program planning.

*Programming should offer variety.* Offer something for the goers-and-doers, something for the stay-at-homers, something for those who enjoy a challenge.

*Programming should be unique to the church.* Adapt ideas you see, read about, or experience to your situation. No two situations are alike. It is OK to add to or take away something from another program and make it your own.

*Programming should not be repetitive.* The death of the best program ever done is to keep doing it over and over the same way. As far as programming goes, variety is truly the spice of life. Change the way things are done once in a while. New favorites might be discovered!

*Programming should offer plenty of time for fellowship.* Folks like to visit with friends. Recreation programming offers the best opportunity for strengthening relationships and forming new ones. The wise programmer will intentionally build fellowship times into the overall program to foster relationships.

*Programming should offer an intentional time of spiritual renewal.* Do not be afraid of offering a time for examining one's spiritual condition. Senior adults need to assess and examine this most important aspect of their lives. Some of them may be grappling with spiritual questions. What better time to allow for introspection than during a devotional or on a retreat in a relaxed setting that is not formal?[39]

Programming is a key ingredient to ministry effectiveness with all ages in the church. Balance should be the planning principle that assures most needs are being met. Involvement of many to plan and carry out the programming will lead to excitement and ensure participation. A well-planned, well-promoted, and well-executed program to all ages offers opportunity to impact the lives of many.

There is value in recreation and fellowship for all ages. Recreation and fellowship offer many opportunities for growth and relationship building that can enrich and enhance all of life. Churches that recognize the values and give all ages the opportunity to recreate will find that they will eagerly take advantage of it. As the differing age populations ebb and flow, the need for leisure services will increase. Churches need to be prepared to reach out in ministry. Recreation is one tool that can help churches meet some real needs of people. A well-planned and balanced program of leisure services will reap great benefits for participants, the culture, and the church itself.

---

### Notes

1. Guy R. Lefrançois, *The Lifespan,* 6th ed. (Belmont, Calif.: Wadsworth Publishing Company, 1999), 189.

2. Kathleen A. Cordes and Hilmi M. Ibrahim, *Applications in Recreation & Leisure for Today and the Future,* 2nd ed. (Boston: WCB/McGraw-Hill, 1999), 59–60.

3. "Playorena the Original Program." Downloaded from http://www.playorena.com. Accessed on 5 March 2002.

4. "What Makes Gymboree Play and Music Unique." Downloaded from http://www.gymboree-hk.com. Accessed on 5 March 2002.

5. Laura Davis and Janis Keyser, *Becoming the Parent You Want to Be: A Sourcebook of Strategies for the First Five Years* (New York: Broadway Books, 1997). Excerpt downloaded from www.parentsplace.com/expert/parenting. Accessed 5 March 2002.

6. Lefrançois, 186.

7. Tamra Orr, "Babies and Books," *Christian Parenting Today,* November/December 2000. Downloaded from www.christianitytoday.com/cpt/2000. Accessed 6 March 2002.

8. American Academy of Pediatrics, "Prescription for Reading," 16 April 1997. Downloaded from www.aap.org/advocacy/washing/readdcpr.htm. Accessed 6 March 2002.

9. Lefrançois, 220–21.

10. Mary Ellen Pellegrini, "Let Them Play: Do You Over-Schedule Your Child?" *Christianity Parenting Today,* March/April 2002. Downloaded from www.christianitytoday.com/cpt/2002. Accessed 6 March 2002.

11. Ibid.

12. David and Teresa Ferguson, Paul and Vicky Warren, and Terri Ferguson, *Parenting with Intimacy Workbook: A Practical Guide to Building and Maintaining Great Family Relationships* (Wheaton, Ill.: Victor Books, 1995), 36.

13. Kenneth H. Cooper, *Fit Kids! The Complete Shape-Up Program from Birth through High School* (Nashville: Broadman & Holman Publishers, 1999), 15.

14. Deane Hartzell, *Recreation for Children* (Nashville: Convention Press, 1988), 9–11.

15. Richard Kraus, *Recreation Today: Program Planning and Leadership* (New York: Meredith Publishing Company, 1966), 271.

16. Ibid., 270.

17. Kelvin L. Seifert and Robert J. Hoffnung, *Child and Adolescent Development,* 4th ed. (Boston: Houghton Mifflin Company, 1997), 349.

18. Cooper, 50.

19. American Heart Association, "Obesity and Overweight in Children." Downloaded from www.americanheart.org. Accessed 15 March 2002.

20. Barri Bronston, "Fit is phat!" *The (New Orleans) Times-Picayune* (28 January 2002): E–8.

21. Ibid.

22. *A Matter of Time: Report of the Task Force on Youth Development* (New York: Carnegie Corp., 1992), quoted in Cordes and Ibrahim, 79.

23. Elmer L. Towns, *Successful Biblical Youth Work,* rev. ed. (Nashville: Impact Books, 1973), 346–50.

24. Robert William Blum, "Lost Children or Lost Parents of Rockdale County?" Downloaded from www.pbs.org/wgbh/pages/frontline/shows/georgia/isolated/blum.html. Accessed 25 March 2002.

25. Towns, 348.

26. Ibid., 349.

27. Ibid.

28. Wes Black, *Introduction to Youth Ministry* (Nashville: Broadman Press, 1991), 214.

29. Cordes and Ibrahim, 101.

30. "ACSM Releases New Position Stand on Losing Weight, Keeping It Off." Downloaded from www.acsm.org. Accessed 27 March 2002.

31. Dick Couey and Tommy Yessick, *Fit to Serve Him Longer and Better* (Nashville: LifeWay Press, 1998), 4.

32. Kenneth H. Cooper, *It's Better to Believe* (Nashville: Thomas Nelson Publishers, 1995), 38.

33. Lefrançois, 459.

34. Mary Grace Kovar, "Health Assessment," *The Encyclopedia of Aging,* George L. Maddox, ed. (New York: Springer Publishing Company, 1995), 433.

35. "Biography of Satchel Paige." Downloaded from www.cmgww.com/baseball/paige/quote2.html. Accessed 8 March 1999 and 28 March 2002.

36. Dail A. Neugarten, *The Meanings of Age: Selected Papers of Bernice L. Neugarten* (Chicago: University of Chicago Press, 1996).

37. Florence Safford and George I. Krell, *Gerontology for Health Professionals,* 2d ed. (Washington, D.C.: NASW Press, 1998), 18.

38. The North American Congress on the Church and the Age Wave, Colorado Springs, May 1997, sponsored by L.I.F.E. (Life Living in Full Effectiveness), Win Arn founder/president.

39. John Garner, *Forward Together, A New Vision for Senior Adult Ministry* (Nashville: LifeWay Press, 1998), 139–40.

# Appendix 1
# *Recreation and Sports Ministry: Positioning for Impact*

Any ministry that impacts culture will have the following characteristics:
1. A defined uniqueness
2. An articulated Christian worldview
3. A focus on quality and hospitality
4. Developed strategy to use the unique giftedness of members to demonstrate Christianity in action
5. Articulated beliefs
6. A place for people to grow roots
7. Promotion plan of what you have to offer to those who need it
8. A plan to meet needs with quality and services
9. Quality, quality, quality!
10. Focus on people
11. World concern
12. Well-articulated kingdom vision
13. Incremental goals, plan for resources, use empowered staff and volunteers
14. Recognition that ministry is effective when multiplied in others

# Appendix 2
# Sources for Lifelong Learning and Networking for Recreation and Sports Ministers

## Faith-Based Training Conferences/ Professional Organizations

**Christian Camping International**
P.O. Box 62189
Colorado Springs, CO 80962-2189
719-260-9400
http://cci.gospelcom.net/ccihome/

**Church Sports and Recreation Ministers Conference**
The Association of Church Sports and Recreation Ministers
5350 Broadmoor Circle NW
Canton, OH 44709
330-493-4824
http://www.csrm.org/

**Church Sports International**
P.O. Box 2237
Los Gatos, CA 95031
408-370-9075
http://www.churchsports.org/

**International Sports Federation**
P.O. Box 13038
Arlington, TX 76094
800-999-2889 ext. 1512
http://www.teamisf.com/

**Outdoor Leadership Lab**
National Outdoor Adventure
Education Institute
4114 W. Lake Sammamish Pkwy. SE
Bellevue, WA 98008
425-746-9110
http://www.caei.net/

**Rec Lab International Conference on Recreation and Sports Ministry**
One LifeWay Plaza
Nashville, TN 37234
615-251-2000
http://www.lifeway.com/staff_r.asp

## Secular Training Conferences/ Professional Organizations

**Amateur Athletic Union**
407-934-7200
http://www.aausports.org/

**American Alliance for Health, Physical Education, Recreation and Dance**
1900 Association Drive
Reston, VA 20192-1598
800-213-7193
http://www.aahperd.org/

**National Association for Sport and Physical Education**
http://www.aahperd.org/naspe/
template.cfm

**American Camping Association**
5000 State Road 67 North
Martinsville, IN 46151
765-342-8456
http://www.acacamps.org/

**American Mountain Guide
Association**
710 Tenth Street, Suite 101
Golden, CO 80401 USA
303-271-0984
http://www.amga.com/

**Association for Challenge Course
Technology**
P.O. Box 255
Martin, MI 49070-0255
616-685-0670
http://www.acctinfo.org/

**Association for Experiential
Education**
2305 Canyon Boulevard, Suite #100
Boulder, CO 80302-5651
303-440-8844
http://www.aee.org/

**National Alliance for Youth Sports**
2050 Vista Parkway
West Palm Beach, FL 33411
561-684-1141
http://www.nays.org/

**National Challenge Course
Facilitators Symposium**
Leahy & Associates
1052 Artemis Circle
Lafayette, CO 80026 USA
303-673-9832
http://www.leahy
inc.com/NCCPS/index.html

**National Intramural-Recreational
Sports Association**
4185 SW Research Way
Corvallis, OR 97333-1067
541-766-8211
http://www.nirsa.org/

**National Outdoor Leadership
School**
288 Main Street
Lander, WY 82520-3140
307-332-5300
http://www.nols.edu/

**National Recreation and Park
Association**
22377 Belmont Ridge Road
Ashburn, VA 20148-4501
703-858-0784
http://www.nrpa.org/

**North American Society for
Sport Management**
PMB 487
Houlton, ME 04730-9001
506-453-5010
http://www.nassm.org/

**Outward Bound**
101 E. Chapman St.
Ely, MN 55731
800-321-HIKE
(There are actually five different
Outward Bound Schools.)
http://www.outwardbound.com/

**Project Adventure**
701 Cabot Street
Beverly, MA 01915
978-524-4500
http://www.pa.org

**Youth Sports Institute**
213 IM Sports Circle Building
Department of Kinesiology
Michigan State University
East Lansing, MI 48824-1049
517-353-6689
http://ed-web3.educ.msu.edu/ysi/

# Appendix 3
# *Membership Survey*

Date _____

Name _____

Phone _____ E-mail _____

Age group ___13–17 ___18–29 ___30–49 ___ 50–65 ___ 65+
  *If you have children under 13, star(\*) the column of their interest.*

Instructions: Check all that apply to you in the appropriate column.

| Activity | Now taking part in | Would like to take part in | Can provide leadership in |
|---|---|---|---|
| **Arts, Crafts, Hobbies** | | | |
| Banner Making | | | |
| Basketry | | | |
| Candle Making | | | |
| Ceramics | | | |
| China Painting | | | |
| Christmas Crafts | | | |
| Creative Writing | | | |
| Drawing | | | |
| Flower Arranging | | | |
| Furniture Refinishing | | | |
| Interior Decorating | | | |
| Leather Crafts | | | |
| Macramé | | | |
| Needlework | | | |
| Painting | | | |
| Photography | | | |
| Pottery | | | |
| Quilting | | | |
| Stained Glass | | | |
| Weaving | | | |
| Woodworking | | | |
| Other: | | | |
| **Social Activities** | | | |
| Parties | | | |
| Banquets | | | |
| Covered-Dish Meals | | | |
| Fellowships | | | |
| Other: | | | |

| Activity (continued) | Now taking part in | Would like to take part in | Can provide leadership in |
|---|---|---|---|
| **Dramatic Activities** | | | |
| Acting | | | |
| Clowning | | | |
| Costuming | | | |
| Directing | | | |
| Lighting | | | |
| Makeup | | | |
| Pantomime | | | |
| Play Writing | | | |
| Props | | | |
| Puppetry | | | |
| Set Building | | | |
| Skits, Stunts | | | |
| Sound | | | |
| Storytelling | | | |
| Street Drama | | | |
| Other: | | | |
| **Music Activities** | | | |
| Choirs | | | |
| Community Sings | | | |
| Folk Singing | | | |
| Fun Songs | | | |
| Instrument | | | |
| Music Leading | | | |
| Other: | | | |
| **Camping/Outdoor Activities** | | | |
| Adventure Recreation | | | |
| Backpacking | | | |
| Bicycle Trips | | | |
| Canoeing | | | |
| Day Camping | | | |
| Family Camping | | | |
| Fishing | | | |
| Hiking | | | |
| Hunter Safety | | | |
| Hunting | | | |
| Kayaking | | | |
| Mountain Biking | | | |
| Rappelling | | | |
| Resident Camping | | | |
| Ropes Courses | | | |
| Travel Camping | | | |
| Other: | | | |
| **Safety/First Aid** | | | |
| Certified Baby-Sitter | | | |
| CPR | | | |
| First Aid | | | |
| Lifeguarding | | | |
| Other: | | | |

| Activity (continued) | Now taking part in | Would like to take part in | Can provide leadership in |
|---|---|---|---|
| **Sports and Games** | | | |
| Badminton | | | |
| Baseball | | | |
| Basketball | | | |
| Boating | | | |
| Bowling | | | |
| Coaching | | | |
| Football | | | |
| Golf | | | |
| Handball/Racquetball | | | |
| Hockey | | | |
| Horseshoes | | | |
| Ice Skating | | | |
| Officiating | | | |
| Skate Boarding | | | |
| Snow Skiing | | | |
| Softball | | | |
| Swimming | | | |
| Table Tennis | | | |
| Tennis | | | |
| Volleyball | | | |
| Water Skiing | | | |
| Other: | | | |
| **Fitness/Wellness** | | | |
| Aerobics | | | |
| First Place | | | |
| Health Screenings | | | |
| Jogging | | | |
| Meal Preparation | | | |
| Nutrition | | | |
| Smoking Cessation | | | |
| Stress Management | | | |
| Walking | | | |
| Weigh Down | | | |
| Weight Lifting | | | |
| Women's Health | | | |
| Other: | | | |
| **Continuing Education** | | | |
| Computer Education | | | |
| Cooking Classes | | | |
| Driver Education | | | |
| Entertaining | | | |
| Financial Management | | | |
| Gardening | | | |
| Home Maintenance | | | |
| Landscaping | | | |
| Literacy Classes | | | |
| Tax Preparation | | | |
| Vocational Guidance | | | |
| Other: | | | |

# Appendix 4
# *The Programmer's Evaluation Cube**

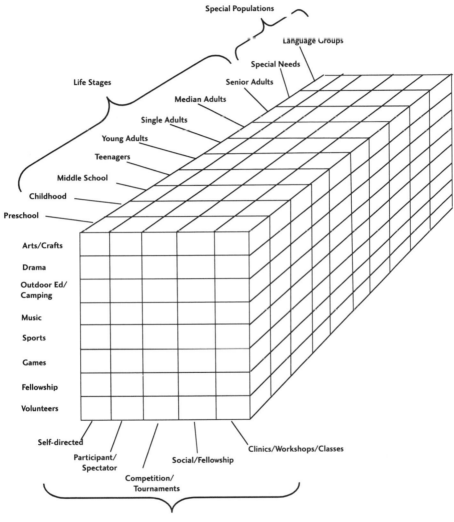

Special Populations

Language Groups

Special Needs

Senior Adults

Life Stages

Median Adults

Single Adults

Young Adults

Teenagers

Middle School

Childhood

Preschool

Arts/Crafts

Drama

Outdoor Ed/
Camping

Music

Sports

Games

Fellowship

Volunteers

Self-directed

Participant/
Spectator

Competition/
Tournaments

Social/Fellowship

Clinics/Workshops/Classes

Programming Formats

*Adapted from Patricia Farrell and Herberta M. Lundegren, *The Process of Recreation Programming:
Theory and Technique*, 3rd ed. (State College, Pa.: Venture Publishing, 1991.)

# Appendix 5
# *Event Cost Projection Worksheet*

Event_____ Year_____

Program/Committee_____ Budget #_____

Date(s)_____ Participant Goal_____

Person in Charge_____ Place_____

| | Total $ | Apr | May | Jun | Jul | Aug | Sep | Oct | Nov | Dec | Jan | Feb | Mar |
|---|---|---|---|---|---|---|---|---|---|---|---|---|---|
| **Expenses/Promotion** | | | | | | | | | | | | | |
| Printing | | | | | | | | | | | | | |
| Newspaper Ads | | | | | | | | | | | | | |
| Mailing/Postage | | | | | | | | | | | | | |
| Other | | | | | | | | | | | | | |
| **Event/Program** | | | | | | | | | | | | | |
| Registration, Tickets | | | | | | | | | | | | | |
| Materials | | | | | | | | | | | | | |
| Supplies | | | | | | | | | | | | | |
| Decorations | | | | | | | | | | | | | |
| Meals | | | | | | | | | | | | | |
| Hotel/Lodging | | | | | | | | | | | | | |
| Transportation | | | | | | | | | | | | | |
| Child Care | | | | | | | | | | | | | |
| Wages | | | | | | | | | | | | | |
| Other | | | | | | | | | | | | | |
| **Leaders/Guests** | | | | | | | | | | | | | |
| Travel | | | | | | | | | | | | | |
| Meals/Lodging | | | | | | | | | | | | | |
| Honorariums | | | | | | | | | | | | | |
| Contract Fees | | | | | | | | | | | | | |
| **Total Expenses** | | | | | | | | | | | | | |

**Income**   (How much will be received: $_____ per person _____ )

| | Total $ | Apr | May | Jun | Jul | Aug | Sep | Oct | Nov | Dec | Jan | Feb | Mar |
|---|---|---|---|---|---|---|---|---|---|---|---|---|---|
| Registrations | | | | | | | | | | | | | |
| Tickets | | | | | | | | | | | | | |
| Fees | | | | | | | | | | | | | |
| Other | | | | | | | | | | | | | |
| **Total Income** | | | | | | | | | | | | | |
| **Net Cost/Budget** | | | | | | | | | | | | | |

# Appendix 6
# *Non-Event Cost Projection Worksheet*

Year_____

Program/Committee_____ Budget #_____

Person in Charge_____

**—PLEASE LIST THE AMOUNT TO BE SPENT EACH MONTH—**

| | Total $ | Apr | May | Jun | Jul | Aug | Sep | Oct | Nov | Dec | Jan | Feb | Mar |
|---|---|---|---|---|---|---|---|---|---|---|---|---|---|
| **Expenses** (Please list the items to be paid—one per line.) | | | | | | | | | | | | | |
| | | | | | | | | | | | | | |
| | | | | | | | | | | | | | |
| | | | | | | | | | | | | | |
| | | | | | | | | | | | | | |
| | | | | | | | | | | | | | |
| | | | | | | | | | | | | | |
| | | | | | | | | | | | | | |
| | | | | | | | | | | | | | |
| | | | | | | | | | | | | | |
| | | | | | | | | | | | | | |
| | | | | | | | | | | | | | |
| | | | | | | | | | | | | | |
| | | | | | | | | | | | | | |
| | | | | | | | | | | | | | |
| | | | | | | | | | | | | | |
| | | | | | | | | | | | | | |
| | | | | | | | | | | | | | |
| | | | | | | | | | | | | | |
| | | | | | | | | | | | | | |
| | | | | | | | | | | | | | |
| **Total Expenses** | | | | | | | | | | | | | |

# Total Cost Projection Worksheet

Year_____

Program/Committee _____ Budget #_____

Person in Charge_____

**— PLEASE LIST THE MONTH IN WHICH THE COST IS ANTICIPATED —**

| | Total $ | Apr | May | Jun | Jul | Aug | Sep | Oct | Nov | Dec | Jan | Feb | Mar |
|---|---|---|---|---|---|---|---|---|---|---|---|---|---|

**Event/Program** (Please copy the Net Cost/Budget line from each Event Cost Projection Sheet. There will be a line for each event.)

| | | | | | | | | | | | | | |
|---|---|---|---|---|---|---|---|---|---|---|---|---|---|
| | | | | | | | | | | | | | |

| Grand Total | | | | | | | | | | | | | |
|---|---|---|---|---|---|---|---|---|---|---|---|---|---|

# Appendix 8
## *Recreation and Sports Ministry Budget Accounts*

Budget Area_____

Monthly Account Total_____

| Acct # | Account | Apr | May | Jun | Jul | Aug | Sep | Oct | Nov | Dec | Jan | Feb | Mar | Total |
|--------|---------|-----|-----|-----|-----|-----|-----|-----|-----|-----|-----|-----|-----|-------|
| | | | | | | | | | | | | | | |
| | | | | | | | | | | | | | | |
| | | | | | | | | | | | | | | |
| | | | | | | | | | | | | | | |
| | | | | | | | | | | | | | | |
| | | | | | | | | | | | | | | |
| | | | | | | | | | | | | | | |
| | | | | | | | | | | | | | | |
| | | | | | | | | | | | | | | |
| | | | | | | | | | | | | | | |
| | | | | | | | | | | | | | | |
| | | | | | | | | | | | | | | |
| | Total | | | | | | | | | | | | | |

# Appendix 9
## *Permission Form*

Child's name _____

Parent(s)/Guardian _____

Address _____

_____

Phone number (work)_____ (home) _____

(cell phone)_____ (beeper #) _____

Emergency contact(s) name _____

address_____ phone number _____

Brief medical history _____

_____

Allergies _____

_____

Medications _____

_____

## Permission to Treat

My permission is granted for _____(name of

caregiver) to obtain necessary medical attention in case of sickness or injury to my child

while participating in _____(name of program/activity).

Family doctor_____

Medical insurance information _____

_____

_____

# Appendix 10
## *Participant Information Card*
(front and back)

_____ **Church**

Name _____ Grade Completed/Age _____

Address _____ Zip_____

Home Phone _____ Birth Date _____

Mother's Name _____ Work Phone _____ Cell Phone _____

Father's Name _____ Work Phone _____ Cell Phone _____

If parents cannot be reached, in an emergency call: _____

_____ Phone _____

Family Doctor _____ Phone _____

Hospital Preference _____

Insurance Carrier _____

**[over]**

My child will arrive at _____ a.m. and be picked up at _____ p.m. by

_____ (name of person to pick up child)

Does your child take daily medication? _____

Does your child have allergies or any other special problems that the camp staff

should be aware of? _____

_____

Should _____ (child's name) need emergency treatment and
neither of the parents or our family doctor can be reached, we hereby give permission
for our child to be transported to the nearest doctor or hospital, and the attending
doctor has our permission to render any treatment he/she feels is necessary.

Signed
(Mother/Guardian) _____ (Date)_____

(Father/Guardian) _____ (Date)_____

# Appendix 11
## *Incident Report Form*

Date_____

Child's name_____

Parent's name _____

Address _____

Phone _____

Emergency contact _____

Time of incident _____

Place of incident_____

Type of incident _____

_____

Nature of injury/illness _____

_____

When and how parents were notified _____

_____

Who was present when incident occurred_____

Name of person handling incident _____

Explanation of how incident happened _____

_____

_____

Action taken_____

　　Treated on sight—treatment given_____ by

whom _____

　　Taken to doctor/hospital—(where and how transported)_____

Date_____

Time _____

Result of follow-up with parent(s)/guardian _____

_____

_____

# Appendix 12
# *Abuse/Neglect Reporting Form*

Report made to _____ Date _____

Child's name _____ Age _____ Sex _____

Child's address _____

_____

Name(s) of parent(s) _____

Address(es) of parents _____

_____

Names, addresses of other care givers _____

_____

Physical indicators observed and when _____

_____

Behavioral indicators observed and when _____

_____

Other indicators observed/known _____

_____

If known, name and address of person responsible for abuse _____

_____

Source of report _____

Action taken by reporting source _____

Parents informed of report being made? ☐ Yes ☐ No

Reporter's name and position _____

# Appendix 13
## *Recreation Ministry Event Possibilities*

**Camping and Outdoors**
Sailing
Senior Adults:
  Chautauqua
  Conferences
  Historic Places
Sightseeing
Snow Skiing
Sporting Events:
  College
  High School
  Professional
Swimming
Tennis Tournament
Tubing
Water Skiing
Zoo

**Activities Away from Church**
Bike Hikes/Trips
Bird Watching
Boating
Camps: Trip, Day
Canoeing
Cycling
Camps:
  Family
  Resident
  Sports
Deep-Sea Fishing
Diving
Fishing Tournament
Float Trip
Golf Tournament
Hiking

Horseback Riding
Horseshoes
Hunting/Hunter Safety
Ice Skating
In-Line Skating
Mission Ideas:
  Concerts
  Craft at Park
  Day Camp
  Mobile Rec Unit
  Volleyball
Nature Study
Playday Picnic
Playgrounds
Putt-Putt Golf
Retreats

**Gymnasium Activities**
Aerobics
After-School Program
  for Children
All-Night Parties
Archery
Badminton
Banquets
Basketball:
  Clinics
  Christmas
  Tournament
  Free-Throw Contest
  Intramurals
  League
  On Skates
  Wheelchair
  Hot-Shot Contest
  Three-Man League
Bike Rodeo

Cheerleading Class
Dinner Theater
Dodgeball
Elementary Fun Day
Fellowships
Fencing
Football:
  Flag
  Touch
Four-Square
Frisbee Fun/Golf
Game Night
Golf Clinic
Gymnastics
Handball
Hockey on Skates
Indoor Track Meet
Jogging
Judo
Karate
Lock-Ins
Men's Noonday
  Exercise
Mother's Day Out
Movies
Officiating
Peanut Patch
Olympics
Ping-Pong
Preschool Recreation
Racquetball
Recreation for
  Children's Choir
Relays
Roller Skating
Roller/In-Line Hockey
Self-Defense Class

Shuffleboard
Skateboards
Sports Clinics
  Basketball
  Soccer
  Volleyball
  Cheerleading
  Baseball
  Football
  Tennis
Superstar Olympics
Tennis:
  Lessons
  Leagues
  Doubles
    Tournament
  Mixed Doubles
    Tournament
  Singles Tournament
Volleyball:
  Clinics
  Intramurals
  League
  Sunday School
  Three-Man
  Blind
Walking
Club/Program
Weight Training
Wiffleball
Wrestling

**Craft Ideas/Classes**
Banners
Batik
Brass Rubbings
Bread Dough Art
Cake Decorating
Calligraphy
Candle Making
Ceramics
China Painting
Chrismons

Christmas Decorations
Coin Collecting
Cooking Classes
Craft Fair
Creative Stitching
Crewel Embroidery
Crochet
Decoupage
Dip and Drape
Drawing
Floral Arranging
Fly Tying
Home Decorating
How to
  Auto Repair
  Furniture
  Refinishing
  Plumbing Repair
Jewelry Making
Knitting
Lace Darning
Leather Craft
Macrame
Magic
Model Building
Needlepoint
Oil Painting
Party Foods
Photography
Pinecone Wreath
Pottery
Puppet Construction
Quilting
Rag Baskets
Recipe Clinic
Sculpture
Seashell Collecting
Sewing
Silk Flowers
Silver Making
Sketching
Smocking
Stained Glass

Stamp Collecting
Stenciling
Taxidermy
Tennis Shoe Art
Tole Painting
Tying Scarves
Wallpaper Hanging
Weaving
Woodworking

**Family Night Ideas/
All-Church Activities**
Children's Cookie Bake
Churchwide Picnic
Covered-Dish Supper
Crafts Fair
Dinner Theatre
Drama Classes
Family Camp-out
Field Day
Game Night
Health Services Night
  Diabetes Test
  Medical Screening
  Blood Donations
  Blood Pressure
    Check
Hobby Show
Home Movies/Slides
Homemade Ice Cream
Men's Cake Bake
  Contest
Movies
Musical Drama
Novelty Band
Pet Show
Pie-Eating Contest
Pizza Party
Senior Adult
  Luncheons
  Monthly Meetings
Skating
Video Night

**Social**
All Church
  Banquet
  Fellowship
  Picnic
Breakfasts
Coffee & Doughnuts
Coffee & Doughnuts
  for Sunday
  Morning
Covered-Dish Supper
Family Night
  at the Church
Hayride
Talent Night
Tasting Bee
Valentine Banquet
Watch Night
Watermelon Cutting
Womanless Wedding

**Team Sports**
Basketball
Soccer
Softball
Volleyball
Walleyball

**Ideas Not Listed**
  **Elsewhere**
Computer Classes
CPR Classes
English Classes for
  Internationals
First-Aid Classes
Health Services
  Weight Monitoring
  Health Fairs
  Nutrition
  Counseling
Language Classes
  Sign
  Foreign

Lifeguard Classes
Mother's Day Out
Officiating Class
Getting On-line
  Classes
Sports Banquet
Tax Preparation
  Seminar
Wild Game Dinner

**Drama Activities**
Acting
Clowning
Costuming
Directing
Improvisation
Lighting
Makeup
Mimes
Monologues
Pageants
Play Writing
Puppets
Sets
Skits
Sound Crew
Speech Choir
Storytelling
Writing

# Appendix 14
# *Playground Equipment Suppliers*

**Aerosling Sling/Parity, Inc.**
Box 3593
Oak Park, IL 60303
800-848-3585

**American Playground Corp.**
Box 2599
Anderson, IN 46018-2599
800-541-1602

**American Swing Products**
1320 Fayette St.
El Cajon, CA 92020
800-433-2573

**BCI Burke Co., Inc.**
Box 549
Fond Du Lac, WI 54936
800-657-0723

**BSN Sports**
Box 7726
Dallas, TX 75209
800-243-7510

**BIGTOYS**
7717 New Market St.
Olympic, WA 98501
800-426-9788

**Bison Recreational Products, Inc.**
603 L Street
Lincoln, NE 68508
800-247-7668

**Children's Playgrounds, Inc.**
55 Whitney St.
Holliston, MA 01746
800-333-2205

**Chime Time**
834 Anderson Ave.
Homer, NY 13077
607-749-7949

**Columbia Cascade Co.**
1975 SW 5th Ave.
Portland, OR 97201
503-223-1157

**Creative Playgrounds, Ltd.**
Box 10
McFarland, WI 53558
800-338-0522

**Dinsmore Sales, Inc.**
35 Loring Dr.
Framingham, MA 01701
508-872-2563

**Flaghouse, Inc.**
150 N MacQuesten Parkway
Mt. Vernon, NY 10550
800-221-5185

**Gametime, Inc.**
101 Kingsburry Rd.
Fort Payne, AL 35967
205-845-5610

**Gerber MFG., Inc.**
2917 Latham Dr.
Madison, WI 53713
608-271-2777

**Grounds For Play, Inc.**
405 Dodson Lake Dr.
Arlington, TX 76012
800-552-7529

**Iron Mt. Forge**
Box 897
Farmington, MO 63640
800-325-8828

**Landscape Structures, Inc.**
601 7th St. South
Delano, MN 55328
612-972-3185

**The Larson Co.**
6701 S. Midvale Park Rd.
Tucson, AZ 85746
602-741-7930

**Miracle Recreation & Equip. Co.**
Box 420
Monett, MO 65708
417-235-6917

**Natural Structures**
Box 727
Sherwood, OR 97140
503-625-2566

**Omni**
5611 N. Peck Rd.
Arcadia, CA 91006
818-579-5600

**PCA Industries**
5642 Natural Bridge
St. Louis, MO 63120
800-727-8180

**Playworld Systems**
Box 505
New Berlin, PA 17855
800-233-8404

**Quality Industries**
Box 765
Hillsdale, MI 49242
800-766-9458

**Rainbow Play Systems**
5980 Rainbow Parkway
Prior Lake, MN 55372
612-447-2554

**Playground Site Amenity
& Surfacing Industry
Reference Directory**
www.world-playground.com
1-800-352-1137

# Appendix 15
# Seven Rules of Gamesmanship

Everyone likes to play games. Children and teenagers like games; and the wilder, crazier, and messier they are, the better they like them. Adults like games too—a little more sedate, but they still like games.

Games for any age group must constantly be updated and adapted to be effective. All games can be adapted to fit the occasion or the age group, from preschool to senior adults. The secret is how the leader comes across in the introduction and instruction of the game to the group. Leaders should convey excitement about the activity.

## Rules for Gamesmanship

*1. No one should be hurt.* When playing games, you should consider the possibility of persons getting hurt. Ask yourself, "Can anyone get hurt doing this?" If so, modify or change the game to lessen the possibility. If you are playing in a rocky field, perhaps you should move to a grassy area. Use your head!

*2. No one should be humiliated.* The idea is to foster togetherness, fellowship, and goodwill. The days of humiliating someone for a laugh are long gone. Youth ministers who humiliate kids soon don't have any to work with. To keep the "jocks" from running over the "non-jocks" and humiliating them, change the rules to level the playing field. Adapt some games so athletic ability is not a factor. Everyone will have a great time—even the jocks.

*3. No one should be forced to play.* Making people play a game they really don't want to play is like making someone pray. You risk loosing that kid. If the game is fun and everyone is enjoying playing, the one who is sitting out usually ends up choosing to give it a try. This is better for everyone.

*4. Games should fit the occasion.* You don't do a really messy game at an event where everyone is dressed formally (like a banquet). Be sure your games are appropriate for the occasion.

*5. Don't mix ages too widely.* Seventh graders usually don't mix well with seniors, and the seventh graders might get hurt. Consider age and ability differences.

**6. Games should not be divisive.** Competition is OK if it does not get out of hand. Watch for signs of a "win at all costs" mentality as your kids participate. Games should foster fellowship and unity. If you get an "us against them" thing going, it can destroy the group.

**7. Know the game.** Know the rules and how you are going to adapt the game before you start playing. It is best if the leader has played the game. The game leader needs to make games come alive and be inclusive.

## Types of Games

Many types of games are suitable to many situations. Some of them are:

1. Indoor Games
2. Outdoor Games
3. Active Games
4. Inactive or Quiet Games
5. Games That Require Props
6. Games with No Props
7. Messy Games
8. "Clean" Games
9. Games That Can Teach
10. Team Games
11. Partner Games
12. Group Games
13. Paper Games
14. Noisy Games
15. Adventure Games

# Appendix 16
# *Qualifications for the Person Who Is Called into Recreation and Sports Ministry*

1. Be a mature, practicing, committed Christian.
2. Have a concept of using recreation as a ministry tool.
3. Have a broad-based knowledge of recreation and ministry in general.
4. Be able to impart vision to one's church as to the ministry and evangelism opportunities of recreation and sports ministry for that community.
5. Be a people person who understands the needs of the many ages that will be ministered to.
6. Have a ministry heart.
7. See recreation and sports as tools that can offer those in the community a nonthreatening introduction to the Christ-life and church participation.
8. A seminary education is helpful but not always necessary—requirements vary from church to church.
9. Be a team player. Good staff relationships with other ministry area staff are important for the smooth coordination of overall ministry efforts.
10. Have good organizational/administrative skills. Juggling class schedules, working with maintenance personnel, working to keep the ministry functioning as a part of the overall church ministry, scheduling volunteers, working with budgets, keeping up with finances, and if a facility is involved: handling facility scheduling, contacting prospects who visit the facility, and doing other ministerial duties that come up are many of the requirements of his ministry position.
11. Understand how the church works and what its mission is.
12. Be an educator, seeking to teach the Kingdom value of recreation and sports used as ministry tools.

# Appendix 17:
# *Game Resources*

**Screamers and Scramblers**
By Michael Caps
LifeWay Press
800-458-2772

**Games That Teach**
By Linda Minyard
Convention Press
800-458-2772

**Fun and Games**
By Rice, Ryberg, and Yaconelli
Zondervan Press
800-727-3480

**A Bunch of Fun Games**
By Wanda Pearce
Broadman Press
800-458-2772

**Right-On Ideas for Youth Groups**
By Rice and Yaconelli
Zondervan Press
800-727-3480

**Adventure Recreation**
By Baack, Hill, and Palmer
Convention Press
615-251-3848

**Adventure Recreation 2**
By Baack and Smith
Convention Press
800-458-2772

**Games with a Purpose**
By George Siler
Convention Press
800-458-2772

**Parachute Games**
By Strong and LeFevre
Human Kinetics Publishers
800-747-4457

**World's Best Indoor Games**
By Brandreth
Pantheon Books
800-733-3000

**The New Games Book
and More New Games**
By Fluegelman
Doubleday & Co.
800-733-3000

**Games**
By Hoenstein
Bethany House
952-829-2500

**Cowtails and Cobras**
By Hohnke
Project Adventure
978-524-4500

**Silver Bullets**
By Hohnke
Project Adventure
978-524-4500

**Everybody Wins**
By Sobel
Walker Publishing Company, Inc.
800-289-2553

**Team Recreation**
By Bill Buchanan
405-598-8844
Game Videos
Camp Leadership

**The Ultimate Playground and
Recess Game Book**
By Educator's Press
800-650-7888